The Silenced Cry

The Silenced Cry

ONE WOMAN'S DIARY OF
A JOURNEY TO AFGHANISTAN

Ana Tortajada

Translated by Ezra E. Fitz

THOMAS DUNNE BOOKS
ST. MARTIN'S PRESS ❦ NEW YORK

THOMAS DUNNE BOOKS.
An imprint of St. Martin's Press.

www.stmartins.com

Library of Congress Cataloging-in-Publication Data

Tortajada, Ana.
    [Grito silenciado. English]
    The silenced cry : one woman's diary of a journey to Afghanistan / Ana Tortajada;
translated by Ezra E. Fitz.— 1st U.S. ed.
      p. cm.
    ISBN 0-312-30351-3
    EAN 978-0312-30351-8
    1. Afghanistan—Description and travel. 2. Women—Afghanistan—Social
conditions—20th century. 3. Afghanistan—Social conditions—20th century.
4. Taliban. 5. Tortajada, Ana—Travel—Afghanistan. I. Title.
    DS352.T6713 2004
    915.8104'46—dc22

2004040543

First published in Spain by Mondadori under the title *El Grito Silenciado* in 2001.

First U.S. Edition: August 2004

10 9 8 7 6 5 4 3 2 1

Contents

The Silenced Cry

Vallirana.

There are those who sell, for two and a quarter reales,
sparrows still cleaving the sky.

It has been just five days since I've returned to Europe. I drift like a distraught soul among the armchairs and corners of my house. I attribute the soreness in my throat to the strong air-conditioning that assaults me at every turn, and to the halfhearted chain-smoking, lighting up a cigarette only for the pleasure of doing so on a whim instead of having to find myself a secluded spot. I cling to the credible excuse that exhaustion (and the disaster that is my insides) offers me, after this voyage to a physical and virtual Afghanistan and to the Pakistani city of Peshawar and its innumerable Afghan refugee population, so as not to leave, so as to see no one, so as to do nothing.

It gives me a certain—if very relative—amount of relief to know that it's not just me who feels strange, out of place, foreign to the world around me. Something similar is happening to Meme and Sara. Since we've returned, it's taxing to relate to our people and environment: they have not been there. Of course, they show interest in our trip, in the things that we have seen, but why won't this vague and frustrating sensation that the echo of our experiences is full of interference leave us? Words and the air through which they travel are morphing into a thick magma and are losing their conductive character that ordinarily permits communication. This doesn't happen when we talk among the three of us. So we take refuge among ourselves, in our own little triangle of common experience, in tune with each other where we feel secure, for those first few days.

We hadn't known each other before it all happened.

It hadn't been three days yet that Afghanistan—the situation that her people suffer under the Taliban's oppression, and the struggle for survival by the Afghans taking refuge in Pakistan—had invaded my life, dominating everything, ever since I received notice that a group of people from the UOC (Universitat Oberta de Catalunya) was organizing a trip. But in reality there was no such group: only Mercè Guilera, a UOC student who had decided to travel to Pakistan in order to better understand the situation of women in that country and who had proposed the trip to Sara Comas, the journalist from *El Punt de Rubí,* whom she had met on several occasions. Each related to themes of cooperation and solidarity. Both had met the same Afghan refugee as I during her time in Barcelona. Sara had interviewed her for her newspaper. I looked up Mercè's—Meme's—phone number. I called, and immediately joined in preparing for the trip.

There was nothing hasty about my decision. It was what I wanted to do. Nevertheless, as I realized the tasks assigned to me via telephone and e-mail, a part of me could not believe what was happening. Three weeks ago, all I knew about Afghanistan could be boiled down to a vague recollection of the invasion of Soviet troops, and the intricate 1998 campaign, "A Flower for the Women of Kabul," had left nary a trace on me. Quickly, though, all my thoughts, efforts, and emotions settled on that forgotten country. I searched for information, I surfed the Internet, I ransacked libraries and bookstores with an insatiable desire for knowledge. The blinders were on: my first thought upon waking was Afghanistan, and I fell asleep at night mulling over everything I had learned and discovered that day. Even my dreams had turned toward that distant country.

Sara Comas, Mercè Guilera, and I got to know each other personally just fifteen days after that first phone call, when we gathered for our first work session. Each of us had her own motivations and personal objectives when we committed to this trip, but all of us coincided on the fundamental: collect as much information as humanly possible, contact the maximum number of organizations, people, and classes, both here and there, in order to gain the most complete vision possible, and thus be able to denounce, upon our return, the situation of the Afghan people with knowledge of the cause itself. I am no expert on foreign politics, international rights, world economics, or anything of the sort. I'm an ordinary citizen. I know that I have rights and obligations. I enjoy life and people. I detest lies and deceit, always preferring the truth.

The trip was, for me, the first consequence of a commitment I had recently acquired with a woman I had never seen before in my life: on March 20, late in the afternoon, I attended a conference in Barcelona featuring an Afghan refugee who was in Catalonia at the invitation of the Lliga dels Drets dels Pobles (the League of People's Rights). The young woman gave her lecture in English, while two interpreters took turns translating her words into Catalan. Back then, my knowledge of English was quite poor, so I was surprised to realize that I could understand nearly every word she said. As her discourse progressed, I became more and more fascinated. The exposition, sober and serene, painted a horrifying reality that captivated me completely. I didn't feel, then nor ever, rage, indignation, or hate for the Afghan oppressors or their accomplices. I don't believe in rage or hate: they are counterproductive.

Nor did I have any qualms about recognizing that what I experienced that day as the conference went on was a growing and inexplicable love for that young woman, for her people and her country. There wasn't an ounce of mawkishness in that feeling; it wasn't a simple emotional reaction. When the talk was over, I went up to introduce myself with a timidity uncharacteristic for me. I wouldn't allow my inability to express myself in English be an obstacle, and asked the translators to convey to her the only thing I wanted to say: "Thank you for working as you do; for not having crawled into a corner to cry."

She replied with a great vivacity: "I refuse to cry for my people's situation. Crying doesn't solve anything, and it takes up energy that ought to be dedicated to changing the way things are."

We said good-bye with three kisses, as is the custom in her country, and she told me between laughs that three was the minimum, and that sometimes it can reach seven, nine, or even more.

"Good luck! *¡Buena suerte!*" I wished her in my awkward, limited English, and we parted ways at a traffic light.

I crossed the street thinking about what I could do, and I came to the conclusion that the only thing I could do even moderately well was write. Maybe I could write a book about this theme, a book that describes the reality just as it is and how it is lived; not a book that reflects, once again, the Western vision but rather the perspective of the Afghan people, of those who know and suffer it. I would document things extensively, so as to be a valuable instrument at her service, but I would write to make her voice the one that is heard.

I placed my offer the following day, via e-mail. I added that were the book to be published and earn royalties, all the money would be donated to the humanitarian projects run by HAWCA (Humanitarian Assistance for the Women and Children of Afghanistan), the organization to which she belonged. There is an Afghan saying—a Persian proverb from the region around Kabul—that reads: "There are those who sell, for two and a quarter reales, sparrows still cleaving the sky." My offer was like the cry of such a vendor who had nothing on hand to sell. But she accepted. It was then that I realized that I didn't know a thing about her other than her name. She offered me all the help that she could, apologizing that her stay in Barcelona was nearing its end and that there wasn't enough time to meet again and talk. But she assured me that she'd answer any and all questions, and that she'd send me all the information that I would need. That was the start of an intense e-mail correspondence, during which I studied English, geography, literature, international relations, antecedents, origins and causes of the conflict, declarations, news reports, articles by experts in the field, and denouncements by Afghan women themselves.

Thus it was that I established a pact with Afghanistan and with the Afghan people: through this woman who symbolized them to me. The account of my time there would be the fruit and expression of this pact. But four days of avoiding the keyboard had flooded me with a sea of nostalgia, and I was shut up in my house like a snail, thanking the gods that everyone else was away on vacation. I didn't feel like seeing or speaking to anybody. I just wanted to be alone so I could savor and assimilate this Afghan sadness that has drawn me out of the shell of memory.

I've already discussed the curiosities and adventures with the whole world. But in reality, everything still remains to be said. I don't know who will be willing to lend an ear to what it is that I have to say, who will know how to put themselves in my shoes and understand this strange mix of emotions and experiences, of desires, joys, and pains. I don't know who will want to accompany me into the depths of that dark and most silent well of peaceful and serene sadness yet not despair. Nor do I know if there will be someone to laugh with me over each of the thousand anecdotes and enjoyable situations that life was offering us, from day to day and throughout our entire existence, even the most dramatic of situations.

In reality, I might even venture to say that life has the same subtle sense of humor as the Afghans, who love to laugh and who—even in the worst of situations, once they have calculated the danger, eliminated options, and made decisions, after thoughtful and interminable deliberations—never fail to take advantage of the chance to smile in the face of the only grotesque detail of a history of terror.

Their secret is that they have no fear.

They recognize the danger, but they don't live in fear. They do what they have to do, they do it with prudence and with taking as many precautions as possible, but nothing stops them. Outwitting the danger spurs them on and is the source of a new round of smiles.

I like the Afghan people. I like them a lot.

I love the perpetual sadness pouring from dry, unflinching eyes. The sadness of Afghan refugees is the profound and sober sadness of a paradise lost, the nostalgia of the country that they ardently love: Afghanistan . . . You hear them pronounce its name and before you can translate what they are saying, the tone and accent of each syllable filters throughout your body and resonates in corners unknown until now. They say "Afghanistan" and this name on their lips tastes of the sweetest kiss, of lost love, of soft lullabies, of a friendly breast, of a protective den, of distant rain.

The contagious sadness of love and nostalgia.

Though I am not Afghan, my eyes cloud over with a yearning for Afghanistan and Kabul. And I wish to be an Afghan woman so that I might have the right to fight alongside them, so that I might stay there—from one edge to the other of that oppressed frontier—defending the rights of my people, establishing a peaceful resistance to the nongovernment of barbarism, contributing pencils and paper and clandestine books to the revolution against those trying to impose ignorance and quash the people's spirit, their intelligence, and all other liberties.

I embarked on my journey to Afghanistan fascinated by her ancient and recent history, by the diversity of her people, the richness of her languages, her cultures, her traditions; enamored of all the myths that embody that thin, dark-haired, and nacre-skinned woman, the Afghan refugee who had come to Barcelona for a day during her tour of several European cities to tell the world about the plight of Afghan women, both within and beyond her borders, and to bring her organization's work to the attention of refugees, building schools, creating jobs for women, and giving aid and assistance to the clandestine networks in Taliban-controlled Afghanistan working to promote literacy and provide health care to those who are denied education and medical attention.

I went to Afghanistan because my heart was touched, and I returned with my heart stolen. Part of the Afghans' sadness has become mine, and I consider it a privilege—a treasure I never want to lose—because this sadness acts like a filter that tinges everything with a new sheen, and when it doesn't drive one to suicide, it is an endless fountain of energy. It is the shadow under which you rest and act, where plans for future hope are hatched: you don't pay it any heed; you don't even realize that it exists. But it is there.

A sadness of love that lives in the heart of every Afghan and in Afghanistan herself, in her mountains, from an almost white ochre to a toasted brown, with her patches of sudden green, in the Kabul River and her varying tonalities, in dusty, treeless, bomb-scarred streets. And in Kabul, "The Silent," where music and laughter are prohibited. Old and New Kabul, both destroyed by bombs, expansive, surrounded by supremely high mountains and climbing through the hills. When you've been in Kabul and hours and hours of sun have filled your eyes with Afghanistan's magnificent landscapes, rough and hard like living rock, you understand the only common lament of this people of easy smiles and re- served sadness, the only complaint that is allowed in the middle of the eternally sultry weather; as one Afghan in Peshawar, the city of his exile, said, in passing, "Ah, the Kabul climate!"

Then his expression lights up and you know that the climate is unimpor- tant, simply a reference, a sort of innocent symbol divested of implications and connotations, where they evoke and translate the memory and nostalgia of a country, a life, a past that was ever theirs until being snatched away.

It is this Afghan sadness of love that today shakes me out of my lethargy and moves me to sit down at my keyboard, animated and full of energy, ready to fulfil my pact.

Peshawar.

The first day that you saw each other, you were friends;
when you saw each other again, you did so as brothers.

We touch down in Pakistan at dawn, at the airport in Islamabad, her capital. On the plane, when our watches indicated that it was midnight in Barcelona, the flight attendants were waking us up to serve breakfast.

It is still dark out when we disembark from the plane, and our first impression is that of entering a pocket of hot air. The kind of heat that comes off a car's engine in the summertime just after you shut it off. Our bodies' cooling systems switch on and cover our skin with a permanent film, a sweat bath that still hasn't left us. But in spite of my usual aversion to heat, all I can think about is that it could be worse.

The airport is full of people. Of men. All dressed in loose pants and long-sleeved shirts that reach down to their knees. White, sky-blue, and beige. The dominant colors of the human wall of Pakistanis who await, behind the gate, the arrival of the passengers coming from the West with whom we've flown since London. Entire, decked-out families: dragging their gauze chadors, laden with gold and children, and those more restrained, in their embroidered caps, some wearing a jacket and tie, perhaps—we suppose—to impress those who will be meeting them. We go on supposing that they are Pakistanis now living in the United Kingdom who come back to visit and who, just as with our country's travelers who return home from trips to Germany, Switzerland, or France, are permitted the pleasure of showing off how good things are there.

We are just passing through Islamabad. A national flight to Peshawar awaits us. Sara, Meme, and I inform the airport employees, and are ordered to gather our bags. To get to Peshawar, we have to check in again. We are caught up in the flood of families surging toward the baggage claim areas. Wheelchair-bound grandparents direct the luggage rescue operation; mothers with strollers, a baby in arms with two more back around in her chador wait next to the suitcases. Youths hawk luggage carts, laden like forklifts, driving them who knows where. Noise. Tumult. Apologetic smiles back and forth.

And Meme's bag doesn't appear.

Another carousel fills with the luggage from a flight full of Pakistanis just arrived from the U.S. The belt spits out huge bags and boxes, including some well-packaged microwaves brought home by travelers for their relatives in Pakistan.

Hidden behind a column and sheltered by the cart carrying our luggage, I light a cigarette, feeling like a transgressor. Among the many things we did during our preparation for this trip, one was to meet several times with a Pakistani woman who was kind enough to instruct us on her country and its customs, on what was considered acceptable and what wouldn't be tolerated. A woman smoking fell under the "very bad" category. I had planned to not smoke for the three weeks that our trip was to last, but my feeble will faltered just hours after the last cigarette.

Although in Barcelona we learned much about urban Pakistani norms, it didn't serve us much, given that despite spending the greater part of our time in Pakistan, it's as if we weren't there at all, and so I can't speak on that country, her people, her traditions, her way of life. Meme, Sara, and I spent all our time immersed in an Afghan world, staying with Afghan families in homes built and distributed in the Afghan manner, ate in Afghan restaurants and locales, Afghan dishes and Afghan ice cream. In the shops, fruit stands, refugee camps, in our interviews with humanitarian organizations, in the streets and markets, among the beggars and drug addicts . . . we spent our time only among those Afghan refugees who comprise this other Afghanistan, stuck at the real and physical border of their country; this other Afghanistan that they felt forced to flee from and whose reign of terror, they hope beyond all hope, will end and enable them to return.

And Meme's bag doesn't appear.

The waiting area has emptied, and only we remain. We try to explain to an airport employee that we've looked high and low, until he finally decides to fill out the appropriate forms and tell us what we have to do. In the meantime, we take turns changing dollars for Pakistani rupees at an airport exchange office. One dollar is worth fifty-three rupees. Then, always following the personnel's instructions, we head for the office of departures and national flights.

Today is the day.

Everyone is watching, but that doesn't bother us. An older woman passes us and smiles. I return the gesture. We've dressed with discretion, in loose-fitting clothing and long-sleeved blouses, but we are still patently out of place among these people who dress so differently from ourselves.

To get our boarding passes for the flight to Peshawar, we have to pay a tax. We weren't expecting this, and offer a bit of protest, in case we're being taken advantage of. The employee who we are lucky enough to bump into isn't the brightest, and has to constantly ask his colleagues for instructions. It takes him awhile to make the conversion, and an impressive line begins to form behind us. When we finally agree to pay, the bill I produce from my travel wallet far exceeds anything the man behind the window is able to change, and he sends someone to the bank. The passenger in line behind us tires of waiting and moves past us with exact change to expedite the process.

Finally we make it out onto the runway. The plane that is to carry us to Peshawar is tiny—forty seats—and is powered by a set of propellers that have to be spun into motion by a man on the ground. All our bags (except Meme's) are at the foot of the steps up to the cabin, and on his way up, each passenger has to confirm and identify his. The plane is not very full at all.

From the sky, Islamabad is a pattern of gray buildings and green spaces. We fly over the mountains, and soon the world changes to an ochre tone. Peshawar, from the air, is the color of bright maroon.

I glance back and cannot understand what force, what sort of magnetism, has brought me here, me, who can't stand heat and who hates to fly.

With us on the plane are a pair of Germans (perhaps members of some NGO), a married Pakistani couple, and a single woman who looks Western and who has already covered her face. Our fountain of information back in Barcelona has told us that Peshawar is a much more conservative city than Islamabad, where one can still go around in short sleeves or sans chadors.

Again we gather our bags, immersed in a mixture of different feelings. Each of us gets off wrapped up in her own thoughts, and we don't speak much. One final time, we tell each other that everything will be fine, and that they're waiting for us. It's our only real concern: if for some reason our friends aren't at the airport to meet us when we arrive, we have no address nor any other way to get in touch with them. The precariousness of fear is such that not even phone numbers are given out. The only thing we would be able to do then would be sit and hope they would eventually be able to find us. In retrospect, I don't know why we were so worried; since we had confirmed the flight number and arrival time so many times over e-mail, our worries were rather boring ones. Plus, the previous day we had received one final message from Azada:

"Dear Ana: I hope you get this message before you leave. Please, don't worry about a thing. We'll be there waiting for you at the Peshawar airport. If for whatever reason we don't find each other, I'll call you on your cell phone."

That wouldn't be necessary.

Soon, amid the waiting crowd, I see her making her way through the sea of people toward us, smiling. It's Azada. In an earlier e-mail I had asked her if her name had some significance. It did. It comes from the Persian word *azadi,* meaning "liberty." Azada is, therefore, a free woman. She hugs us and covers us with kisses. Not the standard three, like in Barcelona, but seven, nine, thousands of kisses. And I knew that at that moment, we were fulfilling the Afghan proverb in the Persian language that affirmed that *"The first day that you saw each other, you were friends; when you saw each other again, you did so as brothers."*

The very next thing that this forward-thinking woman does is to take three chadors out of a plastic bag. One for each of us, and she shows us how to put them on. Some men take our suitcases for us while Azada introduces us to the other women who are waiting with her, if a bit apart, and they greet us warmly. They are named Nasreen and Lala. Both work as teachers at the school HAWCA operates in Peshawar. One of them is carrying a tiny baby in her arms, but explains to us that it's not hers. The men are the drivers who will be taking us to Najiba's house, the woman who would be hosting us during our stay in the city.

Our idea had, from the beginning, been to stay with them. Sara was the staunchest supporter of this option. Meme hadn't ruled out spending a night in a hotel once in a while. We were also aware of the fact that three freshly arrived people staying for three weeks would be a drain on an already naturally precarious economy, which was something we should consider. Contributing to the filling of the house pantry was another option, but given our relative naivete about the Middle Eastern customs and norms, we were afraid that that would be interpreted as an offensive gesture. For that, then, we had no idea what to expect of Afghan hospitality. We knew, from one of the many messages that we exchanged on an almost daily basis, that our hosts had also debated several possibilities for our lodging, and that Najiba's home was one of them. And they added:

"We should tell you that living in our poor homes, where there are restrictions and interruptions in water and electricity, might be difficult for you, especially this time of the year and with the dryness and heat that we're having. If it gets to be too much, don't worry, there's always time to find a hotel."

Don't worry. It's one of the most often repeated expressions in her messages. Something we've all been repeating. As for the difficulties that we were in store for . . . if these people could endure them as a permanent way of life, weren't we going to be able to do so as well, with the knowledge that at the end of three weeks we would be returning to the commodities to which we were accustomed?

While we wait near the cars for Azada to make sure that all the paperwork is in order to recover the lost bag, I can't help but look at the people. I feel rather indiscreet, but everything is so new and unique that I can't fight the temptation.

It's hot. Very hot. But it doesn't bother me.

"Garmi," say the teachers, who don't know a word of English, and they fan themselves, breathing deeply.

Yes, *garmi,* hot. Then we pile into the cars. They're small vehicles with no markings to identify them as taxis, and our bags form a skyscraper on top of the luggage rack.

The taxi crosses the city along avenues and wide streets packed with cars, rickshaws, buses, and trucks laden with chains and dark cloths, decorated with a profusion of colors and decorative motifs. It circles around to the left, and the steering wheel is on the right-hand side. Vestiges of the ancient British Empire. Soon, our car turns onto an unpaved alley. The stoplights, heavy traffic, car horns, and police whistles are all behind us. We find ourselves smack in the middle of one of the many Afghan neighborhoods in Peshawar. Beeping the horn, we make our way down the street so narrow that we could have reached out of the windows and touched the caged chickens, skinned lambs, and piles of fruit that make up the market. It's a swarm of people. Old men in turbans, smiling children, women with faces covered by their chadors, another beneath a glass-green *burka,* still one more draped in a bright sky-blue one. Dogs and carts drawn by donkeys cross our path. A barber shaves a man, both seated on a mat at the edge of the street. A beggar, covered by a *burka,* sits in the shade awaiting alms. A pair of very young children is sleeping around her. In a nearby shop, a man is mending shoes.

The car stops at the entrance to an even narrower alley, which no car could hope to fit down. The driver, outgoing and obliging and a friend of the family who would be hosting us, picks up our bags while the women guides us to Najiba's house. Down the muddy clay street runs a smallish drain that carries off the turbid, frothy sewage from the homes lining both sides of the street off to who knows where.

The doors happen to be closed. Most are metal double doors, but some are merely a hanging cloth. Nasreen, who also lives in the neighborhood, points hers out to us. We continue on, until we stop in front of one door, and the women knock.

"Who is it?"

They respond. The door opens with a metallic squeak, revealing a packed-earth patio. Najiba is there to greet us.

"Salaam!"

Her smile lights up her gray-green eyes. She helps us remove our *shadors* and gestures: indoors, they aren't needed. Then she introduces us to a teenager with great big eyes and braids like rope that reach almost to her waist: Basira, her husband's niece, who was dying of both curiosity and embarrassment, hiding her giggles behind her chador.

Off to the left is an L-shaped porch with three doors. We are invited to take our shoes off and have a seat at the opposite end of the porch, under the shade. Basira brings in an assortment of firm, embroidered red velvet pillows to support our backs as we sit against the wall. The driver sets down our bags and asks Najiba to bring out some *pakas*—rectangular mats of woven straw with wooden handles that look like stiff semaphore flags. They begin to fan us with them. So much attention makes us feel a bit uncomfortable, but it is simply because we do not yet fully understand the concept of Afghan courtesy, of their elevated concept of hospitality that effectively turns a simple houseguest into a king. Gradually we learn to accept these displays of attention with the same casual air that they are offered to us instead of committing the gross offense of refusing them. Playing around with the *pakas,* fanning each other. Nobody present speaks English, and Azada still hasn't arrived yet in a separate car. Communication consists of glances, smiles, and simple gestures. It's a simple topic: the heat. *Garmi.* The curiosity is mutual. They look at us, and we look at them.

The three doors off the porch correspond to the house's three bedrooms. Najiba lives in one with her husband and two children, a girl of nearly two and a four-month-old baby. In the middle room, where we will be set up, live Najiba's husband's parents. The third room, located off the short arm of the L, is her siblings-in-laws'. But none of them are there. Had they temporarily moved out to give us more room? We do not know.

There is no furniture. Only a thick Afghan rug that covers the floor, and a few nails driven into the wall for hanging up clothes. They are protected from the dust by a cloth, also hung from the wall by nails, which serves as a sort of closet.

At the other edge of the patio are three independent rooms. At the moment, all we know is that the rough center door, fashioned out of unsanded wooden planks, is the bathroom: a hole in the ground with a porcelain step for your feet, a faucet in the wall, and a pail. We have to learn to squat. And when we trade in our Western clothing for local garments, it further complicates the issue, given the amount of fabric that has to be gathered up so that it doesn't drag on the floor. There is no paper. The faucet in the wall, apart from filling the pail that serves as the cistern, is for washing off. We use our reserves of toilet paper and hygienic napkins that we have brought for such things, and hang a plastic bag on a corner for disposing of anything that might clog the hole.

We feel relieved when Azada finally arrives. She is our communication bridge, our voice and ears. From now on, she won't have a moment's rest: she'll be our interpreter day and night. I, who know the job well, have no idea how she doesn't drop from exhaustion.

Nasreen bids farewell and heads for her home, a few doors down. The driver does the same. Basira spreads a cloth out on the floor, sets the table, and we eat sitting on the floor of what will be our room. It's rice. A piping hot mountain of special rice, with raisins and carrot shavings: *palau,* one of Afghanistan's most common and popular dishes, served on a brass platter nearly the size of a bicycle wheel. Another bowl has finely chopped chicken in sauce. Contrary to Pakistani cuisine, Afghan dishes are not very hot or garnished with spices. On the side are bowls of natural yogurt, and bread. Nan. Big loaves and flat loaves, long leaf-shaped loaves and diamond-shaped loaves, all toasted in color and with geometric designs covering the outer crust.

Azada, attending to everything, asks them to bring us a few bottles of mineral water. She knows that the tap water, which they all drink, might not be potable to our unaccustomed systems. We all share plates and glasses. At the time, we don't know if it's because there aren't any other utensils in the house, or perhaps it's because, given the scarcity of water, that it's better not to dirty any more things than necessary. Some of the plates are hard plastic, while others are metal, like the camping equipment used in our country for excursions to the mountains. They hand our dishes to us covered. Forks and spoons. No knives. Cutting and shredding chicken, full of bones, with just a spoon is quite an arduous task that is solved only when they tell us that in their culture, eating with your hands (with one hand) is common. I smile at the thought that the proper way to eat here is exactly the opposite of how we've been taught to eat since childhood, where eating with one's hands is considered impolite. We all laugh, they more so at our clumsiness in lifting the food to our mouths.

We aren't permitted to help with clearing the table when the time comes. We are the guests! Our hosts gather up the things while I content myself with watching the kitchen. One gathers up the dirty dishes, another the trays, another consolidates the leftover bread and places it in a plastic bread box on the porch. They wipe down the cloth, fold it up, and stow it underneath the bread box.

Plagued by my habit, I go up to Azada nevertheless ready to comply with her wishes. It couldn't hurt to ask, "Is it very poor manners here for a woman to smoke?"

She smiles and does not answer. Instead she says something in Dari to Najiba who, two seconds later, brings me a crystal ashtray accompanied by a radiant smile. A great weight is lifted off my shoulders. I promise myself not to abuse her tolerance and to contain myself as much as possible. I'll only smoke on the patio, and then only when we're alone in the house.

Nasreen returns that afternoon. And elderly, white-haired woman is with her: her husband's mother. We manage to leave the heat behind us as a topic of conversation.

Nasreen is a young, thin, and tall woman with dark hair and eyes who takes good care of her appearance. Her name means something along the lines of "water flower." Seated next to her mother-in-law, she tells us that she completed her degree in education in 1992. The Soviet invasion never made it as far as Kabul, where life went on with some sense of normalcy. Afterward, and despite the civil war, she worked as a teacher until the Taliban took control of the city in 1996. With that arrival, women were prohibited (among other things) from earning a salary outside of the home. As such, Nasreen, like many other women, felt obligated to renounce her profession. As an early casualty, the sudden dearth of teachers forced many schools to close.

We are drawn deep into the history when this sweet grandmother who looks and smiles at us launches into the story of how she and her family were forced to flee Afghanistan. Azada translates as the woman talks, sitting cross-legged, with her hands folded in her lap or resting on her knees. Sometimes she raises them in a sober gesture. She gets emotional at certain points, but never to the point of crying. She dries her eyes—simply moist—with the tip of her white chador that she has opted not to remove indoors and that she from time to time readjusts around her hair in a series of deft movements.

She and her husband lived in downtown Kabul.

The civil war among the three principal Islamic groups was already taking its toll on the streets of the city.

The year before, in the spring of 1992, General Massoud, who now fights against the Taliban in the north of the country, had occupied Kabul and aligned himself with the forces of the party that brought together the Hazara majority with Dostum's Uzbekistani troops. The president of the pro-Soviet government, Najibullah, after a failed attempt to leave the country, took refuge in the U.N. offices, where four years later he would be dragged out by the Taliban and executed in the street. A provisional government emerged, with Rabbani as president, but the treaties didn't hold up. Gulbuddin Hekmatyar, chief of the other Islamic counterfaction and who also desired power, launched a brutal attack on Kabul. The hostilities among the different factions fighting for control of the capital, bombarding and destroying it, raged incessantly, prompting waves of refugees to flee from the atrocities perpetrated against the civilian population, and each faction was backed by a different foreign power: Iran, Saudi Arabia, Pakistan . . .

The detailed understanding that the Afghan population has of the battles' progression, of the changing alliances, of the barbaric acts committed by soldiers, will not cease to amaze me in the days that follow. The names Massoud, Dostum, Hekmatyar, and Sayyaf are sprinkled all throughout casual conversation. The people detest these crime bosses and their troops, the *yehadis*—Islamic fundamentalists—as much as the Taliban. They remember their bombings, looting, rapes, executions, kidnappings with the same horror: Naheed, a Kabul teenager, threw herself from a fifth-story window when they came for her. Many parents would rather kill their children than let them fall into the *yehadis'* hands, lest they rape them to the point of death before abandoning their broken bodies in the streets.

People scarcely dared to leave their homes, the old woman continues. The city was under siege; the different factions were fighting for control of the various neighborhoods. Anything could happen to the civilian population. Nevertheless, her husband, a cabinetmaker, continued to go to work.

Things were so unbearable that Nasreen's husband decided to move his parents to a peripheral region of the capital, where another of his children lived. There were no rental cars in the city. They had to walk. The old woman tells of how her son carried her the entire way—three long hours—on his back. Once they had the few members of their family all together, they reviewed their options and decided to flee, together, to Pakistan. There were no cars, she repeats. Only a few buses, which took them as far as Jalalabad, the city nearest the border post of Torkham. Only women and the elderly traveled on the buses. For two days, they didn't eat a thing. On the third day, they scrounged up a bit of bread. They split up in Jalalabad. Nasreen and her husband wanted to go back to Kabul. He is a teacher as well and at that point still had a job. In Pakistan, it would be difficult to find work. Becoming a refugee is always the final option to choose. The rest of the family pressed on toward the border. The old woman remembers that once they set foot on Pakistani soil, they were met by a person with cards for the refugees, directing them toward their respective camps. The one to which they were assigned was in the middle of a desert. They were housed in shops, with floor mats to sleep on. There were two stores for every twenty refugees.

We listen in silence, but when the old woman finishes her story, we ask her which part does she harbor the best memories of.

She doesn't even hesitate: the years of Zahir Shah's reign, up until his exile to Italy in 1973 when a coup led by his cousin Muhammad Daoud and supported by the Kremlin forced him from power.

"We had a pretty house in a good neighborhood in Kabul. We didn't even need fans there," she says with a quick gesture at the long-bladed fan hanging from the ceiling that, at that moment, wasn't offering a bit of relief from the heat, the electricity currently suffering from one of its frequent interruptions of service.

"We could eat all the fruit that we wanted . . . fruit of all shapes and sizes, and the tastes and smells were intense." Fruit in Peshawar is prohibitively priced for most Afghan refugees. "Now the homes have been destroyed by bombs. Nothing remains." She sighs. "I didn't work outside of the home, but those women who wanted to, could." After a moment of silence, she continues, shaking her head: "I can never go back to Kabul. There's nothing left for me there. And my house is destroyed."

Nasreen cuts in. She, unlike her mother-in-law, has no memory of a better past. A young woman of about thirty, she was just a baby during the time of the monarchy.

"Afterward, every time was worse than the one before."

Many of the people with whom we speak, especially the older ones, remember fondly the king who, in 1964, bestowed Afghanistan with a modern constitution that laid out the equal rights of men and women and that was approved and ratified by the *Loya Jirga,* the Grand Assembly, an effective Afghan institution where all citizens were represented by elected members.

That night Najiba's husband arrives, who has a shop in the bazaar. The driver accompanies him. He greets us, affectionately and shyly. We aren't sure how to conduct ourselves in front of this reserved and peaceful man who speaks in a soft, slow voice. He sits down on the rug, a bit removed from the rest of us, and takes in his arms his daughter, who ever since seeing him come in the door has been mad with delight. He chats and praises her in the same reserved, muted tone of voice. We are amazed to see the amount of attention and affection that adults give to children, not just in this family but in all the places that we visit, and not only to their own children but to whomever might wander in the house. Najiba's baby is always in her arms, or her neighbor's arms, or the arms of the older children who come by to visit us. There must never be a reason for a baby to cry: they rock it, dance with it, pass it around, talk to it, coo to it. Everybody— men included—is extremely caring of young children, who have any person's lap as their throne.

The driver, much more chatty and extroverted, stays for dinner and to chat with our host, sitting across the rug. The separation between men and women—purdah—exists and manifests itself in this and many other details that we would be discovering.

At dinner we occupy—as we would every night and in every Afghan home we would visit—the noblest place at the table, reserved for guests: on the thin mats set up against the wall, our backs supported by giant pillows. Our hosts occupy the other sides of the square cloth, their backs to the patio, without mats or pillows and sitting directly on the rug. It is a customary courtesy, one of the thousand and one that they would offer us.

As we eat, the driver tells Najiba that we should have some raw onion. It's the best way to alleviate the heat, he says. Najiba immediately sends Basira to the kitchen, and soon enough she reappears with a plate of finely chopped onion.

After dinner comes the nightly conversation that becomes our sheer delight each and every night we spend in the Middle East. It doesn't matter how hard things may be in the days ahead, or how much suffering we may have to bear witness to, the tears we will have to swallow. The night concludes each day with a pool of peace, of shared intimacy, of friendship and laughter.

Liters of sweetened green tea will flow during these gatherings, while family members, friends, or invited guests surrender themselves to the pleasure of conversation. The majority of Afghans who I've met appreciate silence, but give them a word or the seeds of a debate and time will cease to exist while they talk and talk without anyone ever losing the thread of conversation. They are great conversationalists, perhaps because of the millennial tradition of their *jirgas,* those assemblies where people debate, discuss, and decide what is best for the community. In Afghan society, the communal takes precedence over the individual; the needs of the group are given priority, and it is the group that watches out for each individual's needs. The "rugged individualism" of our society is nonexistent here. Decisions are made by consensus.

Our presence makes the stop-and-go intervention of an interpreter necessary, but nobody shows signs of fatigue or boredom, of impatience or discomfort. The conversation is fluid and continues on into the early hours of the morning. When one person is speaking, the others listen respectfully and attentively, without interrupting.

It is our host's turn to speak, and he welcomes us to his home. He apologizes for not being able to offer us all he would like, given the precariousness of the methods at his disposal. He assures us that he is honored to host us, and that everyone will watch over and protect us. He expresses his gratitude to us for wanting to come from so far away just to learn firsthand the situation of the Afghan refugees and people. We must not feel afraid. Nothing bad will happen to us.

His speech is so affecting, so moving, that we feel almost embarrassed. To us, it seems extraordinary: we are nobody, nobody important, at least. We have no influence; we don't control the strings of power, politics, or economics; and we belong to no organization. We are simply three women.

That night, the fan scatters the heat as well as flies and mosquitoes. The electricity has come back on. The moon shows herself over the wall surrounding the house.

The soiree finished, we retire to the bathroom to brush our teeth. It's a small, square room with a tap on one wall, a metal bucket, and a plastic basin for throwing the water outside. Behind the door is a cylindrical depository roughly the height of a person for storing a quantity of water when service is cut off. In a corner of the room, the drain. We hesitate for a moment, and then spit our toothpaste on the ground, washing it away with water. There is a small mirror hanging on the wall.

Meanwhile, in our bedroom, the women have covered the mats in green, printed covers and lined them up on top of the traditional Afghan rug, with its intricate black motifs and designs. They cover it with a sheet and voilà, the bed is made.

"*Shab bajair.* Good night."

We fall asleep exhausted, still not quite fully aware of how scandalous our tight pajamas and shorts are here.

The rattling ceiling fan accompanies us on the road to dream.

I am here.

In the heart of an Afghan neighborhood in the city of Peshawar that, not long ago, formed part of the Afghan territory.

Peshawar, onetime headquarters of the mujahideen and of all those who participated in the war against the Soviet troops, the refuge of whoever fought against the invader.

Peshawar, which shortly thereafter would be the seat of the various Islamic parties as well as the training grounds for their members, the *yehadis,* who jockeyed for power once the Soviet army had been defeated.

Peshawar, the recent birthplace of the Taliban, now genocidal in its power, and the conduit for the drugs that finance their operations.

Peshawar, converted into a giant waiting room where the majority of the population is comprised of the thousands of Afghan refugees surviving on the hope of one day being able to return home.

Peshawar, the stage upon which women demand democracy and respect for human rights in Afghanistan.

I am here.

With all these people. With Azada, sleeping at my side. With Najiba and her family, who have taken us in without knowing a single thing about us. With Meme and with Sara, whom I barely know myself.

And being here is a privilege, a gift from heaven.

MONDAY, JULY 31, 2000.

Peshawar.

Patience is bitter,
but how sweet are her fruits!

We have to buy some clothes.

It's imperative that we don't call undue attention to ourselves. So nobody looks at us, so nobody bothers us nor is quick to accost us, when we go where we go, among the beggars. But above all, it's for the good of our hosts: it would not be good for someone—save for those who are in on the secret—to walk into Najiba's house and find three foreigners there. People would start asking questions. That Najiba had acquaintances in the West would seem quite strange indeed. It's better that nobody know, that we try to pass as imperceptibly as possible because, among other things, Westerners represent money. A lot of money. And it doesn't matter that this is not true in our case. Here, our dollars are worth a fortune. The presence of a few potentially wealthy foreigners would put Najiba's security at risk, living in an already precarious neighborhood.

Thus, for our entire stay in Peshawar, we have to cover our hair and faces with a chador at all times, whether walking down the alley or riding inside a car. It is understood that we cannot return to the local market that we had passed through yesterday upon our arrival.

Further, that very afternoon we would be heading to the refugee camp, and it would do no good there either to call attention to ourselves, considering that not even the police completely control the area there.

Before going shopping, waiting in the patio for the car to arrive, Najiba and Azada try showing us how to put on and wear a chador. We find it so difficult and ourselves so clumsy that we all split our sides laughing. Once again we are introduced (this time as a form of "good morning") to Basira, and to one of her friends. Basira is the shy, cheerful girl from yesterday, and the other a serious, distant teenager who happens to be Nasreen's niece. They watch us hesitantly, not daring to laugh out loud, but the twinkle in their eyes reveals that they are amused.

Azada consoles us with the advice that it's just a matter of practice.

She recalls the night she and her family fled Kabul when the Islamic factions were fighting for control. The *yehadis* were sowing terror through their abuses. Azada was still a teenager. That one fear-filled night when they had to steal past one checkpoint after another to get out of the city and flee to Pakistan, her mother made her put on a chador for the first time. She'd never had to wear one before, and didn't know how to make so that it wouldn't fall. Like we're doing now.

The driver comes looking for us at the agreed upon time.

It will always be like this: at night, we send word through one of the kids who come and go from the house at all hours of the day (the children of the few families who know about our presence) or one of the adults will go and tell the driver what time we need the car. We always use the same three drivers in Peshawar, three men of absolute confidence, friends and sympathizers of the organization, who take turns chauffeuring us from place to place.

Here, taxis are hired by the hour. For quick trips, it's cheaper to take a rickshaw. But in our case we have no choice, since our group would never fit into one of those semicovered, three-wheeled vehicles. The taxi will pick you up, and then wait for as long as is needed to bring you back, or on to your next destination. When you finally return home, the driver will come up to the door with you, calculate the total time, and collect payment.

Another advantage to hiring a taxi is that the driver becomes a sort of personal escort, a guardian angel who accompanies us everywhere, never leaving us for an instant. All this in such a way as to not interfere in our conversations, our plans, our laughter. And he helps with the packages. It's truly a blessing, although at times I feel like a Victorian lady traveling through the Orient. But they're two very different things. Here, the drivers are our accomplices, and the respect is mutual, without a hint of classism, chauvinism, or any other sort of "ism."

As soon as we leave the neighborhood, we uncover our faces. We head for the city center along wide, paved streets full of traffic and awash in a deafening concert: Pakistani drivers scarcely if ever take their hands off their horns. At every intersection and traffic light, children bearing steaming tins assault the car's windows. I don't want to interrupt Azada to ask, and later I forget.

She takes us to a good store on Saddar Road.

In a dressing room that would be quite generous for one person but, with three, becomes a veritable sauna, we each try on the clothing we've selected. We don't know what to make of ourselves in this new style, and nearly die laughing. The very wide cotton pants gathered together at the ankles. Another garment over the top, also of cotton, extending down to the knees, with openings at both sides, long sleeves and tight neckline, and embroidered cuffs and chest. And then the chador to play with: meters of fabric, stiff with newness, which we have no idea how to manage and which seems to have a life of its own.

We exit the dressing room drowning in laughter and the heat. Azada, amused, has us tone down our voices and excitement. She offers her opinion, and fixes our chadors. We try on a few more styles, swapping them between each other, make our choices, and slip back into our original garb. We're sweating so much that I wonder if they'll have to wash our rejected clothes that we leave in a heap on the counter. We also buy a roll of elastic to help tailor the waist of each pair of pants to each set of hips. Azada tries to haggle over the price, but we get no discount.

"This isn't a bazaar, ma'am. The prices are printed right there on the tag."

Next, Azada directs the driver, who had been waiting outside, to take us to a cyber café. The mystery is resolved: for the past several months, we had been quite casually exchanging e-mails with each other, but without knowing how. Was there an Internet connection at the refugee camp? Did Azada have Web access at her house? Evidently not. The car pulls into one of the open spots that, like rectangular bite marks, dot the main streets of Peshawar, where modern shops and supermarkets are located just as they are in Western countries. One of these shops offers Internet access for forty rupees per half hour. If you want to print something out, it's an additional ten rupees per page. There are four computers available; we occupy two. Azada wants to check her messages and answer any urgent correspondence. Besides her contacts in Spain, she has maintained relations with several Italians, who periodically send donations to her organization. Sara, Meme, and I take advantage of the chance to send messages to those back home and others who are interested in our journey. After the half hour is up, the shop manager wants to charge us double the rate advertised by the big sign behind him. Is it because we're foreigners? We haggle, we refuse, we'll only pay for the time we used. But the man is resolute. At least we tried . . .

We return home and show Najiba our recent purchases. Embarrassed, we realize that they have straightened up our room, which we had left in complete disarray, placing our bags and belongings behind the closet-curtain. Najiba enjoys examining every inch of our new clothing, doing so with an approving look. She runs her fingers over the embroidery, inspects the closings of the stitches. She informs us, through facial expressions and gestures, that they are very lovely and well-made clothes. We sit down together on the rug, run the elastic through the waists of the pants, test the size, hem the cuffs; the clothing laid out on the floor, and the girl poking at it all. We spend a good while there together, wrapped up in these household activities.

Then we try on the new clothing. Behind the habitually open curtain to our room, there are no inhibitions. In this walled-off space, on the island marked off by the rug, grows a world of women linked by an easy, natural intimacy of which I am soon aware. It's as if we've always lived together. We feel a bit strange dressed in these new garments, but we have to remember that they're fresh and comfortable.

Dinnertime is upon us: fried eggs and potatoes. It seems that fried potatoes are a universal dish. We mop up the eggs with bread, and devour the potatoes with our fingers. We nibble at a bit of onion and pay homage to the bowls of yogurt. Apparently and according to what they tell us, yogurt is also quite good at combating the heat. But Sara doesn't much like it, and eats it only out of courtesy.

After dinner, Nasreen and her mother-in-law come over. It's not just for the novelty our presence suggests. There is a familiarity between neighbors that we see everywhere we go. Nasreen and the older woman also want to see our new clothes, and we find ourselves talking of fabrics and the differences between Afghan and Pakistani clothing. Afghans are also physically quite distinct from Pakistanis, having eyes, lips, and skin the color of what we in the West would attribute to Indians. The Afghan combination of pants and blouses is more reserved, the fabrics have discreet colors and prints while the Pakistanis have a weakness for vibrant, showy colors, and their clothing is full of embroidery and accessories. What we've bought, then, appears more Pakistani, by virtue of its embroidery and variety of colors.

The truth is that, with practice, it's not hard to distinguish a Pakistani woman from an Afghan woman on the street from the clothes she wears. And also by the *burka*. Because in Peshawar, there are women in *burkas*. As with clothing, the Pakistani *burka* is distinguishable from the Afghan version: it's white, without the gathered pleats cascading from the smooth skullcap that hugs the forehead, and full of tucks at the bottom.

Basira, silent and discreet, has prepared a thermos of green tea as per Najiba's request. The soiree continues. We ask permission, and are obliged to take photos, as many as we want. Nasreen, who always looks nice and sometimes even wears makeup, smooths her hair.

We talk about the school that HAWCA operates, and where Nasreen and Najiba work as teachers. Nasreen had spent three years as a refugee in Pakistan before she learned that her neighbor Najiba was giving classes to children in the slums. Back then there were troubles at home, with three children and the grandparents . . . Her husband was out of work, as was she until she began working at the school. The criterion laid out by the board of directors was clear: given their very limited economic means, wages would only be paid to collaborators whose household economies were most wanting. Najiba, whose husband has a job, makes nothing. There are Afghan children's schools in Pakistan, but they are private; as are the ones for Pakistani children, and the HAWCA students would never have access to these. The day the school gains external funding, given that it is free to attend and therefore could never be self-sufficient, all the teachers will receive pay, so another of the organization's objectives is to create paid positions so that Afghan women will be able to have their own source of income.

The conversation again moves to the topic of the horrors suffered by people in Afghanistan. Nasreen recalls one of the worst nights of her life, back when she was still living in her house in Kabul. She was pregnant and going into labor. Her husband went out in search of a doctor, and didn't return. Hours passed, and she was at home, alone and waiting. A neighbor came and helped her through the birth. Another two days passed without any word from or about her husband. Eventually she found out that he had been arrested in the street that first night by a Taliban squad, under suspicion of being Hazara. The Taliban, who are Pashtun and Sunnis, detest the Shiite Hazara.

It is easy to recognize a Hazara. It's said that this segment of the population are the descendants of the troops of Genghis Khan who remained in the region after the Mongol occupation in the thirteenth century. Their slanted eyes give them away. The Taliban deny their status as Afghans and seek to exterminate them, carrying out a campaign of genocide and massacre, like the one that occurred in August of 1998 in the northern city of Mazar-e Sharif, the first time it was taken over by the Taliban. In three days, they murdered between five and eight thousand Hazara men, women, and children, though the majority were adult males. The Taliban went from door to door, dragging inhabitants out into the street and locking them inside trucks and boxcars and leaving them in the sun to asphyxiate. They shot hospital patients in their beds, leaving their bodies in the streets or in front of their homes, and forbade their burials. Dogs fattened themselves on the bodies.

Nasreen's husband, despite being Tajik, has almond-shaped eyes, and this was enough to get him arrested. They locked him up in a school for forty-eight hours and with nothing to eat. In one miraculous moment, he asked one of his guards for a bit of water so he could wash himself before praying. And this saved him: a Muslim who practiced Sunni rituals could not be Hazara, and he was set free.

Nasreen falls silent.

Then, after a brief silence, they teach us. For as long as we stay, they will spend as much time and energy as possible to make us know, to make us learn, to make us understand. Basira is a good model for showing us the characteristics of the Pashtun factions: dark complexion, thick black hair, and a sharp, finely lined face. The Pashtun have held power in Afghanistan almost without interruption. Nasreen and her husband are Tajik: descendants of the ancient Persians. Azada tells us that she is a mix of Pashtun (from her father) and Tajik (from her mother). Najiba, lying down on the rug so she can breast-feed her baby, raises a finger and smiles:

"Tajik."

At this time of day, under the heat, the ambience is loose. We have all relaxed our posture and are half stretched out on the rug and the pillows as we chat.

Today, Nasreen's mother-in-law has brought a beaded necklace. She explains that there are exactly one hundred beads, one for each of Allah's names. She knows them all. Not all Muslims can say this, and those who do not can only pass over the beads and repeat, "Allah is Great."

From a nearby minaret, a muezzin calls for prayer. The old woman gets up and asks for a prayer mat. Azada lays one out for her in a corner of the patio. When she returns to the group, she confesses, flustered and amused, that she is quite embarrassed, because as she placed the mat she realized that she has no idea in which direction lies Mecca.

"In my house, yes, I know, because I always lay out the mat for my grandmother. But here . . ."

The vast majority of Muslim youth do not pray; only the elders do.

"It's often the same with young Christians," I add.

We have to go. A truck has come for us from the refugee camp where Azada lives with her family.

We stow our Western clothes in the bottom of our luggage, taking only a single, small bag each.

Nasreen invites us to eat at her house when we return from the camp, a couple of days later. We bid that world farewell.

Cloaked in our new chadors, we go out into the street.

The refugee camp is to the north of Peshawar. It's one of 203 registered camps that have existed in Pakistan since the mid-1980s, when Afghan refugees were the center of the international community's efforts and attention, fleeing from the Soviet invasion. They are far from city centers, and have poor communications with the outside world. They spring up out of nowhere. Now, if someone from the camps wants to travel to the city, as was the case with Azada when she wants to send an e-mail or visit the school in Peshawar, it requires a two-hour trip via bus and foot.

We are spared all these hardships. The camp has a few trucks as well as an ambulance available for community use, as was the custom in earlier times, but if someone needs them for personal use, they must pay for gasoline and the driver's time. For us, the camp has decided to send one of these trucks, as well as a bodyguard: they want to be sure that nothing happens to us. As we've been told, some of the areas through which we'll be traveling are not safe.

We load four things into the rear part of the truck: pajamas, toiletry kits, cameras, and notebooks. We leave the city behind us. We pass through small villages that more closely resemble large markets: one based on fruits and vegetables; then one full of scrap metal and spare car parts. The blackened rubber, grease, and metal contrast sharply with the colorful foodstuffs. As we near the camp, Azada asks that we cover our faces with our chadors every time we pass by one of these shantytowns, for the same reasons as back in Najiba's neighborhood: both for our own security and for that of the camp welcoming us. It's the time of day that people are leaving work, and the road is brimming with buses and trucks.

We turn off the paved road. As we near our destination, the road becomes more of a path, and in places it almost disappears entirely. In one of these stretches, the truck gets hung up in some sand. The earth is quite soft in this region: a great source of raw material for the many Pakistani brick factories that have been springing up around the camps since 1995, taking advantage of the abundant cheap labor.

Our driver and bodyguard gets out of the truck and toils happily away for a good while under the oppressive sun and in the middle of a colossal dust cloud, trying to free the wheels with a plank in a display of strength mixed with a certain good-natured pride in his own gallantry. We smile. All of us. We offer to get out and push, but he won't hear of it. He insists, stubborn and soaked and yet with a convincing smile, that he will get the truck through. But in the end, it's not to be. Defeated though still smiling, we retrace our path and find another way to go.

The camp is walled in, and an armed guard stands watch at the gate. Seeing the weapon in his hands silences us for a moment, jerking us back into reality.

The promenading, expansive desert land on which this and other surrounding camps are built is owned by a Pakistani who charges rent for each plot a house is built on.

In the beginning, when the first refugees arrived, there was nothing here. They spent their first year in the shops meted out by the UNHCR, the United Nations High Commissioner for Refugees. Then, as time went on, the families started building one-story earth homes. I'd never seen such houses. For me, "adobe" was a word, evocative as few are, that made me think of Latin American villages and biblical history. In the future, it will remind me of my Afghan friends' homes.

The idea most Westerners have of refugee camps—rows of tents with the Red Cross or Red Crescent logos on the roof that we've seen countless times on television news reports—has nothing to do with this place. At first glance, we appear to be in a smallish town. But that's not quite it. Provisional and emergency stations have been replaced by simple, austere houses built by hand so that life can proceed with some measure of dignity. The refugee condition of these people who have seen fit to flee their country has not waned with the simple passing of time. The inhabitants of this camp form part of the nearly two million Afghan refugees in Pakistan, who even still continue to arrive, wave after wave. Those who live here, in this camp with the outward appearance of a town, are still refugees: Afghans who will never be completely happy in a country that is not theirs.

When we arrive at Azada's house, one of her grandmothers, her uncle's wife, and a young teenage cousin who has just arrived in Pakistan to pursue his studies are waiting for us. The house has the same general layout as that of Najiba's, and most other Afghan homes, with the one exception of having a larger patio complete with young trees that have been planted with a certain eye to the future. Among them is a small lime tree: Azada's favorite. Outside, facing the iron door that opens onto the street is a promenade complete with a rusty swing set and also full of trees, planted years ago to offer some shade and a bit of green to the camp. High up in the branches are some large, brilliantly black birds with blue-gray necks, relatives of our crows. Inside the house, the bathroom lies to the right, the kitchen off to the left. In the back, the main part of the house takes up the full width of the patio, with a porch extending from one side to the other and three bedrooms off the large living room. Hanging from the walls are a number of sand-colored lizards with black, bulging eyes, scaleless and elusive.

We eat early because we're expecting a visit from a member of the camp council. The only thing we know about this council is that it functions as a sort of internal government for the camp, and has approved our visit here and is responsible for us during our stay here, having provided our escort. From now on, anything we might want to do needs their authorization.

The council member arrives promptly at ten. A tall, well-built man in his forties, ceremonious and attentive, bearing the title bestowed to all Muslims who have fulfilled their hajj. He bows ceremoniously to Azada's grandmother, who not long thereafter retires to her room. Then he introduces himself to the rest of us, and takes a seat on a free pillow. Diligently, Azada's cousin appears with a tray of cups, glasses, sugar, spoons, and two big thermoses full of tea. I'm sitting to Azada's left and to our guest's right; Meme and Sara are across from him, seated on the sofa formed by the pillows propped up against the wall.

He welcomes us to the camp in a deep, serious voice. Azada takes notes on a pad, so that she can better perform her job of interpreter. Like a professional. She's doing an exceptional job: quick, precise, fluid, and indefatigable. For a moment, I picture her at meetings, congresses, and international assemblies, wearing her earpiece and translating. If she'd like, she could choose this profession when the nightmare is over, when every Afghan man and woman is able to return to a normal life, tranquil, in peace, and—above all—in liberty.

The council member, after informing us that he is an engineer, begins his exposition, which has that particularly Afghan quality of being quite well constructed. Azada takes notes. The councilman goes on for a good while before she interrupts respectfully to translate, while he sits cross-legged and in silence. Azada now speaks in English, peeking now and then at her notes so as to not leave anything out. Sara takes out her notebook. I do not, needing to focus all my attention on the English. If I try and take notes at the same time, I'll miss half the information. I'll take notes later, that night or the next morning, as I did yesterday, as I will do every day.

The councilman tells everything about the camp that might be of interest to us, and then consents to our questions.

This camp has existed since 1986. The first thing they built was the wall, to protect them from vermin and possible assaults. The first refugees to take up residence were the families of those who were fighting in Afghanistan, the mujahideen who—to the man—took up arms against the Soviet invasion. They lived in tents. There was no electricity, and of course no school nor health clinic. A bit later, many of the families who make up the present population of the camp came in from Afghanistan, fleeing the fundamentalist *yehadis*. They were an educated, professional, and open-minded group, and this fact gave a particular character to the camp, because the level and percentage of literacy here is much higher than the Afghan population in general. If the general rate of literacy in Afghanistan is one of the lowest on earth, in this camp some 80 percent of the inhabitants have received some sort of education and/or professional training. There are some twelve hundred refugee families here, representing all ethnic groups and all twenty-nine Afghan provinces. The unity that prevails over these ethnic and other differences is something that gives an enormous importance to this camp, making it one of the most notable ones in the area.

In the beginning, before the war against the Soviets ended, it received aid from many different international aid organizations. They collaborated and pooled their resources. The contributions of the people would be the means of operation. A German group financed the school and health clinic, and the people volunteered in the construction of both buildings. The channeling of the entire camp, in which the tents were gradually being replaced by the adobe houses that give it the appearance of the town that it now has, was made possible by a Danish group: the camp population portioned itself off into the five hundred thousand meters of zoning. Ten meters was assigned for each home, and the following day, everything was done. The largely female population (including many widows and orphans) worked throughout the night to finish them as soon as possible. The school also received aid: the teachers' salaries, as well as educational materials, were externally financed. The same held true with the clinic.

The war against the Soviets ended. And the civil war began—the bloody struggle for power between the various Islamic factions.

From then on, the politics of military aid on the part of foreign powers, with the United States at the helm, were dedicated to converting these factions into political parties. Every Islamic party had its seat in Peshawar. And the marketing began: aid, as much military as humanitarian, was proportional to the number of affiliates of each party. Refugee camps were gradually aligned with this or that faction. The refugees who continued to filter in from Peshawar had to decide whether to join up or remain outside the camp walls. Those who did not join received no aid.

It was then that the council, our engineer tells us, gathered the entire camp in the central promenade that doubled as a soccer field. During that memorable assembly, the refugees decided that martial law would no longer exist, that nobody would be denied aid or affiliate themselves with one of the various factions. The camp would be a place of unity, with room and respect for any group.

As the civil war dragged on, the international community gradually lost interest in the Afghan refugees, and humanitarian aid also began to wane. Now, the refugees' situation is at its worst, receiving no aid whatsoever.

"There is only one UNHCR program, existing since 1998, which is working toward repatriation," the councilman continues. Some families from here, perhaps a hundred, availed themselves of it. It offered them a chance to rebuild their bombed-out homes, given that the aid consisted of five thousand rupees, three hundred kilos of flour, a floor mat, and building materials. But they couldn't stay. It's just not possible to live in Afghanistan. There is no security, no work, and no schools for the children."

We ask who makes up the camp council, how it is constituted, and if there are women council members.

He tells us that the council is formed of twelve middle-aged men, elected as representatives of the different population groups. It's nothing new: it has to do with the traditional Afghan social structure. Within each home, each extended family, on a street, a neighborhood, a population, in the provinces . . . these elected members, respected and responsible, have existed. It's the same principle as the *jirga*. Often, the refugee groups arriving at the camp from Afghanistan already have a representative, and these men usually end up forming part of the council. These men are respected by the community for their personal qualities, to whom any member of the community can turn when a problem arises, when they want to present a proposal or start a project that in some way affects the community at large. Each member of the council is responsible for a certain field: a doctor, from the clinic; a teacher, from the school; et cetera.

Here, the engineer goes off on a tangent to thank and praise Azada's organization. The activities that they want to realize and promote among women are also subject to the council's approval.

"The council is also responsible for the security of the camp and its guests."

Just then, I am taken by the same feeling that I had back at Najiba's house and which would arise everywhere I went: I feel protected, I feel safe.

Every man takes his turn guarding the gate day and night, armed with an old Kalashnikov, to protect the camp from the wild animals in the region as well as the highwaymen who roam the countryside. The council convenes once a month, discusses the problems affecting the community, resolves any conflicts among the people, and makes decisions affecting the population. Also, they try and secure financing for the various projects that generate work and jobs: once, they enabled the construction of a factory that sold chalk to Afghan schools, but when the Taliban took over the educational system, the factory began to lose clients and was forced to close. Currently, the council is working on cleaning up a stock pond outside the camp so as to convert it into a fish hatchery. They are also working to construct a chicken farm. But money doesn't grow on trees, or anywhere else for that matter.

"We have people with the knowledge and skills necessary to realize any project, but we lack the funds," he says.

Night and the conversation both continue on. We wonder how they are able to live here, in the middle of the expansive desert. The people work. Some run small grocery stores right there in the camp; others have to work in Peshawar factories; while still others run the school, although since UNHCR withdrew its funding they are forced to charge tuition, which has drastically reduced attendance since many families cannot afford this expense. Back when the school was externally funded, the engineer tells us, it was free to attend, and had more than five hundred students. There were two separate sections being taught—morning and afternoon—so that all could be accommodated. Now there is just one section of scarcely a hundred students (including students from neighboring camps) who are still able to attend.

But the majority of men—and some women and children as well—work in one of the various brick factories that have sprung up like mushrooms around the camps.

The councilman goes on soberly explaining the condition of things. Afghans—we will have innumerable opportunities to see and confirm this, day after day—do not lament nor ask for anything. Not one Afghan tries to inspire pity in anyone, because they do not feel sorry for each other, and feel no greater humiliation than the need to ask for charity. They try to come out ahead. Nobody despairs; nobody weeps. The Afghans I have met are a valiant people with a great dignity and an enormous sense of reality. They do not take advantage of each other, but neither have they resigned themselves or flung themselves to the winds of fate. This people's legendary past, which history defines as fierce, formed by numerous, insurmountable wars, zealous with their culture, traditions, and land, repeats itself in the modern age, not just in war but also in peace, in the dignity of their struggle for survival, in their steadfast resolve to return to and regain Afghanistan, no matter how long it takes, because as the Kabuli proverb so well states, *"Patience is bitter, but how sweet are her fruits!"*

The evening's discussion is at an end.

We pass through the embarrassment of having to answer when he—after responding to everything we have asked him—remarks:

"The international community could end the conflict in Afghanistan and contribute to the solving of her problems. But it doesn't . . . And there, in your country, what do the people say about us? What do they think about the situation in Afghanistan? About the plight of the refugees? What stance do Western governments take?"

We have to tell him the truth, however painful it is for us: in our country, Afghanistan is neither spoken of nor understood. The international community turns a deaf ear to the Afghan cry, silenced by the "practical" interests of the great powers who prepare, ostentatiously, to "recognize the fundamentalist Afghan regime" in the face of ignorant silence and the complicit indifference of the rest.

The councilman is immutable.

But I taste a bitterness in my mouth, not of the patience and its eventual fruits, but that of the powerlessness and shame of an entire world: mine.

The Refugee Camp.

All pain passes, save for that caused by hunger.

We sleep in the largest of the house's bedrooms. There is a great matrimonial bed in the center, which we push off to one side. It's Azada's parents' room, who are currently in Kabul visiting family. We're surprised by the relative ease with which Afghans come and go, entering and leaving their country. The border between Afghanistan and Pakistan—as we will come to see firsthand—is absolutely permeable, and regulation—as it pertains to Afghans—is practically nonexistent.

We eat a quick breakfast after washing ourselves with a pail of water in the small room at the other end of the house, just as we did back in Najiba's home.

Azada has brought out a special cheese. It resembles cottage cheese, but is completely dry and hard. It takes some effort to cut it, and it's full of tiny holes: air bubbles formed during the fermentation process. It has a very sharp flavor, and must be eaten with bread. We have our tea on the road, as we are pressed for time.

Azada's grandmother, a very elderly woman with two very long, fine braids that hang down her back and a pair of thick glasses, reminds her of the need to get going early. That way we could take advantage of the cool, early-morning hours to complete the day's more difficult tasks. It's clearly a good idea, but last night—once the council member had left—we stayed up talking until the two thermoses of tea were empty and our eyes were heavy with fatigue. We were a happy group, stretched out on the rug; the temperature was pleasant and the conversation lively.

Azada had to instruct us on another point of courtesy and good Afghan manners: when you are visiting some place or receiving visitors yourself, you must always keep your legs covered up underneath your skirt. You can still change your position, sitting on your side or on your heels, crossing one leg over the other, or bringing one knee up to your chest while the other rests on the ground, but it is unacceptable—in front of a stranger—to spread your legs or stretch them both out in front of you as we are used to doing in our country when sitting on the floor with our backs propped up against a wall.

She hadn't warned us. She told us later, when the councilman had gone, dying of laughter as she recalled the shock and discomfort of that respectable man who had before him, throughout the discussion, Sara and Meme moving their legs in the most inappropriate manner possible. When you're not used to it, it's difficult to find the right posture: your legs go numb and fall asleep. But each time after that it became more comfortable, and the uncomfortable position ended up being seated in a chair without space to shift your weight or cross your legs.

We feel an instant of embarrassment, but are quickly picked back up by Azada's laughing, as she tells us that "You're foreigners; you're not expected to know our customs. Don't worry."

Azada's cousin gathers up the breakfast leftovers. He's a tall, thin teenager, smiling and attentive. Since we arrived, he hasn't said much, but he diligently completes every task he's entrusted with: prepare the tea, set or clear the table, run out for bread or cheese, go out to run errands or send a message to a relative or neighbor. The same tasks that Najiba's husband's niece handled. This seems to be a general custom: in Afghan families, the youngest member—boy or girl—takes care of such household chores, while the elder family members—especially the grandparents—enjoy a great sense of respect and consideration. On more than one occasion, on our visits to different Afghan homes, we see Azada greet elders with a sense of deference: she won't extend her hand or give her usual three kisses; instead, she bows her head (which the elder will take in his or her hands) and kisses their right hand as a sign of respect.

We gather up our cameras and our chadors and head outside, ready to help HAWCA with the various activities they have begun in the refugee camp.

Our first stop is the house where the women's literacy classes are held. The students are a group whose ages range from fifteen to forty. They are learning to read and write in Dari and Pashtun, the two main languages of Afghanistan. The teacher informs us that it's difficult to find unbiased textbooks; at the moment, they're using one published by a German organization in Peshawar. It's considered one of the best, though it does have some ideological errors: images of human beings are prohibited by the Koran and have been deleted, but it does contain a photo of a woman wearing a *burka*. Is the implication that a woman, imprisoned beneath this *burka*, is no longer a human being?

From here, we move on to a house that doubles as an embroidery shop. The camp's streets form a grid. The ground, the walls, and the roofs (both flat and vaulted, the latter of which provide a bit cooler interior) are all the color of toasted earth. The houses are all distinctly Afghan constructions: a high wall that prevents anyone in the street from seeing inside; behind the wall is a patio where some residents raise a few chickens, a goat, or other such animal; to one side or the other are the rooms that constitute the house itself, while the kitchen and the bathroom are set apart from the rest.

We've gone scarcely a hundred meters down the road when the women from the literacy class come out after us. We're surprised to see two of them wearing *burkas*. As we make our way down the street, we run into other women who look, smiling, at us and gesture for us to take photos with their children who, playing in the street, also find us to be a great attraction.

The owner of the embroidery shop tells us that the organization is trying to find a European market for their crafts. The women working there charge by the finished piece, agreeing on a price ahead of time based on the intricacy and difficulty of the embroidery and the size of the piece. We see many examples of their work hanging up on the walls: shirt, blouse, and dress frontpieces, kerchiefs and cloths, and small rugs and tablecloths. All finished products belong to the organization, which tries to get them out to the market. Money generated by their sale goes to the purchase of more material. The problem is, as always, a lack of funds. There are many women in this and the surrounding camps who want to work for the shop, who come to the organization in search of work, but there just isn't enough money or demand for the products. The crafts that these women create are traditional, the same ones you can admire in their trousseaus, their children's clothing, in their chadors and dresses.

Soon, one of the women from the literacy class comes into the shop, covered in her *burka*. Underneath she reveals herself to be a very young, timid, and withdrawn girl. We ask Azada to ask her why she covers herself if here she might enjoy the freedom of doing without this piece of clothing.

The young woman is seventeen. Orphaned by both her father and mother, she has neither brothers nor sisters. One of her cousins living in a nearby refugee camp has taken her in, for which she is very grateful. She stops short of saying that he requires her to wear the *burka,* but does remark that "He's worried about me, he takes care of me, and he doesn't like that I come and go from home or from the camp to take classes without wearing a *burka.* He'd be very sad."

This is why she wears it: so as not to offend her cousin, who has been so kind to her.

Then the discussion begins. The women who fill the little shop begin

to rant and complain about *burkas*. One of them, an expressive and resolute woman of about thirty dressed all in blue, affirms: "I've never worn
one, and I doubt I will as long as I live."

The others nod.

"I marched here from Afghanistan precisely so that nobody could force
me to wear one," exclaims another.

The sad seventeen-year-old keeps silent, embarrassed, her eyes fixed on
the floor while the avalanche of comments continue.

Another woman intervenes: "Of course, the *burka* is part of our tradition. But it ought to be a voluntary part. We don't want to be forced into
suffering, but if someone wants to wear it, then let them do so."

Another of the women admits to donning a *burka* when she has to
leave the camp.

From the other end of the room, where the open door gives way to the
patio, I see a young woman walking in from the street and look at her in
shock: she looks European enough to be just another Spanish woman. Her
hair is a bright chestnut-brown, her eyes are almost green, and her skin is
very fair. She greets us and sits down alongside another, very different
young woman with great, dark, round eyes, black hair, and brown skin,
Azada takes advantage of the opportunity for another lesson: both are
Nuristanis and represent the two main ethnic groups who inhabit that tiny
corner of Afghanistan known as "Land of Light."

It was the last redoubt of resistance to the invasion of Islam when the
Arabs, near the end of the seventh century, came spreading throughout
Central Asia to impose their new language and religion. Until then, the
people of Afghanistan practiced the ancient religion of Zoroaster, Buddhism, and Hinduism. Islam, much more simple in terms of its rituals and
its social and structural elements, innovative in its time, was adopted with
relative ease, although people preserved certain rites and ancient festivals
such as Navrus—"New Days"—the main Islamic spring festival, which
has endured until this day and which the Taliban has condemned and
banned for not forming part of traditional Muslim culture. The Arabs

knew how to impose the new religion, but could not do the same with their language, and Afghanistan—like Iran and other countries in the region—has conserved both their minor and major indigenous languages like Persian and Pashtun, although their vocabularies would incorporate many names and words of Arabic origins, just as has happened in Spain. Only this tiny corner of Afghanistan resisted the adopting of this new religion, and this is why the Arabs call it Kafiristan, or "Land of Infidels." When they finally managed to convert the population, that name would no longer be appropriate, given that the people there had "seen the light of truth," and from that point on, they dubbed that region Nuristan, "Land of Light."

One of the women, seated on the floor like the others, hems some fabric and finishes a bit of embroidery with a black and gold sewing machine that she has on a tiny stool in front of her. She's a dark-skinned woman, obviously Pashtun, with a wide smile and penetrating gaze. She is widowed, with one daughter. She is not passionate about working in the shop, but it is the only position she found that she can live off of, if barely. She wants her daughter to study instead of working, and therefore sends her to the camp school despite having to pay the tuition. Smiling, she remarks that she is lucky enough to have an old, skinny cow whose milk she turns into cheese that she sells to the other refugees.

We enjoy our time with these chatty, smiling women, but resignedly get up to continue the tour that has been prepared for us. Our next stop is a visit to a rug weaver, who is waiting for us.

In one room of her house, just off to the right of the patio, this woman has an upright loom with a bright, wooden bench in front of it. The whole contraption takes up almost the entire room. Seated on the bench between two of her daughters (neither of which can be more than nine), she weaves one line after another, changing the color of the wool from time to time. In her right hand she holds a tool she uses to separate the strands of the warp, thread the wool through, and then cut it once it's been locked off. With a sort of pick or comb, she brushes the weaving so that the fabric comes out thick. One of the girls then passes coarse, undyed wool from side to side of the weft, so as to reinforce the fabric. They work at an incredible rate. The woman shows us the design that she has sketched out on a piece of graph paper. She counts line after line as she weaves, so she will know when to change the color of the wool to reproduce the intended design exactly. In this phase of the process the ultimate design is indistinguishable; the part thus far woven looks simply like a tangled bunch of threads. Once all the knots are made, the rug will be washed and trimmed, leaving stubs so short that, piece by piece, they form a dense mass. The two girls are seated on the bench to each side of her, also tying knots. The elder of the two is quite skillful, and obviously very proud of her speed. A blond-haired boy of perhaps eleven enters the shop with a baby in his arms.

Azada tells us about this weaver of rugs, who has five or six children and is pregnant with yet another. She is alone and responsible for them all. It's been five months since her husband disappeared. He often goes away for long periods of time. Some members of the camp suspect that he is addicted to drugs. From time to time he'll return, sleep with his wife, and then go off again. Weaving rugs for the organization has given this woman an incentive and means of subsistence. Before, she was so hopeless that she was on the verge of a nervous breakdown. Now, however, she weaves rugs and smiles radiantly. She takes her toddler in her arms, and her smile shows her to be a woman of supreme beauty.

Our guide explains to us that the main problem with weaving rugs is the same one that was mentioned earlier in the embroidery shop: they have to find a way to reach the market, to find reliable buyers. We remain silent.

I'm concerned about the fact that these children are helping their mother with her work. The dexterity with which they work—above all the oldest one—leads me to believe that their skills have been many years in the making. I mention this to Azada: that in the West, there is an enormous stigma against child labor. She is aware of this, but here we are not witnessing the exploitation of children by factories for the mass production of products. Here, children belong to families in which all members must chip in and contribute to sustain family life. The girls help their mother at home, taking care of their siblings or helping with the weaving. The children studying at the school HAWCA operates in Peshawar spend their free time panhandling or building birdcages with the rest of their families in order to survive.

But still I ask myself, where is the line, the limit, beyond the flowery rhetoric that prevails in our comfortable society?

After eating, we go out with Sara in search of some place within the camp where our mobile phone will receive a signal. We want to continue with the interviews that we've already set up from Barcelona: with UNHCR, with RAWA (the revolutionary organization of Afghan women with whom we've kept up a correspondence via e-mail), with Nancy Dupree (about whom all we know is that she is known affectionately as "the Afghans' grandmother"), and with the German-Afghan organization based in Germany but with activities going on in both Afghanistan and Pakistan.

Some children are playing in the street. Afghan men are extremely passionate about soccer, and lament the fact that this passion is waning among their children, who are growing up in exile and tend to favor baseball, the most popular sport in Pakistan. It's true: in the streets of the camp, Afghan children armed with stick bats and balls of knotted rags are playing baseball.

Atop a bit of uneven terrain—a bump in the ground large enough for only a single person to stand on it—we manage to get service. Our UNHCR contact is in Islamabad, but he steered us to a colleague of his in Peshawar even before our visit. Considering our desire to go to Afghanistan, he confirms that we should apply for a visa from the Taliban embassy in Islamabad or the consulate in Peshawar.

We hasten back to Azada's house, more determined than ever to make it to Afghanistan. The first thing we will do upon our return to Peshawar is request visas from the Taliban consulate.

It's late. Before long they'll come to pick us up to go tour the brick factories. The council has approved our departure, but has also assigned an armed guard to accompany us. This guard's function is merely to discourage an attack, since what could a single armed man do against a group of attackers? The council has also placed a pickup truck at our disposal. Azada and Meme sit up front with the driver, for they have asthma and should be exposed to as little of the upcoming dust as possible. Sara and I sit in the bed along with the guard, a cheerful young man who seems to enjoy this diversion from routine camp life. He has incredibly blue eyes and a joking, enchanting smile.

We drive by the factories, which extend without a visible end up and down the road where earlier our van was hung up, spinning its wheels in a cloud of sand.

We see people at work in the vast, expansive, golden brown plains. Not a single tree. The only vertical structures are the tall chimneys of the ovens where they fire the bricks before laying miles of them out under the sun to cure and dry. We see men armed with long spades who pile and divide enormous mounds of mud, some of them covered by plastic tarps to keep them moist. Others hunker down on the ground and fill iron molds resembling racks of glasses in a restaurant, carrying them from place to place. Later we learn that those molds, each holding a full complement of four bricks, weighs seventeen and a half kilos—nearly forty pounds—and must be carried to the end of the long, geometric rows of drying bricks, where they have to be flipped over quickly and smoothly, emptied, the final product smoothed and finished before beginning the process all over again: amass, fill, carry, empty, amass, fill, carry, empty . . . What's more, there are also molds that hold just a single brick, which are used by children or those who otherwise lack the strength to carry four.

The work is paid for on commission: a thousand bricks a day for some 80 to 120 rupees, depending on the efficiency of the particular plant. A young, strong, healthy man might theoretically be able to make that, but in reality, such supremely harsh and draining work causes all sorts of injuries and, often, an entire family will have to work at a factory just to earn enough to eat. As one Afghan proverb says, *"All pain passes, save for that caused by hunger."* The average Afghan family has between seven and ten members. Considering that a kilo of flour costs twenty-five rupees; a kilo of rice, thirty; and a kilo of chicken, eighty, it's easy to calculate that 120 rupees still isn't enough to feed everyone. Plus there is rent, water, and electricity to pay for . . . to say nothing of the occasional visit to the health clinic or of sending the children to school, not only because of the additional cost, but also because each hour spent in school is one not spent making bricks and thus earning money.

With the truck bouncing around on the uneven road, it's not possible to take photos. We ask if it would be possible to stop the truck from time to time. The driver doesn't like the idea of stopping along the side of the road on account of the threat of robbers, but he agrees. So from then on, whenever Sara or I see something we want to photograph, we bang on the cab and the driver hits the brakes. When we're ready to proceed, we rap on the cab again. When the workers realize that they've become photo subjects, they stop working and stand up, posing for the camera. Our cheerful guard realizes that for our photos to have significance, they have to show men working, so every time we stop he calls out to them to keep working. The complicity of our smiling escort, his Kalashnikov between his legs, is a source of laughter and diversion.

Our tour comes to an end. We get out of the truck, and our guard and driver come with us. We don't know where we're going next, but we have the utmost faith in Azada, as always.

As it turns out, we go to visit a family she knows. Azada cautions us that a few days ago, the woman's sixteen-year-old daughter committed suicide. She had been married for barely four months. A thousand and one rumors are circulating as to what could have driven her to such a decision. There are some who say that her husband treated her badly; others who contend it was her mother-in-law who did it, but nobody wants to talk about it. Her mother is still grieving when she receives us. She still hasn't set foot in the home of her in-laws, who are actually more direct relatives as well: the girl, as is a custom in Afghanistan, was married to her cousin. We go to the husband's house, accompanied by the entire family, and they immediately send word to the young woman's mother. She arrives, her hands caked with mud, and proceeds to tell us of daily hardships that still don't seem to explain something as drastic as suicide. Everyone wants to find a reason, an understandable motive. Nobody seems to realize that the conditions required to sustain life are so harsh that they could be enough to justify almost anything. But most of the people here endure things, so why didn't she? Many women in Afghanistan are driven to suicide or madness because they can't endure the brutal changes that came into their lives with the arrival of the Taliban. Others continue to fight clandestinely, despite suffering the same horrors. This particular woman did not resist. Any one of a number of seemingly insignificant things could have been the proverbial straw that broke the camel's back. It seems sad and useless to me to accuse the husband of any wrongdoing, especially considering that he has since returned to Afghanistan to live closer to his wife's resting place like some hero from ancient lore. These refugees—if it is at all possible—always bury their dead in the land from which they come. The young man's mother drives us to the now-empty house where the couple once lived and where the young wife shot herself after cleaning the home and making sure everything was in order, and there she shows us a photograph from the day of the wedding.

A young girl—the husband's sister—can't take her eyes off of us. I would like very much to speak with her, but it won't be possible, because the mothers won't let their youngest children participate. They, however, respond to everything. They vie for the right to speak and express their suffering in the name of everyone. The dead girl and the young sister were the ones who stayed at home, preparing food and keeping up the house, while the rest of the family worked day and night at brick making. As to whether or not the two young women were friends, or as to how this young one feels now that she is home alone . . . these things I will never know.

Next we walk to the area where the workers—some twenty-two families all come from Jalalabad—live in houses provided free of charge by their owners. Some of the families we've spoken with once lived inside the refugee camp, but they weren't able to pay the five hundred rupees a day that renting a house with water and electricity costs. Now they live here, near their workplace, and aren't forced to waste valuable time in the commute.

We meet an entire family at work making bricks: three adults and five children. Between the eight of them, they are able to net three thousand bricks per day. But it's a never-ending process; they work day and night. They get up at 1 A.M. and work until noon, when they are afforded a short lunch break. After that, they work until three in the afternoon. From three to four they take a quick nap, and then go back to work until darkness falls. The father tells us that he owned a farm back in Afghanistan and his children didn't have to work like this, but then the Taliban came and burned everything, forcing them to flee.

We continue on through what, for all practical purposes, is a slave camp. We go to see the giant ovens where the bricks are finally cured, after drying for eight days in the sun. They are carried here on burros or in wheelbarrows. The ovens themselves are quite ingenious, excavated out of the ground with the fire situated above. The workers whose job it is to keep the ovens lit use long tongs to open potlike lids and shovel loads of charcoal inside. The fire flares up and spits out tongues of flame. Next to the ovens, the ground beneath one's sandals is quite literally hot enough to fry an egg. They stay lit day and night, with men taking turns to feed the insatiable dragon's mouth. It's getting dark, but the evening brings not a hint of cool air to this inferno. The heat is unbearable. If it's this bad now, we ask ourselves, what could it be like during the long hours of the day, when temperatures can top a hundred degrees without the help of any ovens? We ask the men how they manage to endure it, and I foolishly hope for some answer based on a household remedy or some ancestral trick. But the men simply keep quiet, shrugging their shoulders. Only one answers: "Allah gives us strength."

We return to the camp in silence. A veil of respectful sadness extinguishes any desire to speak. All words suddenly seem banal.

The drive is long and shrouded in darkness. One thought gives way to another, and as we near the camp, I suddenly realize that I miss men. It's an absurd thought, considering all that we've just seen. But I realize that it's been three days now without meeting with a single man. We've set ourselves up in a world of women, and it's been something extremely gratifying. A new level of intimacy has sprung up between us, a complicity I hadn't known before, something completely different from my relationships with my best friends back home, which possess a different sort of richness, profundity, or quality, something born out of mutual understanding, because it's been forged with the strength of confidence, of shared dreams, problems, and satisfactions. Here, we know precious little about any of these women; nevertheless, a separate, rich, and comfortable world has been created where everyone—origins, pasts, and presents being what they may—moves so naturally and with such confidence that there are no barriers. Perhaps this has happened precisely because no man has played a part in it. But I am surprised at myself with how much I miss the natural ease with which we relate with men in the West, with their ways of doing, speaking, and thinking about things. Also the ways in which they are present in our day-to-day life, in working, traveling, shopping, among friends and family. In Najiba's home, her husband keeps himself distant. The driver does as well. They are attentive, courteous, and their appreciation is sincere, but although they dine with us, sharing both rug and conversation, there is a certain distance—an infinite abyss—between them and us. It's not because we hardly know each other; the barrier is neither linguistic nor cultural. It's because they are men. Because we—whether Western or Afghan—are women. And this is not to imply any pejorative connotation or discriminatory attitude. If, in the West, I've often thought that men come from a different planet, then here in the Middle East they seem to come from an altogether different galaxy. If, in the West, relations between men and women have seemed to me by turns complex, fun, enervating, and always distinct from the relationships that exist between women, then here in the Middle East it seems to me that men and women live in isolated bubbles. Perhaps they are tangential, intersecting at some superficial point of shared space and time, but true life is made deep within the nucleus of our own, airtight compartment. Until now, this hadn't seemed important to me. Great, I thought. We have so many things to talk about with Azada and the other Afghan women . . . Coming from a world as heterogeneous as mine, this seemed perfect—almost a relief—this world free from masculine interference. I had succumbed to an authentic sense of pleasure, with scarcely a flicker of realization about what was happening to them in this absolutely and exclusively feminine universe. But soon I realized that I missed them. It's nothing physical; it's not the idea of machismo that I miss. It's the difference, that particular quality that we so often curse but that now, to me, seems like a blessing.

A surprise is waiting for us back at Azada's house. As we are eating the delicious meal prepared for us by Azada's aunt, her cousin—who up until now has scarcely opened his mouth—breaks out talking in magnificent English. Even Azada is dumbstruck.

Now past the boundaries of embarrassment or whatever it was that kept him silent for the entire time we had thus far spent in his home, the young man speaks effusively, pleasantly, and enthusiastically, sprinkling the conversation with observations and commentaries. Like all good Afghans, he seems unstoppable. He smiles, radiating satisfaction at seeing the effect of his words, and his eyes shine with contentment and that healthy, teenage pride that comes from having left his cousin and her invited foreign guests simply flabbergasted. We tousle his hair, joking with him about his unveiled surprise and admitting our admiration—especially Meme and I, who are hard-pressed to express ourselves in English. Then he tells us how impossible it is to study in Afghanistan. The Taliban are converting all the schools into madras factories or institutes for studying the Koran. Girls' schools closed first, once girls were prohibited from attending. Boys' schools took a bit longer; time dedicated to teaching religion was increased (as were teachers' salaries who promoted this subject) while other disciplines were gradually phased out. English teachers, for example, were driven to seek other work out of the need to support their families.

After dinner we watch a videotaped report on the destruction of Kabul. It reaffirms our dedication to visit that city, and the need to get the necessary visas to do it. We contemplate the images in silence. Both those from before and those from after the civil war, the latter of which don't correspond to the current situation, since the Taliban would then rise to power and reduce the ruins to pure rubble. Historic monuments, emblematic sites, installations, and institutions. Nothing is spared.

It's a chronicle of desolation.

The Refugee Camp.

The world lives on hope.

At first light, the owner of the embroidery shop comes knocking. The women, thanks to our presence in the camp and our visit to the shop the other day, have grown bolder. Rumors that we are potential buyers and represent this or that organization abound, enough so that they are driving up the prices of their goods.

"Nothing's wrong. Don't worry," Azada calms us upon noticing our concern.

The shop owner has explained time and time again to these women just who we are and why we are here. That we have no money, that we haven't come for souvenirs. She has also informed them that they are free to keep on working at the shop, or they may leave.

But our feelings of discomfort persist. The last thing we want to do is to undermine the normal camp life and create expectations we can't satisfy.

We take advantage of the opportunity to talk with Azada and the shop owner about the possibility of finding a market for their products in our country. In Barcelona, we had been advised to recommend smallish things at affordable prices, which could find a niche as inexpensive gifts: bags, glasses cases, coin purses, vanity kits. Nobody would be willing to pay a lot for such things, even though they are made completely by hand. There are also the added problems posed by taxes and the difficulties in finding a middleman who would work in complete accordance with the organization's best interests. We are not trade experts; none of us have the slightest idea of how to start such a business. We talk simply for the sake of talking.

We've seated ourselves on the porch, on a small, hard old wooden bed covered by a coarse rug. Azada's other grandmother arrives to greet us; she is a petite, sparkling woman with brilliant eyes and white hair. She's accompanied by another elderly woman with great, green cat's eyes whose hands and hair are red with henna. They greet us enthusiastically, and Azada's grandmother takes some rectangular objects wrapped in kerchiefs from her purse: framed pictures of her family. The largest one has a small crack in the corner. As she talks, she points out each person appearing in one of the pictures. She pauses after each sentence and motions for Azada to translate. They are her children. Four of them are dead, lost to the war. There's not a family in Afghanistan that hasn't lost someone to the war. Azada has lost seven of her aunts and uncles. Her grandmother smooths out the pieces of cloth, places each photograph face up in the center, and folds it up meticulously yet with firm, rapid movements, full of life. Then she returns them to her purse. I'm taken with the care with which she does this. These few photographs are her treasure, the only things that remains of her children.

During all this, the elderly widow who owns the skinny old cow has arrived and gone into the living room where Azada's other grandmother is waiting. She's brought a beautiful dress she wants to show us. It's made of dark blue velvet and adorned with intricate gold piping: a typical Pashtun festival dress. We admire its beauty and the richness of the workmanship. Then they suggest—insist, amid much laughter—that I try it on. I do, and spark quite the uproar. I'm being fixed up like a doll. Azada's second grandmother removes her white chador. The other one takes some bobby pins out of her red hair. They put the chador on me, securing it so it doesn't slip and trying to straighten it out, which doesn't quite work, so they let it fall down my back and instead try to gather it about my shoulders.

"You're missing your pants!"

"You look like a bride!"

Everyone's having a grand old time of it. I am as well. Meme and Sara are dying of laughter. Azada smooths out my hair while she glows over the dress, explaining to me how every ethnic group has their own manner of dressing, typical and traditional, for things ranging from festivals to daily life. The Hazara are distinguished by the many tiny mirrors sewn into the fabric, and the Baluchs are special as well. The widow and the school-teacher (who has also dropped by) contemplate the scene from their seat next to the first grandmother. They have me go out on the patio to take a photo. When I finally take off the dress, I'm drenched in sweat. One of the women asks if I'd like to buy her festival dress that she's got back at her house. I thank her for her offer and say that the dresses are indeed precious but that I wouldn't be able to make use of it where I live, and it would be too much of a shame to keep it hung up in a closet.

Azada brings the commotion to a close. The camp doctor is waiting for us at the health clinic, and it's getting late. The first guest to say good-bye is the second grandmother, who goes off with her friend, her purse secured with both hands and her gait lively, as if she were a young woman of perhaps twenty.

Then we gather up our chadors and our cameras and head off down the street for what the refugees call "the clinic."

On the way we run into a group of ducks, a goat, and a turkey. The animals range free, as they do at Azada's house where her grandmother's four chickens have the run of the porch and patio, pecking at everything.

We arrive at the clinic, and the doctor is attending to a patient. We wait in the vestibule overlooking a patio. From the street, the only thing to distinguish this building from all the others is the sign hung up on the door.

The appointment is over, and the doctor invites us into his office. He is perhaps fifty years old, with thick, black, curly hair, a neatly trimmed beard, and a rectangular face. Pashtun. He sits down behind his desk while the rest of us take a seat on a narrow wooden bench save for Azada, who sits down on a steel bed marked by rust and chipped white paint. We start the conversation. Azada never refers to the doctor by his name, always by his title: "doctor." The nurse, a tall and corpulent woman, interrupts us. The doctor gets up and invites us to accompany him to the treatment room. A young man has come in, someone who was until just recently fighting at the front, until being injured in the leg. He is no longer an inpatient, but still has to come in once a day to check on the wound's progress.

Meme, who works in a doctor's office in Barcelona, examines the instruments laid out there: glass syringes, suture needles.

"The bare minimum."

We go into the treatment room, which we can barely all fit into. The patient's surprise is obvious. He's a young man, gaunt and emaciated, with markedly dark circles under his eyes. He's seated on a stool. Next to him, up against the wall, is a pair of crutches. Azada informs us that he speaks one of the less-represented languages in Afghanistan, and that he can barely understand Dari or Pashtun. The conversation is confusing. We try to stay out of the way while the doctor examines the wound: a hole the size of a fifty-cent piece and of indeterminate depth. With the aid of a pair of tweezers, the nurse inserts bits of gauze deep into the wound. The doctor informs us that the loss of muscle mass to the extremity, coupled with the difficulty in stitching a ragged wound caused by shrapnel, will at the very least result in much scarring. It's still not clear whether the young man will lose his leg entirely. But this young man of twenty-some years (though he appears twice as old) is more concerned about whether he will be able to support his family. His father is quite old.

We ask permission to take photographs. I'm concerned about invading the privacy of a medical operation. But Sara insists, and is the first to get up close and personal with the wound in order to snap a picture, while Meme is content to take a quick, professional glance and make her diagnosis: "They're lacking in everything here."

Then Sara sits down on a stool, white as a sheet. We realize then that blood, wounds, even the mere verbal description of a disease or surgical procedure unnerves her. But she's a professional: she takes the picture, which won't come out, because a bit later she realizes that her roll of film has been snagged since the first day. When we go over to her to see if she's alright, to see if she needs us to take her outside, she only asks, "Do me the favor of taking some pictures for me."

Which I do, though none of mine will turn out masterfully either. The nurse continues to swab the puncture wound with sterile gauze, while the doctor probes the flesh around the injury. There's nowhere to focus the camera, something which I'm not entirely unhappy about.

We go back out into the doctor's office. He's been here in the camp, running the clinic, for over ten years. Before, when they received aid from various organizations channeled through UNHCR—well, that was another thing. The doctor, the nurses, the pharmacist . . . everyone had a paid position. There was even a pathologist on the payroll. In the laboratory, which today is practically abandoned, many tests and diagnoses were carried out. Now, the clinic simply does what it can. Before, a doctor earned something on the order of four thousand rupees a month, and nurses two thousand. Now they charge patients five rupees a visit, though some can't even afford that. The council has a fund for use in cases involving poverty, and when there is a serious enough situation, the whole camp will take up a collection to cover the patient's hospital visit or pay for a surgical procedure.

At first the doctor tries to speak to us in English, but soon he stops, shaking his head and laughing at himself. He stops, looking to Azada to translate, and the conversation is very pleasant and drawn out. He is the first man to speak with us without the invisible yet palpable barrier separating men from women springing up. He tells us that he got his degree at the medical institute in Jalalabad, where the classes are given in Pashtun. For students who speak Persian, there is—or was, he corrects himself—an institute in Kabul, where classes are conducted in Dari. Speaking of

Afghanistan, the doctor, who seems to enjoy peppering his speech with proverbs and imagery, says, "Be careful when attacking the fox, because you might become a lion."

Azada and I simultaneously ask, "And in this case, who is the fox?"

"The people of Afghanistan," he replies, a bit surprised at having to explain what is for him painfully obvious.

I feel the same pride I would feel if I were an Afghan woman myself. The now clarified metaphor requires no more explanation, but I want to know more, and though I don't want to rub salt in the wound, I can't help but ask, "What's happened to the lion?"

The doctor looks at me. And perhaps this is a figment of my imagination, but at that moment, I feel as if we are speaking the same language.

"The lion is very tired," he says.

We both nod, and fall silent.

Later the conversation moves on to the dual themes of history and literature. He recommends a book on Afghan history written by a Pakistani friend of his. I'm excited to visit this friend, who lives not far from Peshawar. I ask the doctor to write down the author's name and the title of his book in the notebook I carry with me at all times. (Tragically, during our time in Afghanistan, we will have to destroy all our records, and I fear that this information has now been lost.) I ask him, also, why it is that a Pakistani writer wrote a history of Afghanistan, and not an Afghan one. The doctor smiles at me and replies, "My friend is Pashtun."

I smile at myself too. The Pashtun population of Afghanistan occupies the eastern part of the country, but the actual Pashtunistan also encompassed the whole western part of Pakistan, and it ended up divided when the British established the Durand Line to mark the boundaries of their colonies in Asia, the same way that Baluchistan was divided up when Iran drew up its boundaries. The creation of Pakistan therefore ratified these divisions that Afghanistan never actually accepted. Ever since then, Baluchs and Pakistanis alike have periodically staked claim to these territories.

The conversation resists conclusion, and eventually Azada invites the doctor to dinner at her house. We joke that the doctor comes and goes from all homes without anybody worrying about it. The entire camp knows and respects this man, his open and spontaneous character, his passion for conversation. And since he's also a married man, nobody would ever suspect him of any illicitness in treating his patients or in making spontaneous house calls.

The doctor brightens up both the food and the conversation. He tells us of the principal difficulties that arise in the daily practice of medicine here, including a lack of instruments, supplies, and medications, and how things are simply done as best they can be. Gynecology and the related fields is a problem. If there were a specialist in the camp, perhaps things would be different, for as things stand now, most women won't submit to being examined by a male doctor. Other problems stem from the people's superstitions and the competition from the mosques.

Superstition is the greatest problem. Less cultured people continue to believe that diseases are the result of a jinn—a sort of evil spirit or duende—that strikes a person and that cannot be dispelled by any earthly force, least of all by science or medicine. These people prefer to go see a mullah instead of a doctor. The mullah, enveloped in his sacred aura, writes a few prayers from the Koran down on a slip of paper that the affected person will then have to dissolve in water and drink in order to recover. It seems ridiculous, but there are still those people who seek such recourses. For a period of time, the competition between the mullah in the camp and the doctors was fierce. Now, his attitude has softened a bit, to the point where he once allowed his daughter to see the doctor. He was desperate; his child was very sick, and his remedies were proving ineffectual. Fortunately, it was not too late for him to save the child. Even since then, when a person's condition does not improve with the mullah's help, he will then refer them to the doctor. It's a step in the right direction.

After eating, we go out for a walk through the camp. The doctor accompanies us, as does Azada's uncle's wife. We pass through a small door in the wall to the exterior. To our right is the stock tank (the size of a swimming pool) that the council wants to convert into a fish hatchery. We cross a green field where a group of children are playing, near the path leading to the spring that supplies the camp with fresh water. The spring is protected by a wooden structure and around it a group of men is toiling away, including the engineer with whom we spoke on our first night here. We say hello, thank him for his hospitality, and take advantage of the chance to also bid farewell: we will be leaving for Peshawar that same afternoon.

He tells us about the problem that's come up: the pipe for drawing water up out of the spring—a fairly new acquisition—has fallen down into the well, and they're now trying to recover it. If they can't manage to retrieve it, it will be a great loss for all. Not only because of the problems it would create in terms of access to the water (which is a difficult process in any regard) but also because to get yet another one, they would have to take up a collection among the entire camp in order to be able to pay for it.

He tells us all this without exaggeration, with that characteristic Afghan calmness in the face of adversity, halfway between fatalism and the greatness of spirit.

Eventually we pass through a vegetable garden roughly the size of a basketball court. The doctor greets the owner, a gaunt man with gray hair and beard, who proudly guides us among the rows of peppers, tomatoes, potatoes, onions, and zucchinis, among many other vegetables typical of the region but which we've never seen before, even in our supermarkets supposedly offering foods from "every corner of the world." This garden is the private enterprise of this energetic farmer. He cultivates this little plot of land so he can sell his produce around the camp and pay his rent.

We loop back around, and just as we go back through the smallish gate, a group of children chasing after a young calf runs past us like a gust of wind. Near the door, Azada shows us what looks to be a small mound of earth, a sort of elevated platform reachable by a pair of ladders and capped with a thatched roof. It's the communal oven where women bake the day's bread each morning before the sun's heat becomes too oppressive.

I touch the surface, captivated. As with the adobe homes, these ovens with their thousands of years of history hold a great sense of fascination for me. My interest in the quotidian life of ancient towns—unrelated to the great deeds and exploits that make up history—comes from afar, and to find its vestiges, enduring where they do, always amazes me. I feel that this oven is not so different from the ones that women used to bake their daily bread thousands of years ago. But it's almost noon now, and nobody is baking bread. I wish I had known about this ritual in advance, so I could have woken up in time to see it. How right Azada's grandmother was in saying one always has to get up early! Still, though, I must say that I will have the great luck to see my wish fulfilled when we return to the camp, just before departing for the West.

The truck is waiting for us. We gather our things. Azada's other grand-mother is there, for Azada has gone to fix herself up because she wants to take a photo with her grandchildren and us. A photo that in all likelihood will be kept with the others, wrapped up in a handkerchief and tucked away inside her brown cloth bag. We bid them all farewell: her grand-mother, her cousin, her uncle's wife, and the doctor, and then we head off to Peshawar.

On our way, we stop by the airport to see if Meme's lost bag has finally arrived.

"Do you think we'll pass the test, given our clothes and the fact that these people treat us like local women?" Sara asks me as we cross the street. I look at her and am taken with a fit of laughter: her chador is dragging on the ground behind her. No, I think, we're not fooling anybody.

We make our way to the claim office, but it's now after six, and the at-tendant is inflexible: nobody can check the baggage until 9 A.M. tomorrow morning. Meme understands everything: we appeal to the attendant's good nature, we offer him a tip, we threaten to file a complaint. All is in vain. See-ing her so dignified, so Western in her arguments, but dressed as a Pakistani and with the chador framing her face, prompts a smattering of uncontrol-lable laughter from Sara and me.

We go back to Najiba's house and receive a round of hugs and kisses. Najiba tells us that she and her daughter have missed us dearly, that the house has seemed so empty without us. We leave our things on the floor and go out to chat on the porch. Basira sits with us, smiling and expectant, as she peels and slices vegetables. Then they tell us that tomorrow Rustam will arrive from Islamabad.

Rustam is another unsolved mystery, similar to our earlier question about access to the Internet. Until only three weeks ago, we knew nothing about his existence. For three months, our only correspondence was with Azada. But then she told us she had to leave Peshawar for a bit, and wrote: "Don't worry, if you need any sort of information at all, my colleagues will help you with anything."

But we couldn't help but worry. We had thought that she was the only one who spoke English. However much her colleagues wanted to help us, how would we be able to understand each other? And what if she didn't return by the time that we landed in Peshawar? We were on tenterhooks for the better part of two weeks. We wrote e-mails with the distinct sensation that when we hit the SEND button, they would vanish into sidereal space where they would be sucked into some deep, black hole.

And then, a response finally arrived. In impeccable, concise English, dispelling doubts, clarifying points, providing needed information. We were elated. A typographical error and our unawareness of the Afghan names led us to think that it was from a woman who could understand us very well, who got to the point and explained things with crystal clarity. I even remember thinking, "This woman really plays her masculine role well!" It's just that I hadn't read much on the dual masculine and feminine components that each person possesses, or of the necessity to nurture both such that they can enrich and complement each other. And soon, of course, we learned that our interlocutor was a man. I admit that this bothered me at first. Until then, in our correspondence we had maintained the ambience of a female world (as we did in Najiba's home) and I would write liberally, without mincing words, expressions, or thoughts as I wrote to Azada. It bothered me that I had to pick and choose my words now that the person at the other end of the E-mails was a man. An Afghan man whom I did not know. And above all it bothered me because I didn't know what was considered proper there when dealing with a man. For example, how should I sign my notes? "Sincerely"? I remember feeling suddenly alarmed at the realization that I had been sending them with "kisses." But he seemed at ease, and our correspondence continued to be fluid and constant. He provided me with much valuable information and we discussed my proposed book on Afghanistan. He offered his thoughts and insights on traditions and customs. It was a pleasure.

The three of us were intrigued by this man. And now he was about to arrive, and we were finally going to meet.

We joked around nervously.

We had learned to speak a few words in Dari, and I set the scene: "Knock, knock!" *"Ki ast?"* I'll say it's me there behind the door, as is the custom when someone comes knocking. "Rustam," he'll say. And then I'll open the creaky door and greet him with a quick *"Chetor ast, Rustam?"* Just a simple, "What's up, how are you?" Not the long string of questions and answers about health, family, etc., etc., as Afghans usually will do amid friendly kisses and the shaking of hands.

We laugh for a while at the reception that awaits Rustam the following day.

It's dark already. In Pakistan, the night comes quickly.

A bit later, a young man comes by. We're introduced: he is the school's night watchman. After greeting one another, he sits down, away from us, barely on the edge of the rug. Azada and Najiba proceed to tell us how the school began.

The streets of Peshawar are full of Afghan boys and girls. Beggars, children who rummage through the trash in search of boxes, bits of cloth, and scraps of metal . . . From the inception of their activities, for Azada and all the members of HAWCA, the objective was clear: give women and children the tools they need to realize a better and more dignified future.

Work for the women and schools for the children. And so they centered their efforts on the most ignored places, the neighborhoods into which the refugees have been pouring over the past few years, where nobody saw fit to register their arrival or afford them the most basic living conditions, where they have managed to settle together and form small communities, living in shantytowns built out of cloth and plastic recovered from the trash. They started by simply stopping children on the streets and asking them if they wouldn't like to go to school, asking them where they lived and where they were going. Then they spoke with their parents and with the community representatives, who shared their enthusiasm. Everyone was ready to sacrifice the hours of work and the wages that they would be losing in order for their children to go to school. They understood full well the opportunity and the future that the simple ability to read and write could offer their children—the opportunity to become educated young men and women. The next step was to find a place where they could hold the classes. They couldn't even dream of gaining access to a local place. They didn't have a single rupee to their name. They discussed the issue during one of the meetings of the children's parents. And the solution presented itself easily and naturally, the fruit of the simple yet deep-seated generosity and desire for the community's well-being that pervades Afghan society. The grandfather of one of the children offered up his shack as a place to serve as the schoolhouse. The old man knew that it was more important for the children to have a place to meet and learn than it was for him to enjoy the relative comforts that having his own shop offered him. He had already spoken with one of his children, and would be able to move in with his family.

This was barely one year ago.

The teachers worked voluntarily and without pay, and even basic materials were nonexistent until some timely donations from Italy and Spain enabled them to rent a house in the neighborhood. They began with sixty students. After just a few months, the number had risen near 100. Now they total some 150 students, and are sadly forced to turn down the requests of many parents simply because they don't have the means to meet the demand of new students. They need funds to pay for materials and to pay the teachers a salary, since they are refugees too and living in difficult straits themselves.

Najiba's husband returns from work. I notice a fleeting expression of joy flash across Najiba's face on seeing him come in through the door. I'm a bit embarrassed to have noticed this look, because in front of us (and, I suppose, in front of anyone), there are no displays of effusion or contact between men or women, even husbands and wives. He greets us, happy to see us there. He greets the watchman, who seems relieved by his presence. The two men move the TV out onto the porch to watch the evening news, while Najiba disappears into the kitchen, which we still have yet to see.

Meanwhile, Azada tells us about the watchman. First of all, she tells us why he is needed: in Peshawar, a closed door is seen as an invitation to the roving bands of robbers. They recruited the young man when they rented the building to guard against someone breaking in to their makeshift school. There isn't much to take from there, but still . . . They looked for a confident man, and found one in him. He had been working in a brick factory up until eight months ago, when he suffered a back injury that also affected his right leg. He was twenty-five years old, and already had a large family to take care of: his wife and three children, his elderly father, and his brother's widow and her own two small children. It was up to him and his eighteen-year-old brother to work and carry the family forward. Azada tells us with pride how he recently asked for permission to use one of the classrooms at night, so that he could organize a literacy course that young men could attend when they returned from work in the evening. He offered to teach it himself, and the school board had no objections.

After dinner, when tea is served, the ambience seems more distended. The watchman dared to look in on us once in a while, and even smiled once. We wonder, sincerely interested, about these men. Later that night, when we are alone, we ask Azada. Surrounded by a group of women engaged in animated conversation, men seem quite timid, afraid to disturb the atmosphere. But no, this can't be it . . . It's something more profound, the sensation of belonging to distinct worlds, and not because we are foreigners. It's because we're women. Perhaps the ancient, traditional purdah—the physical and palpable separation between men and women—has left its imprint on this invisible wall that seems almost insurmountable in terms of the relationships between men and women who work together, who have the same objectives, who respect each other, talk and even joke with each other, but dare not to cross this subtle barrier that has interposed itself between the genders like a crystal. With Azada, men do not show this timidity. For example, the camp doctor showed nothing of the sort in his dealings with women.

"Well, it's because the doctor is a very special person."

We talk about what we've done the past few days that we were away; Najiba's husband smiles as we explain how the formal, solemn council member was shocked by our ignorance and lack of composure. How gratifying it was to bring a smile to this man's lips; this man who is so affable and affectionate and yet still so profoundly sad! Najiba sheds quiet tears of laughter while her baby lies, sleeping, on the rug at her side.

The watchman interjects politely and asks our permission to stretch out his injured leg. We look at each other: this is customary behavior.

The laughter and relaxed conversation gives way to more serious themes, and Najiba's husband chimes in.

He tells us of children, of the new generation of Afghans who are growing apathetic, who give in to a passive resignation, losing interest in the country's future because they no longer believe it possible that one day peace will come to Afghanistan. Nor do they believe in freedom. The problem is that Pakistan is not interested in Afghan peace; on the contrary, it is in Pakistan's interest that the war continues so it can test its weapons on the field of battle and thus train its soldiers for the conflict over Kashmir. No—Pakistan is absolutely not interested in a strong, free, and democratic Afghanistan that could potentially reclaim Pashtunistan, for without Pashtunistan and Kashmir, Pakistan would be left without a thing.

Azada translates.

Everything in Afghanistan has collapsed, from the economy to social life. There is just a single flower that—when it blooms each spring—turns the country into an enormous scarlet rug: it is the opium flower, which the Taliban trafficks. Anyone visiting Peshawar can see with their own eyes the containers full of Afghan opiates seized by Pakistani police. It is in Pakistani laboratories located along the border that these opiates are then distilled into raw heroin. From Peshawar, it is shipped to the port city of Karachi and eventually to Europe.

This young man, who was a student when the Soviet troops invaded, suspected (as do many other people) that the purported, charismatic leader of the Taliban, Mullah Omar, did not even exist; that he was an invention.

"Nobody has ever seen him, he never gives interviews, never appears in the various media . . ."

Najiba picks up the conversation, and transforms herself in the process: the sweet, calm woman who we've come to know now metamorphoses into a woman who speaks passionately, with a firmness and conviction that we find striking. She speaks concisely, and knows exactly what she wants to say.

"While the war against the Soviets was going on, there was an avalanche of journalists who permeated the country, covering the events and reporting on everything that happened. Then, the entire world closed its doors to Afghanistan. Now, many have lost hope. Before the arrival of the Taliban, I would never have thought it possible that people would be stoned to death or have their hands and feet cut off in soccer stadiums. We are living in nightmarish times. But we cannot stop. We must continue on until we have achieved democracy for Afghanistan. Now, perhaps, all we can do is educate those around us, and to convince others who are able to teach those around them as well. This we can do. Certainly, life here is difficult, but we press on, for we are dedicated to achieving our goals, and our determination is unwavering."

We fall silent, a bit unsettled. I think about her name, Najiba, which means "upstanding" or "noble."

"The world lives on hope," says a certain Afghan proverb.

Afghanistan lives on hope.

And Najiba is that hope.

THURSDAY, AUGUST 3, 2000.

Peshawar.

A river is made drop by drop.

Rustam arrives as we are eating breakfast. He is a thin young man, dressed as if Western. I give up trying to limit the number of greetings. The car comes to pick us up for the day's journey. The first thing to do (after, of course, retrieving Meme's suitcase from the airport) is obtain visas from the Taliban consulate so we can travel to Afghanistan. The five of us pile into the car: the four women in the back and Rustam up front, next to the driver. Shutting the door after packing the backseat with our bodies, long clothes, chadors, bags, and bottles of water takes a minor miracle. We're like sardines in a can. To the constant Peshawar heat, we add the internal heat of our tightly pressed bodies. We roll down the windows, secure our chadors so as to cover our faces, and we are ready to leave.

To Meme's relief, we pick up the missing suitcase at the airport without any further complications. We stow it in the trunk, and continue on toward the day's main objective.

The Taliban consulate is located in one of the city's residential zones. Wide, peaceful streets. The driver has to stop and ask directions twice, but we finally arrive and park on a little side street. We get out of the car, panting heavily and ready to stretch our legs. We gather ourselves a bit before going in, so as to make as good an impression as possible. The guard at the door directs us to an office down to the right. Our driver goes with us. There, a half dozen or so people have formed a line in the hallway, and we sit down on a bench to await our turn. The driver goes up to the window to inquire, then comes back for us and we all file into the office. We are met by a civil servant who speaks a bit of English. Seated behind a desk is a Taliban official, whose fierce, clear eyes fill me with a sudden chill. He is a young, supremely handsome man dressed impeccably in his uniform and turban, and he sports a long, thick, black beard and dark lines underneath his eyes. If the old Afghan legends and superstitions that talk about genies, devils, and other malignant spirits were true, this Taliban official would be a prime example. Only his eyes could betray him.

"Don't look at him," Meme cautions.

We're asked to fill out a questionnaire. Name, address, nationality, profession . . . purpose of trip: tourism; cities the visa is requested for: Kabul; place of residence while there. We vaguely know of a hotel in Kabul, and put its name down. Later we find out that we got it wrong; that instead of "Hotel Intercontinental," we wrote "Hotel International." Lastly, at the bottom of the form, we have to list our traveling companions: a driver and an interpreter.

We return the forms, and again have to wait. The guard frisks certain men coming in. Others he greets with a handshake, hug, or kiss. After a bit, the civil servant directs us to another room. Our driver waits in the hallway while we cross the patio toward the main building. Once there, we are ushered into a carpeted office complete with upholstered chairs and a broad, dark, wooden office desk. Sitting behind this desk is a Taliban official dressed in sky-blue clothes and a white turban. He has our applications in front of him, and invites us to sit down. He speaks a singsong English, and converses with us as he looks over the forms. Upon seeing I've listed my profession as "translator," he asks me what languages I work with.

"From the German," I say.

Sara explains our situation to him: we're on vacation, and we've come to spend the next three weeks in Pakistan so as to get to know the country. And since we're such tireless travelers, and since we're so close by, we wanted to take advantage of the opportunity to see Kabul.

How long do we want to spend in the city?

Not long, perhaps three days, just an excursion.

Where are you staying in Peshawar?

We give the name of the only hotel we know in the city. He glances back at our applications. Spain. He asks us something about the monuments there.

The Alhambra de Granada, the Mezquita de Córdoba, the Giralda de Sevilla.

I, concerned that we will appear to be ingratiating ourselves to him by mentioning only examples of Spain's Islamic past, list some other typically Spanish items: the running of the bulls, the Fallas de Valencia . . . Sara translates for me with a look of amazement on her face.

The Taliban official writes a few indecipherable lines down on one of the forms and bids us good day. As we exit, Sara turns to me and says, "Are you crazy? 'The Fallas de Valencia . . .'?"

"Didn't he ask about festivals and monuments characteristic of Spain?"

"Islamic ones, girl, Islamic ones! 'The Fallas de Valencia' indeed!"

Somehow this had escaped me. It sparks in us yet another uncontrollable fit of laughter.

"We shouldn't be joking around like this; they're going to think we're laughing at them," Meme cautions. She's right. We compose ourselves and return to the office with our forms in hand. What could this scribbled writing mean?

The older man sends Sara over to another building to stamp the applications. She goes alone, save for our driver who accompanies her. We are told that they will review the information and that we should return in a week, at which point we'll be told whether our visas have been granted. A week! We exit the office in a dignified and serious manner, and even when we meet with Azada and Rustam in the car we can't give free rein to our hilarity. Sara tells them about my blunder:

"And when the consul—"

"That was the consul?"

"It's true, you didn't learn anything there. But yes, he was the consul."

I am dumbstruck. I had been speaking with the consul himself without even realizing it. Looking back, it all makes sense: the luxurious office, his elegant dress, his manners . . . But the thought that we might be in the consul's office had never crossed my mind. My thoughts had strayed down other paths. Seeing Meme and Sara in their Pakistani clothing and chadors, chatting politely away with the Taliban in the white turban, sitting on those couches as if they were thrones . . . I felt like a film protagonist or the heroine of some mystery novel: three English governesses on a journey through the East. And I had completely forgotten the essential. The real.

"They're not going to grant us the visas," Meme says. "Let's be realistic."

"Of course they're going to grant us them. A week from now we'll be on our way."

"I don't think so. But if you all are right, I'm taking you out to a nice dinner."

From here, we go to the market—one of the big Peshawar bazaars—where Afghan women and children come to panhandle. We've only just stopped when a woman covered in a dirty *burka,* dark green and striped, comes up to the window. Only her hands are visible under the fabric. They are the hands of a middle-aged woman. With a gesture, she removes the other strip of cloth that covers her face to be able to see better through the thick gauze veil. Azada strikes up a conversation with her. She speaks to her with respect, calls her "mother," or *"maadar,"* and surprises us yet again with her ability to ask people questions, to relate with whoever approaches her and strike up conversations, to connect and immerse herself in their lives, their difficulties, their circumstances. She offers them nothing—she can't—save for respect, time, and the counsel of listening to their troubles.

Already along the bazaar's colonnades and alleyways, we are approached by another woman begging, suppressing her shame beneath a yellow *burka*. Another woman in a darker *burka* joins the group. Their stories and those of thousands of women like her form a mosaic of uniform color and pattern: Afghan women, widowed, alone, with families to care for, with sick parents or children, with hunger their only *muhrram*—their faithful companion—with a dignified, even happy past, with no other future than the uncertainty of being able to live another day or not. *"A river is made drop by drop."* And although the proverb refers to the tiny grain of sand that each one of us can bear, I can't help but think also that, drop by drop and life by life, the river grows into a sea salty with pain. But what help could crying be to these women? These beggar women, obscured beneath their *burkas,* talk only of what lies within the comprehension of transients: hunger, sick children, husbands who disappeared during a bombardment or were killed during a raid or while on the front. They don't talk about their solitude or their powerlessness as single Afghan women. Because for a moderately young Afghan woman (their hands give them away) out begging in the streets, the situation must be desperate. The extended Afghan families take in their widows, their orphans, their sick . . . they keep watch over each other. Young women don't go out among the Afghan refugees to ask for charity; it's the elderly and the children who do so. When a young woman has to resort to the compassion of whoever might be passing down the street, it's because she has hit rock bottom: she is on her own and in charge of caring for those who depend on her. Who depend on the shameful act of begging. Nobody speaks of this solitude. Nor of fear. But they do speak of the shame.

Today we do give out alms, as Azada indicates.

We continue on through the bazaar's narrow streets. Children mob the car, trying to sell us pens, lighters, and other sundry items. In the windows of a tailor's shop, several festive Afghan, Pashtun, Uzbeki, and Baluch dresses are hung up for display. Sara interviews a boy who watches over the crowd from behind one of the shop windows. He's also Afghan; the store belongs to his father. Then he turns back to help his uncle, who has also fled here from the Taliban terror.

While stopped at an intersection, a tall and thin man approaches us. His cheekbones jut out above hollow, sunken cheeks covered by his beard. Dark, curly hair pokes out from beneath his small, round, simple cap. Slung over his shoulder is the traditional large kerchief that Afghan men use either as a turban or as a bundle for carrying things. He wants to sell us a pair of small statues he carries in his hands: two metallic birds, their wings spread above a wooden foot. He says they're silver, from the museum in Kabul, and that he paid a woman who works there to steal them for him. Then, after throwing a suspicious glance over his shoulder, he produces two daggers in finely wrought sheathes from within the folds of his clothing. He assures us that these are all authentic pieces, predating the reign of King Zahir, and that he's come to Peshawar just to sell them. As soon as he is done here, he'll return to Afghanistan where his wife and children are waiting for him. He asks for six hundred rupees for each dagger. They're worth much more, he says, but he only needs six hundred. And then, without waiting for an answer, he tells us about his asthma, and about the fig trees that cause it.

No, we're not looking to buy anything. Thank you. *Tashakor.*

We continue on. Rustam doubts that the pieces were authentic. Nevertheless, it saddens us to see the legacy of an entire people reduced to selling trinkets on the streets of this or that market. Maybe these particular pieces weren't in fact authentic, but this is how countless real artifacts and treasures have disappeared, one by one, from the museum in Kabul, where years ago visitors could go to see priceless works of art, now lost and irreplaceable.

Rustam invites us to dine with him at the Kabul, an Afghan restaurant located on one of Peshawar's main avenues. Azada bubbles with childlike excitement at the idea. The driver parks our car out front. We wash our hands before going in, and Azada takes a small cotton towel out of her bag for us to dry with. Back in the market we'd seen vendors roaming the streets, laden with veritable multicolored mountains of such towels. I take note of the practicality of always carrying a towel with you in your purse, to have in case of need. Inside, the dining room is empty; we are the only customers. In the back of the room is a raised dais with four seats upholstered in red velvet, making them seem almost like thrones.

"They're for hosting weddings here," our Afghan friends inform us. "The traditional thing is to hold the reception at home, but if there are a lot of invited guests or the home isn't big enough, these days more and more people opt to hold the ceremony at a restaurant such as this."

In traditional Afghan society, marriage continues to be arranged by the two families, especially in rural areas, though this old custom is gradually being abandoned in big cities and by educated families who respect young adults' freedom of choice. Marriages of love are becoming more and more common.

The eldest women of the family—mothers, aunts, and grandmothers—are the ones who discuss the different options in the beginning. In some cases, weddings can take place between members of the same family (who have known each other since early infancy) or potential spouses can be chosen from a wider circle of friends. The women then agree on a list of who might make a good pair, based on personality, interests, and affinities, and then propose their choice to the rest of the family, including any possible future spouses. If everyone is in agreement—including the young potentials—the families will celebrate the first official step on the road to marriage, called the *Jasgari,* which is something akin to what we might call "the asking of the hand": the elders of the young man's family approach the elders of the young lady's family with the proposition. In this first encounter, the response is always "no," but the door is left open for a second and perhaps a third petition. If the potential bride's family does not know the suitor or his family well, they may perform their own investigations. If they don't like what they find out, they will reject the proposal once again and definitively, but if they are pleased with the idea, then they will send the petitioning family a gift of candies or chocolates wrapped up in a kerchief. This is called the *Sharin-e-Dadan;* literally "the giving of sweets."

The next step is for the groom's family to begin preparations for the *Sharin-e-Joree,* the aforementioned engagement ceremony, which is held in the bride-to-be's house, although the costs of the event are borne by the groom's family. Today, a couple will exchange rings and seal their vows by giving each other a spoonful of some sweet liquid while the women and children sing and dance to the rhythm of the Afghan *daria,* a musical instrument similar to the tambourine. During the ceremony, the couple receives gifts—including the *jaiz* or dowry—which are displayed for all the guests to admire. The couple's closest friends and family will receive certain gifts as well. Then, a grand variety of dishes are served (always including the *qabalee palau*—savory spiced rice) as in any celebration. Finally, the bride's family will present the groom's family with a large, ornately decorated basket of candies.

During the next year that leads up to the actual wedding itself, the two families will continue to exchange gifts, especially on major holidays. The couple—if they are progressive in the sense of belonging to urban or educated families—can see each other and go out together whenever they please, but in the more conservative rural situations, this is not allowed, and the couple cannot even see each other until the day of the wedding.

The actual marriage ceremony—called an *Aroosee*—is very similar to the engagement ceremony, save for the fact that the number of invited guests is much greater, and the singing and dancing continue on without interruption.

The night before the wedding, the bride and groom each hold a small celebration in his or her home. There, the female friends and family of the bride decorate her hands and feet with henna, and the groom's male friends and family do the same for him. In both cases, the decoration is accompanied by much singing, dancing, and merrymaking.

The *Aroosee* itself begins in two separate places: the bride's house and the groom's. After the respective guests have arrived at each home, the singing and dancing begins. Here, even young children will often participate, with even boys and girls dancing together, something usually frowned upon in society. Guests will toss coins at the dancers, which the children will rush to catch or scoop up off the floor. Eventually, the formal ceremony will take place, at the bride's house. The couple, professionally made up and decked out, waits in separate rooms. The bride selects one of her aunts, uncles, grandparents, or in-laws to give the definitive "yes" answer. An elderly mullah recites the *Nekah* (the passages from the Koran pertaining to marriage) and asks the couple if they take each other as husband and wife. The groom answers for himself, while the bride answers through her chosen representative. After this brief ceremony, the bride and groom are presented to each other and—still in the bride's house—the two of them sit together while a representative of the bride's family presents them with the dowry that the two families have provided for their new marriage. The ceremony concludes when the groom's parents escort the couple out into the street while singing the popular song *"Ahista Biro,"* where a decorated car is waiting to take them to their new home, in the groom's parents' house. Once there, the festival continues on into the late hours of the night, and doesn't conclude until the newlyweds finally retire to their room, which has been completely remodeled and decorated, to consummate their marriage and begin their new life together.

One week after the wedding, the *Tajt Jamee* is celebrated at the groom's house—a banquet attended by the closest family members of the new couple. The first time the couple will "go out," so to speak, will be to visit the bride's parents. After that, the bride can visit her family at any time, and her friends and family can invite her over to dine at any time.

Rustam has ordered for us, and we have the distinct feeling of being at one of these nuptial banquets when the waiter starts bringing out plate after plate of food: seasoned rice, grilled chicken, bits of lamb on skewers, salads, bowls of yogurt and custard, and bottles of mineral water and Coca-Cola. Afghans wine and dine their guests with enormous amounts of food, insisting on second and third helpings, refilling plates without taking "no" for an answer. The polite thing to do is for the guest to accept the generous helpings, so as to properly honor the banquet. But we can't physically eat it all, and it seems a shame to leave so much food heaped upon the platters. I suggest that we at least take some of this delicious mountain of rice (which, for all our efforts, we have scarcely made even a dent in) with us, but the restaurant has no carry-out containers, and we have to leave with our hearts heavy at the waste of so much good food.

We have an appointment.

We've managed to secure an interview with a representative of RAWA, the organization that, besides providing humanitarian aid in Afghanistan and to Afghan refugees living in Pakistan, also engages in political activities aimed at denouncing the situation of Afghan women. We've arranged to meet in the lobby of one of Peshawar's many hotels, for reasons of security. While we wait, we sip cups of coffee: a glorious indulgence after so many days of abstinence. In Pakistan, coffee is something of a luxury, and served only in hotels that cater specifically to tourists. Nevertheless, the waiter is hesitant to bring us some. Rustam intervenes with an authoritative gesture: is it because we are women? Is it because my English is so bad that you can't even understand me when I order a cup of coffee?

Finally our liaison appears: a very young woman, elegant and beautiful, accompanied by a tall, elderly man. It is her *muhrram*—her guardian, and very nearly a true bodyguard—a vital figure when considering the persecution these women are subject to, both by the Taliban and by other fundamentalist groups, even here in Pakistan where Taliban members move about freely. The young woman paints the picture for us:

RAWA was formed in 1977 by a group of educated Afghan women in order to defend the rights of women in their country. During the war against the Soviet invasion, the Afghan Islamic fundamentalist parties received help and support from Iran, Pakistan, the United States, and France. When these parties took Kabul in 1992, there began—especially for women—one of the worst periods in Afghanistan's history. And it has yet to end. The women of RAWA published reports and organized conferences all over the world, including Pakistan, where the authorities often tried to break them up by means of force.

She goes on to explain her organization's objectives, and gives us a brief description of the actual situation.

Regarding the future of Afghanistan, only a democratic government can be considered acceptable, with the stipulation that each and every fundamentalist party that receives support from Pakistan and/or Iran be excluded from participation. They are conscious of the fact that at this time it would be simply impossible to hold elections in Afghanistan, even if the United Nations (which is currently doing nothing for the country) were to intervene with peacekeeping forces. First, hope and confidence must be returned to the population.

She insists that their objectives are not those of a privileged few: the remnants of the country's intellectuals or the small group of women who have had access to education. Her organization is defending the rights of all Afghans, because everyone wants the same basic things: every woman who requires medical attention must have access to a doctor, whether she can read or not; any woman may reject traditions that threaten her basic human rights; any woman can speak out against restrictions and impositions that curtail her freedom . . . For these things, the meaning of words like "democracy" and documents such as the Universal Declaration of Human Rights are not lost on RAWA members. Other Afghan women may not know of such things—may not know how to put words to these ideals—but they all know full well what it is that they want.

This woman, who has put her very life in jeopardy for the simple reason that she belongs to an organization clamoring for democracy for her country, continues: "In Afghanistan, the most pressing thing is to disarm the parties in power; not just the Taliban, but also the fundamentalist forces in the north, the troops that control Massud and who are supported by France, who happens to have interests in the region." She insists that, for this to happen, an intervention by U.N. peacekeepers will be necessary. The U.N. must take a position and act, swiftly and decisively.

We tell her about our desire to help denounce what is currently taking place in Afghanistan. One of our journey's primary objectives is to get to know the country's reality through its own people, through their eyes and their organizations. We set up another meeting with her for a few days later.

Upon arriving back at the house, after paying the driver and bidding him farewell, we inform Najiba (who has been looking quite tired lately) of the decision we made in the car on the way there: tonight we will make dinner. We even have the menu all planned out: chicken with garlic and potato tortillas. This prompts a mild commotion: we are the guests! But we settle it all by saying that we've been made to feel like family, and thus should have our turn to cook. We give Najiba a smiling order: go out on the porch and relax. We draw up the shopping list and send Rustam out to the market. He complies happily, if a bit surprised at the amount of oil, potatoes, and onions that we'll need. We tell him not to worry; if something is left over, we'll simply use it one of the following days. We also ask him to pick out a ripe Afghan melon for our dessert.

Not one of the innumerable books I've read on Afghanistan has failed to make reference to Afghan melons. We've seen them piled high on fruit vendors' stands throughout the city, enormous and golden. Now is the time to finally try one.

Finally, we have gained control of the kitchen. It's a square, suffocating room with a counter, a stone basin, a drain set in the floor, and a large drum full of water and with a spigot at the bottom. Hanging on the wall is a plastic dish drainer piled high with clean plates, glasses, and lids. On the cement floor is a small camping stove with a single burner that will have to be used for everything. Among the sparse furnishings, we find a pot and a frying pan missing its handle, and we set ourselves to work.

We sit down out on the porch with Najiba, Azada, and Rustam to peel and slice the potatoes and onions. Azada soaks the onions in a pot of water so they can be more easily peeled. There are only two knives, and neither is very sharp. Luckily, we asked Rustam to buy precut chicken.

Meme is the tortilla expert. Sara is in charge of the chicken with garlic, which she promises will leave us licking our fingers. I'm left with the role of kitchen assistant.

I heat up the oil in a large pot so it will be ready to fry the potatoes. Here in Pakistan, the oil is a quasi-solid greaselike substance that comes in two-liter cans. It has to be scooped out with spoons like shortening, but once it is heated, it takes on the smell and consistency of sunflower seed oil, and it cooks the potatoes, onions, and chicken perfectly. We work, hunkering down on the ground next to the stove, handling the pots and pans with cloths to keep from burning our hands or dropping them on the floor, draining the fried potatoes and setting them aside. We have to wash the pans after each batch so that we can use them over and over again, scrubbing them under the spigot with soap and water and a small plastic bag as a scouring pad. The dirty, soapy water runs over the floor and down into the drain. Flipping the tortillas is the trickiest part of the whole operation, but Meme is a true expert and none of her creations come out either burnt or broken.

Azada dips in from time to time to lend a hand. We're sweating like convicts in the close, stuffy kitchen and under our long clothing, and take turns stepping out onto the patio for a breath of fresh air.

Dinner is a huge success. The tortillas are moist, and the chicken is browned to perfection. Afterward, our hosts insist on doing the dishes for us. We don't want to press our case any further, and concede.

Smiling, Najiba's husband slices the melon while telling us that he could arrange for us a visit to Peshawar's largest refugee camp, the one folks here call "Camp Kabul," since almost all of its inhabitants come from that city. We thank him kindly as we dive into the tray of melon slices that he's put together. The flesh is firm, pale and dry, and extremely delicious. The books I've read weren't lying.

We chat about Afghan humanitarian organizations, the work they're doing, their financing (or rather, their lack thereof), the help they receive from Europe, and the sense of ignorance the rest of the world seems mired in.

Later that evening, on the porch and under the light of the Peshawar moon, Rustam gives us a brief summary of Afghanistan's recent history. I listen carefully to the story this man weaves out of today's reality that—like so much of yesterday's—with roots in a very recent past, determines and forms something that, at first glance, seems like a grand imbroglio.

We're surprised by the cry of a mullah in a nearby mosque calling followers to the next morning's prayer. It's still dark out, but if the mullah continues to call out, it's because there has appeared on the horizon the first clear light that heralds the start of a new day.

As Rustam moves through his story, I recall the months of study in which I tried to formulate a manageable outline of Afghan history, and the pieces of the puzzle finally begin to fall into place, finally start to form a picture I can grasp. The intellectual pleasure of understanding that I have right now is comparable to the pleasure of finally getting to taste the legendary Afghan melon.

I realize with a heightened sensitivity, my nerves on fire, that he is making reality a dream. A dream that does not deceive, but rather lives with all the powers of the spirit and the energetic body working at full tilt.

FRIDAY, AUGUST 4, 2000.

Peshawar.

Who will admit that their own milk has spoiled?

I wake up early. Very early. So early, in fact, that it's still relatively cool outside, and everyone else in the house is still asleep. Dawn's light floods the patio. I try to reconcile the dream once more, but I know I won't be able to. Despite having slept for only a few hours I feel rested, my mind clear and alert. I get out of bed carefully so as not to disturb anybody. I bathe and dress myself. I retrieve my particular ashtray from the kitchen and sit down on the patio steps to smoke a cigarette and enjoy this rare moment of silence and solitude. To think about everything and nothing. Because for all the enjoyment I take in living here—communally—I don't think that I could do without some personal time for any extended period. Bit by bit, the house comes to life. Najiba's baby whimpers.

Today will be an intense day. Our agenda is full of interesting appointments. They've been so easy to set up. In Barcelona, in the midst of a flurry of e-mail replies from the various contacts that we'd been establishing, we got a bit concerned: they all had something in common, an offer of "we'd be delighted for you to stay with us. Call us when you get to Pakistan." Our Western minds couldn't see any possible way to incorporate all such requests. We would be there for exactly three weeks . . . why not set up dates and times beforehand, and thus arrive in Pakistan with some sort of plan, a moderately organized calendar of our time in each city? But this idea never took shape: "Call us when you get there" was the only plan we had. We thought that we wouldn't be able to see anybody, but we were wrong. Meeting up with our contacts—even those who were far busier than we—proved simpler than we could have imagined. We would call, and set up a meeting for the following day. Two days later, at the most.

Our first interview is with Nancy Dupree, an American woman who has lived in Afghanistan for over thirty years and has authored many published works. Her husband is an archaeologist and historian who contributed much to the splendor that is the Kabul Museum. Actually, this elderly woman, after seeing the need to abandon Afghanistan, remained in Peshawar and dedicated her efforts to recovering the country's artistic and historical legacy. Plus, the center that she serves as director is in charge of coordinating several aid organizations that work for Afghanistan and with many Afghan refugees in the region. She meets us in a room stacked thick with books and periodicals. We explain the reason for our visit and introduce Azada, who tells her about the activities in which HAWCA is engaged, and the difficulties that the Pakistani government poses for the legal establishment of any type of aid organization.

The woman nods. She knows the problem full well. Pakistan hasn't approved the registration of a single organization in the past five years. Many functioning groups are even being closed down. In the next six months, another thirty are expected to close for any number of reasons: some, despite receiving money, have become ineffectual; others because they were discovered to be fronts for terrorist organizations. Add to that the fact that terrorism is one of the major problems plaguing Pakistan and Afghanistan. The idea of the Pakistani government isn't bad: in theory it attempts to expose the mountain of purportedly "humanitarian" organizations that actually perform no real functions, but this creates a prejudice against those that are serving a purpose. Those that aren't properly registered encounter serious difficulties with fund-raising and other activities, and operate under the constant threat of being shut down by the police.

"Pakistani bureaucracy is very British," the woman remarks, smiling. "The only recourse available to Afghan organizations that really are working (and working hard, believe you me) is to get legal documentation."

Azada and Rustam are heartened to hear about this recourse apparently available to the school and other activities pertaining to the refugee camp: going to the Pakistani government's High Council for Refugees. Nancy suggests their first step be to open an office in the city, as there is a high degree of suspicion among the authorities toward organizations with no physical base of operations. They should also be prepared to provide reports, statutes, etc. . . . anything to use bureaucracy to their advantage.

"I've lived in Afghanistan for quite some time, and I know that your people are valiant and courageous."

Later she tells us about ACBAR, the Agency Coordinating Body on Afghan Refugees. It's made up of over sixty members, both Afghan and international, and their efforts are focused specifically on education, health, and agriculture in the cities of Jalalabad, Herat, and especially Kabul, where they coordinate all activities in the city. When the last earthquake struck the region, they were on hand to control the damage. Currently, they're doing what they can for the victims of the drought, whose effects will continue to be felt for at least another year or two. The drought has prompted a mass migration into the center of the country, which is better irrigated. Here, and in some northern cities such as Mazar-e Sharif, there is an abundance of food but a lack of money, and this is putting quite a damper on commerce. Wells are currently being dug to water livestock, but these are long-term plans, not of much help to the immediate situation. On the other hand, it functions as the focal point for gathering and publishing information—in English, French, Dari, and Pashtun—from all the disparate aid organizations working with Afghan refugees.

ACIR, the ACBAR's Center for Information and Resources (which works to reclaim Afghanistan's "cultural patrimony"), is the other project this elderly woman dedicates her time and efforts to. Books, magazines, maps, pamphlets, videos, audiotapes, even a curious collection of mujahideen brochures. All this material—rescued from barbarism—is cataloged and archived by the Center in a huge database available to researchers, along with the Center's large lecture hall.

"Ignorance is the worst affront to culture," she affirms.

Through 1996, when the Taliban rose to power and banned music, reading, and all other cultural manifestations, smashing televisions, theaters, cassettes, and videotapes, and burning books in the streets, the ACIR spread its services throughout Afghanistan. By 1999, there were already thirty-one traveling libraries in twenty-two of the country's twenty-nine provinces, with a total of over ten thousand books in circulation. Technical books on health, medicine, maternity, child care, agriculture, and livestock; books on Islam, poetry, history, and literature; specialized books and even pleasure-reading books would appear from time to time. Other organizations followed the ACIR example, and now there are some four hundred libraries scattered across Afghanistan. I presume they operate clandestinely.

"Do you all have a half a million dollars?" she asks us while taking a sheaf of articles from a bookshelf, which she'll give to us to take with us.

Noting our shock, she tells us that that is the amount that would be necessary to recover all the pieces that have been stolen from the museum in Kabul. They weren't stolen by the general population, but rather by fundamentalist groups. The museum is located on the outskirts of Kabul, some eight kilometers from the downtown area. During the clash between the Hazara majority party and the Sunni fundamentalists, "no-man's-land" gradually shifted toward the museum. Nobody knows who stole what pieces. After the fighting died down, the Taliban took what pieces remained and relocated them to the city center, to be guarded in the Ministry of Information.

Nancy shows us some of the Center's publications pertaining to the restoration of certain ancient works of architecture destroyed by the war.

One contains a photo of a supremely beautiful tower or minaret rising defiantly over an expansive desert. Its outer surface is covered with a profusion of motifs and enamel mosaics; its very existence is a filigree in stone and baked clay. Nothing beside it remains but a pile of ruins; Shelley's "Ozymandias" immediately comes to mind.

"It's gone."

I feel a disconcerting lump rise in my throat, but I can't will it away. My eyes well up with so many tears that I can't blink or swallow them away, and I feign concentration on the little pamphlet. Then I move to examine the rest of the material stacked on the bookshelves, trying to think of anything to prevent me from breaking down into tears. I tell myself, "How important can a tower in the middle of a desert be, especially when so many human beings are being victimized by barbarism and ignored by the world?" But this terrible sense of loss still plagues me, because this symbol of all good things that humanity is capable of no longer exists. Eventually, I regain my composure enough to return to the group.

We move on to the Center's archives, including the library and the map room. I feel better surrounded by rows of shelves filled with books saved from the bonfires. I am eternally grateful to this woman and her team—to their work—for books are my life. The past and a knowledge of history are the keys to our present, and this thousand-year patrimony is broadened and enriched by each new century; each town is a book where we can learn of past mistakes and recover lost knowledge, where hope and faith in a humanity that occasionally loses it can be nourished.

We leave feeling contented. For our Afghan friends, the meeting has been a positive one. For us, it has been instructive. For me, it's been a revelation.

Rustam and Azada take us to a local spot for an ice cream. "No untreated water, no salads, no unpeeled fruit, no ice cubes, no ice cream" was every doctor's order before we embarked on our journey. Until now we've done our best to follow them, but today we'll digress. Afghan ice cream tastes like milk-meringue. It's frozen in rotating metal cylinders surrounded by crushed ice, and served in crystal dishes rising out of a bed of ice like a sweet and creamy tower. Delicious! Here, for the first time on our trip, we sit at a "private" table. We know that restaurants often have such tables and even dining rooms for women. Once again, the purdah—the segregation of the genders—shows us another of its faces. At some establishments, the tables will even be enclosed by curtains, with only an opening for the waiter to have access. There, women are sheltered from the gaze of the rest of the (male) clientele. It's a strange sensation: you go in an establishment—some even have separate entrances for men and women—and are instantly whisked away by a host through the crowd to your private table. But once there, behind the curtain, you can do whatever it is that you came there to do; you can even take off your chador and smoke.

Our next meeting is with the UNHCR member from Islamabad. We compose ourselves and go into the office, dressed in our Pakistani garb that is only now starting to obey us. A relatively young man gets up from the armchair behind his desk and extends his hand. Then he makes a motion for us to remove our chadors, saying, "Please, we're not in Afghanistan."

We do so, and settle into the chairs he offers us. He sits back down behind his desk, rocking slightly every time he pauses to change the subject or answer one of our questions. At first he seems distant and aloof, almost bored by our presence. But gradually (though without losing this apparent air of discipline) he begins to tell us things that sound surprising coming from the mouth of a member of an organization like UNHCR, in an official office in the United Nations building. During one of these curious pauses—his hands occupied by a paper clip and his head rocking slightly with the movement of his swiveling desk chair—we ask what his nationality is. "American," he replies. And he goes on talking about the issue of refugees, asserting that this is the lowest point in the twenty-year history of Afghan refugees. UNHCR's main function in all of its interventions is the protection of the refugee population. This protection usually takes the form of health care programs, elementary education, and vocational training, though UNHCR does not directly manage the camps, opting instead to outsource such tasks to other humanitarian organizations. The Afghan refugee population is quite numerous. Some 50 percent of Peshawar inhabitants are Afghans, and it can certainly be argued that some of these have successfully integrated themselves. All over the city, entire Afghan neighborhoods have started to spring up, with their own bazaars, restaurants, and shops. Some city streets are such that someone who knows Afghanistan well might feel as if he or she were walking down a street in Kabul. Nevertheless, it's obvious that the great majority of Afghans don't want to remain in Pakistan. Their greatest desire for the duration of their time in Pakistan is to one day return home.

"We will never feel completely happy here," affirms Azada.

Our UNHCR representative goes on: if the Afghan population was ever to leave Peshawar, the local economy would collapse. This is highly improbable, though, as the situation in Afghanistan is constantly deteriorating with no easy solutions in sight. Poverty is worsening, there are no jobs, no schools, no sanitation, and no freedom ever since the Taliban rose to power. Those who flee to Pakistan do so to avoid persecution by the Taliban and are seeking protection, but UNHCR lacks the economic resources to provide it. Fifteen years ago, during the war against the Soviet Union, the funds earmarked for Afghan refugees were near a hundred million dollars annually. Today it is twelve million. Several months ago, the only active program was one of voluntary repatriation. Now, even that has been suspended, owing to the drought that has devastated the country and prompted a new avalanche of refugees. The man rocks back and forth. Repatriation programs don't make sense. The people may go back and try rebuilding their homes, but a short time later almost always finds them returning to Pakistan.

Through UNHCR we learn that most of the money the U.N. dedicates to aiding Afghan refugees is being wasted; its true objective being to placate the Pakistani government.

When the Soviet invasion began, and during the first years of the ensuing civil war, the Pakistani government—despite never having signed the agreements and international resolutions pertaining to refugees—voluntarily received any and all Afghans that crossed over its borders. It did so for religious reasons: Islamic law guarantees that anyone fleeing a war has the right to refuge and shelter. But the situation has changed now that the Taliban—allied with Pakistan—controls almost the entire country. The Pakistani government now sees no reason why the refugees should not return to Afghanistan. The Taliban is, effectively, a Pakistani mercenary unit used to occupy Afghanistan.

"In Afghanistan, it's all about playing dirty."

The man again rocks back and forth in silence before going on. The United States wanted to make Afghanistan into a Russian Vietnam, and after the Cold War it kept on arming and financing Islamic groups. The U.S. government has never fully informed its citizens about the fact that, up until very recently, it supported the Taliban, and condemns them now largely as a matter of image. If the U.S. wanted to, it could end Afghanistan's deplorable situation tomorrow. The Taliban regime could be gone in a week. But for the United States, things like democracy, human rights, and the United Nations are simply tools to be used when they want, and for their own benefit. If the U.S. wanted to end the Taliban regime, it would be enough to simply put pressure on Pakistan and unconditionally condemn their support of such criminals. But they don't want to jeopardize the tenuous equilibrium that currently exists between Pakistan and India; if the U.S. were to press Pakistan on the Afghanistan issue, this equilibrium would shatter, much to the dismay of the Pakistani government. One must realize that some 80 percent of this country's budget is put toward its armaments, and that all its bridges, highways, and other infrastructure have been built with loans that have to be paid back.

Another pensive rock in the chair. Perhaps the drought that is currently devastating the Afghan countryside will also bring the cultivation of opium to an end, something that has risen sharply since the Taliban came to power, and perhaps this will provoke a total catastrophe in Afghanistan and Pakistan. Still, it's highly doubtful that the U.S. would ever let Pakistan be affected by such a collapse.

We are silently shocked. Rustam nods. I can't believe what I'm hearing.

Maybe I've misunderstood the man's English, but I don't dare ask for clarification, out of embarrassment. But I've understood it correctly. This is the truth. And here are people ready to speak it. I'm reminded of the Persian proverb that explains our tendency to be silent about our own mistakes, defects, and wrongdoings: *"Who will admit that their own milk has spoiled?"* And I feel an enormous amount of respect for this man who is willing and able to call a spade a spade.

He concludes with the remark that Afghanistan is the only country to have never recognized India's partitioning, because to do so would be tantamount to recognizing and accepting its current border with Pakistan.

We bid farewell by talking about other things. We mention a few of the problems facing the various aid organizations in Pakistan, and he confirms for us what Nancy Dupree has already said. He offers to lend a hand to HAWCA in any way he can, and then says good-bye and wishes us a good stay in Pakistan with the same disconcerting aloofness and coolness as we felt before. As if he hadn't told us anything, as if he hadn't told us about problems that the world ignores, or at least pretends to.

"He's an honest man; he knows what things are like, and doesn't try to cover them up," Rustam solemnly affirms.

We eat hastily in an Afghan restaurant; there's no time to return to the house. Sara and Meme order grilled chicken; the rest of us have lamb kebabs. Our tastes haven't changed much. We pass on the rice so there will be fewer leftovers, but we do order salads, yogurt, bottled water, and five Cokes.

We arrive promptly at our next appointment, this time with the person in charge of a Peshawar Afghan-German organization. Once again, the meeting takes place in the lobby of a well-known hotel. Two doors down is a patently Afghan arts-and-crafts shop. We go in to poke around, as we've got some time to kill. Right away, I'm drawn to a display case containing earrings, the only pieces of jewelry I like. Everything else— necklaces, bracelets, rings—I've never been attracted to, but earrings I enjoy. I try on a few. Long, silver, dangling ones. Some are even equipped with tiny bells. I'm intrigued; I'd like very much to buy a pair. They cost only five hundred rupees; barely ten dollars. In Barcelona, it would be a bargain, but here it's expensive. It could pay a teacher's weekly salary, buy two hundred kilos of flour (enough to bake bread every day for nearly a year), or send e-mails from an Internet café for six and a half hours. And so in the end, I can't bring myself to buy them. Just trying them on in front of the mirror is enough for me.

Once again, we're anxiously looking forward to having a cup of coffee.

We're beginning to understand that punctuality isn't particularly high on Afghanistan's list of virtues. At the very least, thus far in our trip, not one meeting has started on time. We enter the hotel discussing the day's interviews, and occupy ourselves by trying to guess which person entering the lobby might be our man.

"He's not coming," Rustam says, very seriously. "He's Afghan."

A rather facile explanation, but finally he does appear, if quite fashionably late. He speaks quickly in English, in a barely audible tone of voice. I stop trying to listen and understand. Sara will pose all the questions and get all the information we're interested in about his organization. Given the similarity of their objectives, this information may prove useful to Azada and Rustam. The man answers all our questions quickly, doesn't invite us to see his school or office, says good-bye, and leaves. Sara gives us the highlights: his organization operates free schools in Peshawar as well as offering classes in Afghanistan, and they also run a carpet shop. They receive some support from UNHCR, and are subsidized by grants from German organizations as well as private donations. UNESCO helps them out with books.

It's now too late for Najiba's husband to accompany us to the refugee camp he told us about last night; tonight he has a festival, for it's Friday, the Islamic holy day. We're also late in getting to the bazaar, where we need to buy more fabric: we don't have a change of clothes, and laundry must be done. Plus, we'll be able to have a tailor make them into traditional Afghan garb.

Back at the house, we take notes, tell Najiba how the day went, and leaf through the pamphlets we've brought back from the ACBAR offices. Rustam notices that one of them is sprinkled with quotes taken from classic Persian poetry. He selects a few at random to translate and read to us. Then I ask him to go back and read them in the original Persian, just as they were written, so I can close my eyes and listen to the sound of the words. Rustam recites the lines well, rendering them passionately. The others laugh, but I don't see the humor. For me, it's a magical moment. Rustam has resurrected, through the original language, that which, in the best of cases, I could only have read in English or perhaps Catalan. Thus ends a brief, magical literary seminar, of which I am the only spellbound alumnus.

Rustam goes on to tell us about the great poets and writers of the past thousand years, such as Affis Sherazi, an ascetic who protested many things through his writing, but above all he wrote against institutionalized religion, as Fariduddin Attar. Rustam also tells us about Abnisinal de Balch, an atheistic and scientific doctor who penned important works on medicine, utilized the therapeutic properties of certain plants to treat diseases, and who—according to legend—once used his art and abilities to resuscitate an apparently dead man. And there is Zekria Rasi, the doctor, astronomer, and poet, as well as Jayyam, who was also a critic of institutionalized religion, wrote poetry about the people's everyday life, and espoused a philosophy of "If life and its many pleasures are here at hand, why wait for heaven?" He also tells me about Saddi, the current king's official (laudatory) poet; about Amashu Baba, the poet-king who wrote in Pashtun; about Rabia Balji, the female poet; and about the great Firdausi who wrote the *Shah-nameh,* or *The Book of Kings:* three thousand pages of verse written according to the strictest rules of Persian grammar to steel it against the Arab influence brought in by the conquerors. Rustam is the name of a legendary hero who appears in this book; he was a powerful and generous man who fought bravely against his enemies and always stood for the simple man. As the days go by and I get to know the flesh-and-bone Rustam better, I begin to realize just how well he has honored his namesake.

Nasreen has invited us over for dinner tonight before we leave for the refugee camp. We're tired after a long, hot day of interviews, but we muster the energy to bathe and ready ourselves to head over to her house. Najiba tells us that there was quite a commotion earlier when one of her nieces found out that we had taken photos of her grandmother. The poor thing had been horrified: if a Taliban official had happened to come in while they were talking and taking pictures with foreigners, the whole family would have been detained. Najiba's husband intervened, explaining that we were in no way spies working for the Taliban. Azada, as always, told us not to worry about it. But we decide to leave our cameras behind anyway. None of us wants to make any of these people feel uncomfortable, or exacerbate the fears of these youths, who have grown up dealing with terror on a daily basis.

The fact of the matter is that the Taliban has prohibited anyone from taking photos or from being photographed, citing the religious prohibition against reproducing the likeness of the human body. They only make one exception: photos for identification documents. These are off-limits to the general public, but I've seen reports published in magazines where Taliban officials not only let themselves be photographed, but they do so smiling. Contact with foreigners is also highly punishable. The Taliban has condemned the West and the "pernicious" influence it has exerted over the region in the past. These are the two primary reasons why televisions, movie theaters, and videos have been banned: to prevent the reproduction of human images, and to prevent corrupt, Western ideology from being beamed into the region via satellite. Of course, the Taliban allow themselves to maintain a Web site as well as a New York office.

We're greeted wonderfully at Nasreen's house by a throng of people. We all sit down inside on mats, pillows supporting our backs, legs properly situated, like educated people. Everyone is there: Nasreen's husband, whose eyes—narrow and almond-shaped—remind me of what happened in Kabul, his brother, his brother's wife and kids, their grandmother, the five of us, Najiba's husband, and their daughter. Najiba has stayed at home with the baby. It is terribly hot, stifling any conversation. The women filter in and out of the room bearing plates and trays. By their excited glances, attentive movements, radiant smiles, and the pains they take to attend to us, it is obvious that our visit—their opportunity to wine and dine us—is a big event and the cause for much happiness and celebration. We're not sure just how to respond.

With the tea comes the time to chat at length about any and all things. Nasreen's brother-in-law is an engineer. His wife studied education in Afghanistan and worked there for three years, until they were forced to flee from the fundamentalism and war. Now the engineer has a job in the local bazaar. The women of the family—with the exception of Nasreen, who works in the school—stay at home. The children—quite a handful—all go to an Afghan school. The tall, distant teenager who we've already gotten to know through her many visits to the house tells us that she started out attending a Pakistani school, but she had such a difficult time with the language and her classmates (and her teachers showed little interest in helping her) that she transferred to an Afghan one. She would like to one day study medicine, but her family doesn't have the money for such things right now.

Najiba's daughter has fallen asleep in her father's arms, and so he gets up to take her home. A short while later, Najiba arrives. With her husband at home with the children, she is free to participate in the discussion.

Nasreen's sister-in-law tells us that after they fled Afghanistan, they set up in one of the official refugee camps in Peshawar, but it wasn't safe there. The roving bandits acted with total impunity and the connivance of the local Pakistani police, which was supposed to keep watch over the camp. The police would either close their eyes or simply look away when night fell and the bandits went into action. When her family was the victim of one of these attacks, they filed a formal complaint. Later that same night, the bandits returned—their faces masked—and forced them to withdraw the complaint under threat of violence. The police had given them up. It was then that they decided to leave the camp and move to the city. There, at least, they would live in less fear.

The children bring in the reading book they use in school. Their mother, the teacher, then recovered from her initial shock at having us there in the house, indignantly shows us the page containing a drawing of a *burka*. The corresponding text refers to a sick woman who buys medicine to make herself better.

"What medicine?" the woman exclaims, vehemently.

The picture and the text are indeed cause for anger: there is no medicine for sick women in Afghanistan. What's more, a *burka* is not a woman; it's a piece of clothing. But even if it were, is this illustration implying that women are not living human beings? And don't the Taliban zealously enforce the laws prohibiting the likenesses of any person, man or woman? Why has this picture not been censored along with so many others in this same book? She leafs through the pages and shows us another drawing: someone cutting grass in a field with a sickle. At least, that's what's implied here, for only the sickle and the grass are visible, while the *burka*-woman is discernible only as a blank silhouette.

"Don't they realize that we're human beings? Even in censored books, we're made to seem like mere objects."

They give us the book to take with us. The truth is that even in censorship, the Taliban are sloppy: another page shows a serpent—a cobra's raised head—which, as a living thing, should technically have been censored as well.

We go back to our house, thanking Nasreen and all her family for their generous hospitality. Once back home and on the porch, nobody can even think of sleep: throughout the day, we'd been compiling a list of things we wanted to discuss. Najiba tends to her hungry baby; her daughter wakes up and comes out to the porch as well. Then Najiba sets up a rectangular mosquito net in the corner of the porch, near where we're all chatting, and settled down inside with her two children. Soon, all three are sleeping peacefully. The rest of us go on talking in low voices, until once again the cry of the mullah floats in.

The sand-colored lizards emerge from the walls and perch themselves near the warmth of the glowing lightbulb.

Peshawar.

Blood cannot be washed away with blood.

It's six-thirty in the morning, and I'm awake. From my bed on the rug, I can see Najiba taking down the mosquito netting. Then she helps her daughter to the bathroom. The little girl is still learning how to control things, and once in a while she doesn't quite make it, forcing her mother to get a bucket of water to clean up the floor. It occurs to me that I have yet to see (nor will I see) a baby wearing diapers here. When a baby soils itself, the mother simply washes it off under a faucet. Life here, given the precarious conditions, is one of simplicity and small surprises. There are no major problems in terms of daily life here. After washing, Najiba dresses the child in pants and a shirt, and then washes the dirty clothes, hanging them up to dry on the patio. Then, hunkering down, she proceeds to sweep the porch rug with a bundle of thin, woody branches about the length of a person's arm.

I get up.

Sobh bajair. Good morning.

I freshen up and, like Najiba, take the opportunity to wash some of my underwear. I remember that in Barcelona, while we were preparing for our trip and thinking of the things we would need to live in new, dangerous conditions, it was either Sara or Meme who said: "As long as I have a pail of water so I can wash up every day, nothing else matters."

And our wish has become a reality: every day we have a pail of water to wash with. We can even bathe more than once a day if we want. And wash our hair each morning. What more could we ask? During our trip, we've become patently aware of just how full of excess our privileged lives back home really are. Here, not much is truly lacking. We've learned how to bathe with very little water, and how to manage our laundry with extra soaking. A cup of water can really go a long way.

After hanging up my laundry to dry, I feel like sitting on the patio steps to write, and I think again about just how right Azada's grandmother is: there's nothing like waking up early to start off your day well.

The clotheslines are hung with drying laundry from wall to wall. Yesterday, after returning home from our many appointments, we had created quite a jungle with our clothes and Pakistani chadors. Najiba brings an odd-looking contraption out from the corner of the porch, where the refrigerator is also located: a washing machine. It reminds me of the first washing machine we had in my house when I was a child: it would turn the clothes over and over, but everything was done manually. You filled up the tumbler with soap and water from the hose, washed your clothes, emptied out the dirty, soapy water onto the ground, and then refilled it with fresh water for the rinse. The two of us wring every last drop of water out of the clothes, and the whole process becomes something of a party for us. Splashing around, getting wet and spattered, stepping in puddles . . . there is a very youthful joy in the work. In me, at least, it produces a curious and profound joy, as if I had just been reconciled with life, land, and the universe. We wash and laugh. We're drenched by the time we finish it all, but in the middle of the Peshawar heat, it matters not.

Last night had drawn out to be quite long indeed. And there was still much that had been left unsaid. Reminiscing and reflecting upon the day's events while night crept in has become something of a habit for us. A custom, even: a nocturnal round table where each of us brings up something to discuss.

Yesterday, while we were running from place to place and meeting to meeting, there was one topic that we joked about to no end: Rustam's life. We wanted him to tell us everything, and when we finally returned home at the end of a long day, we refused to go to bed right away.

And Rustam had no other choice but to tell us his story.

He studied history and literature at the University of Kabul. Thus the mystery of his overwhelming knowledge was unveiled: in the short amount of time we've spent together, we've noticed a distinct passion that he puts into casual conversation and his answers to our questions on just about any subject. When the Afghan capital became the main objective of the Islamic factions and the bombings and skirmishes descended on the city from all four cardinal directions, devastating the city, Rustam's family—like so many others—fled for Pakistan and her capital, Islamabad. A short while later, the family emigrated from there to the West. Besides the some two million refugees estimated to be in Pakistan and the other two million who have fled to Iran, approximately another million have spread into Australia, Europe, and the United States. Rustam's family was among this group, and Rustam therefore grew up in the West. There, he took classes in computer science, and started a new life for himself. That is, until a couple of years ago, when he returned to Kabul to visit some relatives. The Taliban had already reared its head, and was gaining ground every day, advancing territory by territory. Rustam also visited other refugee families who were still living in Pakistan. At some point, his path crossed with that of Azada. They had known each other many years ago, in that dim, distant past when they were both children living in Kabul. But Azada had by then begun her humanitarian work, organizing literacy courses that became so popular that she was forced to expand her network of coconspirators.

And Rustam never returned to the West.

"My people needed me. I couldn't turn my back on them. I won't be a traitor to my country. I've met many Afghans who have taken refuge in the West, and now don't want to know anything about Afghanistan. All they want to do is cut off their roots and start a completely new life, full of comforts and pleasures, that has nothing to do with their country or people."

I understand this young man's heartbreaking condition, being torn between two worlds, having lived in both and coming to know the best and the worst that each has to offer. The hedonism, frivolity, materialism, and individualism of the West inspired him to reject it. The archaic traditions, immutable customs, and outdated social and familial structures of the East disgust him as well. He wants to be able to marry out of love, with a woman he has come to know on his own; he wants Afghan women and girls to enjoy the freedom to study, work, make friends with each other—including men and boys of their own ages—but at the same time, he finds unrestrained sexuality in the West to be off-putting as well, especially the way so many women are treated merely as objects of desire by men. How could people come to understand that a woman shouldn't be ashamed for enjoying her sexuality? If a man can have many sexual relationships, why can't a woman? Where does freedom and personal choice lie in this scenario?

Azada, much more even-keeled and reflective, admits that both worlds— both East and West—have both good and bad aspects. Her philosophy is to incorporate the best of other cultures into her own way of life. The ideal thing would be for each to learn about the other. The East could appropriate many positive Western ideas.

She is, of course, right.

We move from sexuality to homosexuality, and Rustam goes off. He views it as an aberration. Of course, he doesn't agree that such behavior should be punished (the Taliban are extreme in their prejudice, executing homosexual pairs by collapsing walls on top of them), but he himself cannot understand such a relationship.

We chat for a good while. Their arguments are basically the same that were brandished in our society years ago, and good enough to frustrate us. Still, the conversation is rather loose, despite the passionate subject matter, and it even becomes mildly amusing to provoke Rustam and prod him a bit.

"Just for a moment, imagine that things were reversed: that heterosexual relations were the ones that were condemned, and that you fell in love with a woman—wanted to marry her, share your lives together, have children—but that you were persecuted for it. How would you feel?"

Again it's the open-minded Azada who elects the right conclusion, the one we've been unable to express despite all our arguments and examples. I've come to admire greatly this woman who, at such a young age, possesses a wisdom and equanimity that takes some people a century to gain. Azada: the free woman.

"The truth is that never before in my life have I discussed such things so openly—or in front of a man—but I think that in the end, if we want to defend human rights to the fullest, then each individual's sexual orientation forms a part of these rights."

From this, we move on to the idea of polygamy, which Islam permits. In the beginning, polygamy was conceived of as a way to protect the many widows left in the wake of war in a world where a single woman had no means of subsistence, and this may conceivably be justification. Later, during Islam's period of expansion, it was considered imperative to bring as many Muslims as possible into a world rife with infidels. The simple satisfying of a man's desires has been rejected as a defense, but—just to provoke Rustam—I can't resist making a comment: "Polygamy wouldn't seem so bad to me if women were also allowed to have multiple husbands."

Azada tells us that polygamy—despite being legal—has grown increasingly uncommon in Afghanistan, though there was a time (even during the reign of Zahir Shah) in which it was considered fashionable in some social circles to take a second wife. But if Islam does permit the taking of up to four separate wives, one must bear in mind that this requires that all four be taken care of with the same respect and attention to their well-being.

The Taliban have done their part to return polygamy to Afghanistan, and the majority of them have four wives. I highly doubt (given the misogyny and hatred with which they treat women in general) that their wives are treated with respect, as human beings. I can't even begin to imagine what the relationship might be like between a Taliban man and his wife, other than one of repression, humiliation, slavery, and hell at home. I do realize that there are some women who support the Taliban, who unconditionally accept their vision of the world and the life that they would lead in such a world—but I can't understand it. It's quite difficult to get any information about these women; they don't appear anywhere on the Taliban's official Web page. Perhaps these women accede to the Taliban solely out of fear or necessity. I don't know.

Toward the end of our little soiree, we talk about our meeting the next day with our RAWA representative, who wants to take us to see several different activities, and whether it would be advisable to bring Rustam and Azada with us. They are extremely concerned about our safety, and worried that any one of a number of things will happen to us if we're alone, but somehow we manage to allay their fears. We'll be fine; nothing will happen. They don't need to come with us.

Finally we get to bed very late, but here I am—awake, rested, and enthusiastic—sitting on the patio steps.

Najiba's husband got up awhile ago to head to work. On his way out, he greeted me with a nod and a smile. The whole world is awake. Azada insists that we iron our new clothes. It's true; they are quite wrinkled after being washed, but the idea of ironing . . . In the end, I have no choice. Najiba smooths a bit of fabric out on the rug and plugs in the iron. She warns us not to touch the metallic parts; we'll get quite a shock. On our knees, using our fingers to sprinkle the clothes with water from a bowl, rolling them up to conserve the moisture . . . this also reminds me of the ironing sessions of my youth, when there was no such thing as a steam iron. Thus, each of us ironed out her dresses, pants, and chador.

Azada and Rustam accompany us to our scheduled meeting place.

Although they won't be coming with us, they won't leave us on our own until our contact and her *muhrram* from the other day arrive promptly at eleven, again in a hotel lobby. Still hesitant to leave us in others' hands, our friends insist that it be our driver who takes us there. Azada hugs and kisses us as if she were never going to see us again.

"Don't worry, don't worry!" It is now our turn to say these words to her.

We're taken to a house where the organization has established a seamstress and rug-weaving shop, but none of the neighbors know what else goes on inside these walls. For all intents and purposes, it's a common, everyday family house that happens to get a lot of visits from relatives. These women are in constant danger because of the political nature of their activities, and it's important to remember that fundamentalism is still the law of the land in Peshawar, and that Taliban operatives are everywhere. Today, in this house, several women from several different refugee camps scattered throughout the city have come here to meet and talk with us. They're all sitting down in a circle in a large room, waiting for us. We take off our shoes at the door and greet them as we enter, before taking our place at the crown of the circle, which they've reserved for us.

"*Salaam.*"

The women look expectantly at us. Bit by bit, they begin to tell us their stories, getting more and more animated. In broad brushstrokes, they paint for us a picture of their lives, the circumstances that forced them to flee Afghanistan, their families, their experiences, and their aspirations.

The first to speak is a smiling, relatively young woman. It's short and sweet: she's been in Peshawar for the past eight years, she's widowed and has a daughter and two sons ages nine, eleven, and twelve, all of whom attend school at one of the organization's orphanages. She also takes care of her elderly mother.

The next to take up the conch is the woman sitting at her side. She's practically just arrived: it's only been a year since she fled Kabul, where she was a professor until the Taliban rose to power and closed down the schools.

"I've been a widow for twelve years. My husband was killed in the war.

I have a son who's eighteen, and a daughter who's sixteen. Of course, we lived much better before Massoud—and later the Taliban—attacked Kabul. There was war going on before the arrival of the Taliban, but when they came to power is when most of the women left the city. They would beat women in the streets if they weren't wearing a *burka*. I wanted to ask for documentation from UNHCR to be able to legally flee the city, but some Taliban operatives beat me up to terrorize me into not doing so. We lived in constant fear. We still do. The Taliban cut off people's hands and kill them for so-called religious reasons. I finally decided to flee Kabul when I found out that the Taliban were planning to take my son to the front lines to fight against Massoud. We crossed the border that same night. I had heard of an organization that offered help to women and widows, and thought that maybe I could work for them. I have a degree, I'm a professor, and here I can continue to teach other women. I want to help . . . my greatest wish is for the war to be over, for Afghanistan to gain a government democratically elected by its people. Massoud, the Taliban, Gulbuddin Hekmatyar . . . they have all reduced the country to little more than a cemetery."

A thin, tiny woman seated to our right—her head covered by a dark chador marked by a golden yellow stripe—is next to speak.

"I had a good life in Afghanistan. We lived in a town, far from the city, and the war hadn't reached us yet. But the Taliban had. They separated the men from the women and children, and sent them to the front to fight. Later, they packed young women into vehicles and took them away. None of them was ever seen or heard from again. The Taliban destroyed every home in the village, and burned all the fields as well. They burned down my house right in front of my own eyes."

To our left, the sister of the woman who has just finished speaking adds:

"I was pregnant when the Taliban came to our town. They piled all our clothes and other belongings in the middle of the house, doused them with gasoline, and set fire to it all. We had to grab what we could and run. This was eight months ago. We left on foot. The Taliban offered to take me with them, but of course I wouldn't, since I have two teenage daughters. So we started walking in the middle of the night: me, my sick husband, and our nine children. Around dawn, I went into labor, and gave birth to my son in the middle of the road. Then we picked up and started walking again, heading for the city, which we reached somewhere around nine in the morning.

"When the Taliban came, I told them that I was a widow, but they didn't believe me. They chose three of my small sons—ages five, eight, and ten—and started to beat them on their fingers with wooden rods to make them say where their father was and where he was keeping his weapons. They beat my sons until they lost consciousness."

A dark, stout woman, expressive and emotional, a native of the city of Herat, speaks of the hatred she feels for the *burka*. Her voice soon breaks down into a sob, but she recovers:

"It was four years ago that I fled Afghanistan with my three children, who are now seven, ten, and twelve years old and who attend a school run by the organization. A group of Taliban—some ten men—showed up at my house one day and carried off my husband. As an afterthought, they beat me so severely that I still carry scars on my back. I never saw my husband again, nor heard any news about him." Then, she playfully yet honestly adds, "I hope they're shaking in their boots. I hope one day women return to Afghanistan. We'll rip them apart with our own bare hands."

The other women laugh and smile. When it all calms down, a woman with a look of deep perdition wrought on her face begins to speak:

"My husband died some three years ago, in a bombing during one of the battles between Massoud and the Taliban. The Taliban barricaded the elderly in their own homes, and then set fire to the buildings. I fled for the mountains with my children and neighbors. The Taliban were there, offering us trucks to take us away from the fighting, but we chose to go on foot. We spent ten or twelve days up in the mountains, in very harsh conditions."

"The Taliban beat and tortured me to try and get me to tell them where my husband and oldest son were hiding."

"My husband died ten years ago, during the war with the Russians."

"The *yehadis* came to my home in the middle of the night. They killed my husband, then tried to take me with them. I resisted, and they beat me savagely. Terrified, I fled to a nearby house without even thinking of my children; then I went back for them, accompanied by a few of my neighbors. The *yehadis* had caught my three-year-old daughter, and she was screaming and crying. We confronted them, and I ended up in a hospital for a month, both because of what they did to me, and because of the things I saw and still can't forget."

"Before coming to Pakistan and abandoning Afghanistan once and for all, I took refuge at a relative's house in Kabul. This was after the Taliban killed my husband and were looking to take my son. We left at night and reached Kabul after spending the entire next day on the road. Now I live here with my husband's mother and my sister. All three of us are widows. My husband's father was killed by the Russians, my sister's husband was killed by the *yehadis,* and my husband was murdered by the Taliban. We survive however we can; my son sells vegetables, and my daughter gathers firewood."

We are struck speechless. These women tell story after tragic story without cessation. They show us their scarred and burned bodies. One still has a piece of shrapnel embedded in her side. Our young contact translates into English each history, each life, each pain, and still we've heard only a handful of the women there in the room. A handful of histories. Similar yet distinct, for each is the story of an individual woman, with a name, a face, and an age, with a memory, a present, and who knows what future. Histories that must be multiplied by a hundred—a thousand— until reaching and encompassing all the millions of women who make up the population of Afghanistan. Because each and every Afghan woman has a story of pain and suffering to tell. They don't want revenge because, as the proverb states: *"Blood cannot be washed away with blood."* They want justice. They want peace. They want freedom.

We thank them for their time, and bid them farewell. Our contact then takes us into a different part of the house, where a woman is teaching a group of children the art of rug weaving on a big, horizontal loom.

Afghan rugs are noted for being woven entirely of wool, whereas other oriental rugs incorporate silk, cotton, or even camel hair fibers. Depending on the region and the group to which the weavers belong, the rugs may be of either a single or double weft, and as a general rule they are secured using Persian knots, also known as *sennah*. Another characteristic has to do with the rectangular orientation of the designs. The dominant colors are reds obtained from the roots of a particular bush that grows in abundance in the regions most famous for their rugs; the dark brown of walnut tree bark and the light brown of a pomegranate's skin; yellow is given by a wildflower from the steppe; and for blue, they usually use indigo. All are natural pigments, though sometimes an artificial dye will be employed. The entire process—from shearing the sheep to the carding and spinning of the wool and, of course, the weaving—is still done completely by hand.

Traditionally, women weave the rugs on horizontal looms. The designs are done by memory and contain elements and touches characteristic of the different groups, tribes, and clans. They are heavily laden with symbols whose origins and meanings are so remote that today scarcely anyone can recall them. In reality, there are shops that use patterns and templates sketched out on paper for the weavers to copy. The regions with the greatest sense of history to them are that of the northern part of the country, whose population is largely from Turkmenistan, and also the region around Herat, to the east of Afghanistan, where they weave rugs and kilims according to the traditions laid down by the nomadic tribes who lived in the region. The rugs from the former region are perhaps the best known of all, as they are woven from the wool of the famous karakul sheep, which produce two types of wool simultaneously: a long, external hair over a softer layer right next to the skin. The Herat weavers generally use local sheep, like the *ghiljan* and *gaadi* breeds.

One of the most common and easy to recognize elements of a rug's appearance is the *fil poi*—or "elephant's foot"—the big, stylized, central design. Plus, each city, clan, and tribe has its own distinctive design, which allows you to tell with a simple glance whether the rug was made by the Tekke, the Kepsi, or the Yamouds; or perhaps it contains some designs indicative of Beshir: the multicolored, geometric design known as a *bagh-e-shinar*, or "leaf of the poplar tree." Maybe it contains none of these trademarks, but rather is defined by the tiny, colorful geometry of Afghanistan's Chichaktou nomads. They may serve also as a door or curtain, in which case they are known as a purdah or *Hatchlou*: a vertical partition, with fringe hanging from the bottom while the top portion hangs from a cord supporting the framework.

And through these rugs, bags, harnesses, lintels, and door decorations, hampers, general-use saddlebags, the weaving tradition is maintained.

The expressive woman from Herat has gathered the three of us together, and we try to communicate with gestures, but we end up just laughing a lot with her. Another woman comes over to say something to our contact: the food is ready. We're quite surprised; we had no idea that we'd be invited to eat. Our driver is waiting for us. The young woman says we should stay and eat for a while, unless (she adds discreetly) we're in a hurry because we have another meeting to get to. No, of course we can stay. They'll wait for us back at the house, though of course worried and thinking that every possible thing has happened to us. But we calm ourselves anyway and accept the invitation. It's a feast fit for kings: a giant mountain of *qabalee palau*, salad, chicken in sauce, and pudding. We thank the cook, who comes in to say hello, and the woman from Herat fills up her plate time and again, inspiring us to eat more as well.

Finally, we bid a hearty farewell. We let our contact know that we may, in the next few days, be heading to Islamabad. Her reaction is immediate: she'll try and arrange things so we can also see some of RAWA's activities in the region. The woman from Herat hugs and kisses us good-bye, and everyone escorts us outside to where the truck and our driver are waiting.

Back home, we are greeted as if returning from a long voyage to Hindu

Kush. Azada greets us as if it has been centuries since she's seen us last. The heat is suffocating today, and the five of us retire to our bedroom to rest for a while. We draw the curtains that sometimes double as a door (a purdah, we now know) leaving Rustam outside. Although the room's lone window is at floor level, it's almost like being out on the porch.

In midafternoon, we get up and have our driver get ready. Azada wants to take us to the market to buy some more fabric. It's been days since we brought up the need to get something else to wear, but we haven't yet found the time. Plus, when we finally get to Kabul, we'll have to dress in the Afghan mode.

"Let's be honest, girls, they're not going to grant us our visas," Meme insists.

We talk about our trip to Afghanistan as if we already have our visas in hand. And while we wait for our driver out on the porch, we talk about our different clothing options, though there isn't much we can do. The only real variation is in the neckline: rounded or squared, embroidered or in some other style that strikes us as awful. The only other possibilities include sleeves bunched up at the upper arms, or a stripe of false buttons that runs from the neckline down to the waist, and is rather in style these days in Basira. Rustam doesn't like the button idea. He offers his opinion without being asked for it, and I can't resist pointing out that dresses aren't for him. Azada applauds, and Rustam decides to stay home rather than accompany us to the bazaar.

The fabric shops in the bazaar are thronged with people. We walk up and down stairs, and go in and out of an endless number of shops. The storefronts are stacked almost to the roof with bolts of cloth, and the vendors are either perched on top of them, surveying the scene, or diligently attending to customers. One of the shops has a small bench where we sit down while a man shows us cloth after roll of cloth so that we can feel the fabric and inspect the design and workmanship. They make no complaints about bringing out sample after sample; outside, the bolts fall steadily with a dull thud. Our attendant then separates the double-weft fabrics from the rest, so we can fully appreciate both sides of the workmanship. We continue to amble through the bazaar. We buy fabric for one outfit at one store; at another, we get fabric for another; and then we go back to look at that one piece that we weren't sure about, but still . . .

In one of the packed alleyways, we come across a young girl begging for alms. She can't be more than eight years old. Clenched in her fist are a few small bills that she's managed to obtain. Azada talks with her for a good while. Then, we take a few photos with her, and give her a few rupees.

Our driver is getting anxious. His wife is going into labor, and he hasn't been able to locate any of the other drivers to substitute for him. We'll have to be quick.

Meme chooses an ornately embroidered bright pink linen cloth for her outfit, another straight piece for her pants, and a few other meters of plain cloth for her chador. Both the color and the material are exquisite. Sara buys cloth for two outfits: one, a dark blue, while the other is the color of red wine with tiny designs appearing in a lighter shade of red. In another shop that sells only chadors, she picks just one: a lovely, deep garnet color with gold highlights. I buy a length of blue cloth sporting a floral print and fringed with black, and another piece of fabric checked with green, black, and yellow squares that I combine with a pair of yellow pants. The chador I select is smooth and white.

As we're walking over to where our driver has parked the car, we poke around some more, and Sara stops to buy a paper. Back at the house, Rustam ignores our little purchases. Azada sends word to the dressmaker for her to come first thing tomorrow morning.

We find out then that Azada has decided to spend the rest of the day at the refugee camp to be with her grandmother. It's the anniversary of her uncle's death—her grandmother's oldest son. And yet she took the time to go to the bazaar with us! We feel guilty; sometimes this prevailing sense of hospitality—this way of converting the guest's every whim into an order—seems awful. Forget our clothes! We tell Azada how sorry we are that she didn't go to spend the entire day with her grandmother, to keep her company on this day of remembrance of so much pain. And we ask that, in the future, she not put her own plans on hold just to attend to ours.

"*Don't worry.* She'll understand. She knows you're my guests, and that I'm going to be taking care of you."

And once again, we have to swallow our uneasiness and simply accept this people's extraordinary generosity.

For dinner, we eat a stew of potatoes, onions, and tomatoes with bread, and then get ready for the film session that's been prepared for us. Najiba sends one of the driver's children off to rent a VCR. We move the TV out onto the porch, set everything up, and start the show.

The first film shown is a concert by an Afghan singer, who caters to refugees or other Afghans who have emigrated here. Her repertoire is made up primarily of traditional songs, especially (and as the grand finale) the *atan,* the most emblematic of all Afghan songs and dances. The crowd loves it. At first they are relatively calm, but then a person here and a person there begins to snap their fingers or clap their hands along with the music. The most adventurous ones, occupying a slightly more open space behind the regular rows of seating in the concert hall, start to dance. Both men and women. The *atan* is a loose, free dance, with each person moving as the music so moves him or her. Often, people will form together and dance in a circle. Shoulders pump up and down in time with the music, the feet follow the swaying of the hips. The rest of the body can go forward, backward, from side to side, spin, or scarcely move at all and just vibrate along with the highly distinctive rhythm. The dance can be rather sensual and unrestrained, depending on the dancer, but the amount of emotion he or she puts into it is always a personal choice. And its call is irresistible. The body begs to join in the dance. Everyone there, Afghan or not, watching the dance on TV and listening to the enchanting music, joins in either knowingly or subconsciously, tapping their feet, clapping their hands, or nodding their head. It's incredibly moving to see such a radiant expression of happiness there on the screen; to see so many exiles dancing without a care through the halls, in every corner of the room, in every town, everywhere.

We finish watching the video, which includes a second concert. It's getting late, but there's still another feature: a documentary on Afghanistan's recent history. The detailed rendition—from the ratification of the constitution and the reign of Zahir Shah, through the successive conflicts, governments, and coup d'etats—contains powerful images, symbolic of the Soviet invasion and subsequent defeat: the last defeated tank limping back across the border into Russia. And then comes the civil war. The documentary concludes with footage of the ongoing radio conversation that Gulbuddin Hekmatyar and Massoud maintained before each launched his respective army on Kabul: one looking to conquer it; the other hoping to defend it. Between the two of them, the city was destroyed.

The documentary is narrated in Persian, and Rustam translates for us. Soon, we are able to put faces to all these names implicated in the destruction of Afghanistan: the Communist leaders, the Islamic leaders, and the warlords. It lasts for over three hours. A few days later, we decide to get a copy to bring home with us: we want to preserve these images and replay them, immediately and everywhere, to move more Westerners to denounce the situation in Afghanistan.

By the time the documentary has finished, the mullah has already sounded his daily call. Everyone is getting ready to go, but I want the night to go on. I'm about to strike up a conversation with Rustam about what we've just seen, when Najiba's husband comes over and sits down next to us, his legs crossed.

"How long do people sleep in your country?"

The question troubles me. "Six, seven, eight . . . it depends."

"Do you think people sleep out of habit or out of necessity?"

"I suppose it's a bit of both."

"For me, it's a necessity. When I don't get enough sleep, I don't feel either well or happy. I feel down, I can't work, can't find joy in anything."

I have no idea where this is going.

"We're all starting to get a bit worried, because since you've arrived, you've slept very little."

I'm touched by his concern, his delicate interest in our well-being, and the roundabout way he broached the subject. Once again, I feel a great tenderness for this discreet, sensitive man. I assure him that I'm fine; I point out that I'm so thrilled to be here that I don't want to lose a moment of my time, and then I thank him profusely for his concern and apologize for having been the cause of any worry. He sits and smiles while Rustam translates my words.

"Tashakor," I tell him wholeheartedly, and then get up to go straight to bed. *"Shab bajair."* Good night.

SUNDAY, AUGUST 6, 2000.

Peshawar.

---

*If the water is already over your head,
one fathom is as good as a hundred.*

I hear the doorbell ring. It's still very early. Could there be a visitor at this hour? I get out of bed, and from inside my room I can see Najiba out on the porch. She sees me as well, and starts motioning to get dressed and come on out. I wake the others up and tell them to get dressed as well.

Seated on the rug is a tiny, very pretty woman with dark hair and rounded cheekbones. It's Nasreen's neighbor, who has offered to make our new clothes. She takes all our measurements, unfurls the fabric, and begins to hash out her cuts. She asks one question—what type of neckline each of us wants—and goes to work. While she does, we wash up and have a breakfast of cheese, bread, and tea.

Rustam has gone off to Islamabad to attend to some work he has there.

Azada will finally go this afternoon to visit her grandmother, for there isn't much for her to help us with today: we'll be meeting with the families of some of the school's students. Lala, one of the teachers, will be gone, but Najiba is leaving the children in Basira's care.

We drive to a neighborhood on the outskirts of the city, where the roads are unpaved. We park on a dusty promenade and continue on foot.

The teachers point to a wooden door framed by an adobe wall marking an otherwise featureless plot of land. Inside the premises and under the simple canopy that they built themselves live some twenty families. The living accommodations are marked out in six-meter squares, and posts support the roof of pieces of plastic and cloth stitched together.

We're greeted by the group's main representative: a middle-aged man. Children flock around; their happy, curious eyes are fixed on us. They're obviously thrilled to see their teachers and anxious to start up the classes again. The school's watchman tells us that they've been checking in every day to see if it was time to return to school. Here, vacations can be tough to endure.

We're invited into a room where we are greeted by a group of women, the youngest of whom carry their babies in their arms. A short while later, some elderly women come in as well, and Azada gets up to greet them respectfully. They offer us tea and sweet little candies shaped like aniseeds. Flies swoop in to attack them in droves, and Azada has to ask for some round cloths with which to cover them. There is no fan.

This walled-in, covered structure belongs to a Pakistani man. Refugee families pay him a small monthly fee (about one hundred rupees) to rent out one of the small rooms inside. The generator, which must have cost several thousand rupees, is shared communally. When they're not able to pay, the electrical supply is reduced. For water, they have reached an agreement with a nearby mosque, which allows them to pipe in a certain amount to a spigot and wash area near the outer door of the structure. In exchange for this service, each family pays two hundred rupees per year to the mosque. Not far from there is the clay furnace, which is fed with wood taken from the boxes of fruit and vegetable shipments, which are also communal.

All of these families come from the same region of Afghanistan: one of the country's eastern provinces. There, they were farmers, businessmen, and butchers. That is, until the Taliban arrived and destroyed everything.

"We had to leave with what we could carry. Our life back in Afghanistan was by no means easy, but compared with the way things are now, it was a golden age," the head of the family tells us.

Another way they raise money to live on is to build birdcages. Each family builds their own, and sells them to Pakistanis. Small cages bring in twenty-five rupees; the big ones can command sixty. Small cages take a day to construct, while the big ones take two. Everyone—men, women, and children—works, cage by cage. To add to this meager income, children and the elderly go out every day to beg.

We strike up a conversation with some of the women, and sip some tea with them. They call our attention to a thin, listless baby in its mother's arms. But then we realize that it's not a baby at all, but rather a two-year-old child, malnourished to an unimaginable degree. Another woman comes up to us, carrying a child of a few months. Its blotchy, red-and-black hands send chills up and down our spines. Meme, who knows something of childhood diseases, examines it, while the baby's mother tells of how a pot of boiling water was accidentally spilled on the baby's hands. The black is the dead skin (which she trims off with a pair of scissors), and the red is from being treated with henna. But the hand is badly swollen, and the burns are worse in the folds of the wrist. They have yet to scar over. Meme is horrified.

"This child has to get to a doctor."

But there are no doctors available to Afghan refugees. They have no way to pay for treatment. Pakistan has public health care, but not for Afghans.

"And this child here is suffering from severe malnutrition."

Other women start bringing in their children for consultations. One very young, pregnant girl doesn't feel well. Another young mother. More children. Another woman covers an enormous goiter with her chador. Diseases of both hunger and misery.

We speak with the group's representative. Is everyone in agreement that the foreigners will pay for the baby with the burns to see a doctor, and that they will also leave some money to help feed the one suffering from malnutrition?

The man promises that the money we leave will be used to take care of these two children. This quickly prompts an avalanche of mothers and sicknesses. But the foreigners don't have money for everything. This isn't what they've come here for.

I admit that the situation made me uncomfortable. I don't like what's going on here. I'd prefer to work and contribute all my time, energy, and money to address the origins of these problems, though that is a long-term outlook. Still, I understand that there are specific, urgent cases that would soon turn hopeless if it weren't for an emergency intervention. But this isn't what I've come to Pakistan for, and seeing all this makes me quite sad indeed, because a handful of rupees solves nothing in the face of so much overwhelming poverty. True, the burned child will get to see a doctor. But what will be next? What will happen the next time someone needs money for medicine? Where will it come from? What good will a visit to a doctor really do, knowing how severe the burns are, and knowing also that the mother will probably be unable to treat it with anything other than more henna? *"If the water is already over your head, one fathom is as good as a hundred,"* says another old Afghan proverb. For me, it's a conflict. Why this child and not another? Why is his blackened hand demanding of the most attention? How many other children are sick? How many are deathly so? Still, we can't deny them a chance at hope: maybe a doctor will be able to save the child's hand. Nevertheless, my uneasiness continues to grow. The mothers are surrounding us, all talking at once. I get the distinct impression that we are no longer the friends of the women who brought us here to meet with these people. We have metamorphosed back into foreigners, Westerners who have money.

There's a boy who keeps himself separate from the commotion going on around us as the rupees change hands. He introduced himself to us before; he's a student at the school as well. Najiba's told us that he's among the best, brightest, and most dedicated to his studies. I admire him for his dignity. He obviously doesn't want to participate in this spectacle.

We leave the room to go look at the rest of the site, and so the children can show us the cages they've built. The group representative will allow us to take pictures of the facilities and the children, but not of the women. There's a chalkboard set up in one of the rooms, which one of the teachers uses to teach literacy to the students' mothers. The children are like little actors, posing happily for us at their workplaces.

More women with children in arms come up to us: this child also has to see a doctor, that one is also undernourished. Of course, they're all telling the truth. All of a sudden, one of the elderly women falls senseless to the floor.

"It's the heat . . . *Garmi!*" cry the women who rush to her side, fanning her and moistening her face with water.

We've got to get out of here; we've got to bring this visit to a close before it degenerates completely into a competition between neighbors as to whose pain is greater and who will get the foreigners' help.

I have no problems with contributing money to a worthy cause, but I don't support simple panhandling. I abhor that shoddy form of charity; it reminds me of the high-society ladies who would tour the poor neighborhoods once a week, handing out old clothes, food, and money to the poor, but in actuality it was their own husbands who created their state of poverty by not paying them fair wages. I look at handouts as an impulsive act designed to pacify a person's conscience when he or she is confronted with the harsh side of reality. People become ashamed—if only for an instant—of what they have, and think nothing of tossing out a few coins to quell this sense of remorse and replace it with a sense of generosity and well-being. What the poor really need is not generosity; they need justice.

The women ask us if we can get them UNHCR food stamps. They don't know that program came to an end awhile ago. Nor do they realize the lack of importance the rest of the world places on whether or not Afghan refugees have enough to eat. Greater visibility is what they need; not handouts. The international community must act. Over the past fifty years, we have developed many tools that, in theory, have made the world a better place to live in: there is the Red Cross and the Red Crescent, the

United Nations, the Haya Tribunal, UNHCR, and the concept of "human rights." All that's left is to make sure they operate the way they should, that no power can corrupt these organizations, that personal interests and motivations don't tie their proverbial hands, and that hypocrisy and greed don't become empty words or facades preventing virtue from spreading.

We say good-bye to the families and head toward the schoolhouse, which offers the handful of children who are able to attend the chance at a better future. It is in dire need of additional funding, so that it can continue to admit more and more students and also offer other Afghan refugees (like their mothers) a place to work and make a living on their own. The boys and girls who once attended class here are now men and women who can move on to better-paying jobs and the freedom from poverty, hunger, exploitation, and the shame of having to beg for handouts. If more funding does arrive in time, they are hoping to build a school kitchen that—besides offering a couple of new jobs—would also vastly improve the nutrition that children are receiving here.

On the door is a blue sign with white lettering: "Primary School." The watchman opens the door for us. Out on the patio are several very tall trees, proffering some very welcome shade. Across the way is a one-story building with a porch built onto the front. Another one sits off to the left. There are four classrooms in all. Each is equipped with a mat on the floor and a chalkboard. A main room serves as an office, distinguished only by a large desk and a map of Afghanistan hanging on the wall. The watchman brings out some folding chairs so we can sit and rest in the shade. Off in one corner of the patio is a stone basin outfitted with a spigot. Right next to it is a large clay vat for holding and storing the drinking water.

We speculate about the expenses required to maintain such a school. There's rent, electricity, water, and wages for the guard and the two teachers who were chosen because otherwise they had no other family members able to earn a living. Also, there's the expense of busing in the other teachers who have other jobs but also work as volunteers. The school provides materials to its students: books, paper, pencils . . . Each student has his or her own textbook, but has to return it at the end of each course for the next students to use. They are bought wherever they can be found and found cheap, everywhere from the local bazaar to secondhand book sales. The donations that come in from Italy and Spain are enough to keep the school open for five months out of the year; then, when the money runs out, classes are over. It's August now.

We sit out on the patio and chat for a while. Najiba talks about her student, the teenage boy whom we've met. He was admitted to the school despite his age for two reasons: one, for his steadfast desire to learn, and two, because he's seriously ill and can't do hard labor to support his elderly father and three younger sisters. Meme is quite taken with his case, and decides to look into flying him to Barcelona for an operation that may indeed save his life, and improve his enjoyment of it.

We suggest that the whole group go out to eat together. Our driver has to make two trips to get us all there, but we are able to all meet at an Afghan restaurant with a large dining room and wedding reception area. We try the *manty*, a type of dumpling filled with lamb meat and something spicy. We also invited the school watchman, but he and our driver prefer to sit apart from the rest of us, who again find ourselves seated at one of the draped booths. Purdah. They'd feel uncomfortable surrounded by so many women.

The school continues to be the main topic of conversation throughout dinner. Afterward, Azada leaves for the refugee camp to visit her grandmother. We take advantage of the cool evening air to visit the famous Peshawar museum, renowned for its collection of Buddhist art. Our driver again makes two trips: the first to take Azada and Najiba home, and the second to take Lala and us to the museum. But at the last moment, Lala—who is a timid sort and doesn't speak English—decides to go home instead.

It's almost five when we get to the museum, and they're about to close. We're on the verge of turning around, dispirited, but the guards offer to stay open a bit longer. How long? We agree on 5:15, and we pay our three fees on our way out.

"But there are four of us." Our driver is coming in with us.

"This man is your driver, no?"

"Yes."

He doesn't have to pay. It's assumed that he would be going in with us. Of course, he's our *muhrram,* our attendant. Certain things still surprise us in this society; we see them with each passing day.

The museum isn't very large. The majority of the works on display are examples of Gandhara art: statues, reliefs, figures sculpted out of black stone, seated Buddhas, standing Buddhas, smiling Buddhas, and serious Buddhas. Everything is finely rendered, rich, and full of movement and detail. The large statues are secured up against the walls with iron bands around their necks. Knowing we're pressed for time, we make our way hastily through the exhibits. Just a quick tour. Not much information is offered with the exhibits, and I think about buying a little book (in English) explaining in detail the characteristics of this culture and its art, but our driver intervenes immediately, protesting the book's "excessive" price. In the end, I leave without the book, thanks to his overzealous haggling. The information would have been nice to have, I think. But I'll find it via different avenues. Among the bas-reliefs and etchings, I am surprised to find references to Atlantis and other mythical places and beings, like the half-man, half-fish merman. In Nancy Dupree's book, I read that the discovery, in the Ai Janoum deposits, of a statue that dates back to the second or third century B.C. debunks the (until recently) prevailing theory that the Hellenic influence on Gandhara art came from Rome. I also learn that this particular art has its roots in Central Asia, specifically the region known as Bactria.

They start to shut off the lights, signaling that they're locking up, and we hurry to make it out in time.

We stop on the way home to buy mangoes, a melon, and our daily supply of bottled water. Najiba is there to greet us, chatty and effervescent. The driver's son—with his baby brother in arms—goes running off in search of his teenage brother, who knows English and will serve as our interpreter now that Azada and Rustam have gone. Najiba tries to teach us a few words in Dari, but we prove to be rather poor students. The nightly conversation floats between song and dance: the two ingredients of the concert film we watched last night. Again, Najiba sends her children off to rent a VCR and a couple of tapes. We set everything up, pop in a tape, and immediately recognize the distinctive rhythm of the *atan*. We ask our hostess if she'll teach us to dance it, but she refuses, opting instead to simply snap or clap in time with the beat. We are alone again in that curious world of women, ruled by a relaxed sense of intimacy. The driver's sons don't talk much; they're still quite young. Sans Najiba, we stand up and attempt to mimic the arm and hip movements we see on the screen. Najiba laughs, alternatingly applauding or disapproving with a grimace when our swaying goes beyond what might be called a dance. We go at it for a good while. Then, Najiba asks us about the dancing in our country. Besides the myth and stereotype of the folkloric Spanish dances, we consider ourselves *Sevillanas:* Meme and Sara, who know how to dance properly, take the lead, while I hang back in the wings to sing and clap. It turns into quite an enjoyable evening.

It's already dark out by the time Najiba remembers that we still have to take the material for the other two sets of clothes to the tailor. She looks at us pensively, and decides that Sara will go with her. Of the three of us, her complexion is the most likely to pass as Afghan; she'll just have to remain silent. Najiba will do all the speaking for her. I'm dying of envy as I watch them head out the door, carrying the plastic bag that contains our fabric. We're left at home to take care of Nasreen's eldest niece, who's sitting on the porch with her younger sisters and us. Nobody says a thing.

Najiba and Sara return a short while later, dying of laughter. Najiba had told the tailor that Sara harkened from a distant region of Afghanistan where they speak an extremely obscure dialect, and that she didn't understand a word of Dari or Pashto. The man then took all her measurements—more than were necessary, they said—and then showed her an amazing array of styles for the neckline.

"*Ne, ne*" was all Sara could respond to each of the tailor's "suggestions."

We wash the vegetables while Najiba prepares to cook. Our driver's younger sons are off busying themselves with the children, while the eldest stays with us to translate, if needed. We stretch out on the porch, exhausted. The gastrointestinal problems that have made Sara and Meme the butt of recent joking are now starting to affect me as well. Every couple of minutes, one of us goes running for the bathroom.

Najiba's husband arrives a bit later on, shortly followed by Nasreen's husband. We all eat dinner together. Everyone enjoys a good laugh over Sara's encounter with the tailor. Then, Nasreen shows up with her daughter, and the driver drops by with his wife and teenage daughter, neither of whom we've met yet. During the course of the ensuing conversation, Najiba mentions our first, experimental flirting with the *atan*. This proves to be quite a riot, and of course we're asked to show off our newfound "skills." Someone mentions that Najiba really is a very good dancer, but again she refuses to take the stage, claiming that it's really her husband who knows what he's doing. We put on the new tape and the driver—easily the most extroverted Afghan male we've met thus far—gets right into it. He starts off dancing in the middle of the rug while the rest of us clap along with the beat. He spins around, his arms held up high and a look of rapture on his face. He makes his way (somehow it seems as if he isn't even moving his feet) over to his daughter, who blushes deeply but obligingly takes her father's place in the center of the rug and the ring of spectators. Then everyone joins in, save Najiba. Her husband dances, though, his movements more restrained than our driver's, but with such feeling that I begin to tremble. He seems so happy while dancing that it almost moves me to tears. Even the children start in, as does Nasreen's husband, opening up a bit. As a way of thanks, we give our rendition of the *Sevillana*.

At the height of merriment, the lights go out.

We try waiting out the darkness for a bit. Someone goes for a lantern. When it seems like the lights aren't going to come back on for a while, the families begin saying good night to each other.

There is a great plant out on the patio and underneath the clotheslines; it looks like a crest of broad, light green palm leaves minus the trunk. Before retiring to our room, I pause to gaze at it for a moment. And this is the first time I have noticed it, but a brand-new leaf—until now rolled up like a giant blanket—has unfurled and spread out over the others.

MONDAY, AUGUST 7, 2000.

Peshawar.

To an anthill, even a gentle rain can be a flood.

We get up late. The night has been a long string of trips from the bedroom to the bathroom and back again. It's hot. We've been dozing all day.

Najiba's baby is crying uncontrollably. Nothing seems to calm him down. Najiba tries feeding him, nursing him, cooling him under the faucet, rocking him gently. Her daughter isn't much better: they both have come down with a fever. Najiba is worried; although she doesn't say anything, her concern is evident.

Azada returns in the afternoon. We chat for a bit; we tell her about what we've seen and done, but the general concern for the two little ones dominates everything. The crying continues; the fevers are worsening. It does nothing to remind ourselves that babies occasionally go through bouts of fever; the mothers are always and ever worried. It's not healthy for a fever to go on too long, and the frequent baths and cool cloths don't seem to be helping to break it. There's nothing else we can do; there are no thermometers, no pills, no nothing.

The tailor and our neighbor return with our finished clothes.

"Tabrik!" Azada exclaims. When someone tries on a new set of clothes

for the first time, it's customary to congratulate them with this expression.

"*Tashakor.*"

Najiba is waiting for her husband to get home from work. When he does, the two of them will take the babies to the doctor. They'll take a taxi there, and spend the night at Najiba's mother's house, who lives near the clinic. I'm afraid to even think about what this might do to the household budget. *"To an anthill, even a gentle rain can be a flood"* goes another proverb.

We fix dinner ourselves. Azada lets us help her. We've missed her terribly. Her grandmother, along with the rest of the refugees in her camp, sends us their memories.

We are alone in the house, and have no need to hide our indecent nightgowns. Tonight we sleep outside, on the porch.

TUESDAY, AUGUST 8, 2000.

Islamabad.

You won't seem like a stranger if you adapt to what's in front of you.

We get up at five in the morning. As has been the plan, today we leave for Islamabad. It's a five-hour road trip, and so we decide to take the bus, on account of its air-conditioning, even if it's a relatively expensive mode of transportation here: a dollar per passenger.

We pack our bags for the two-night trip. Our driver comes to pick us up and takes us to the station, where he'll wait until he's sure we're safely on the bus, loaded mostly with Pakistani businessmen who will be making the trip with us. We are the only women on board. Dark curtains are drawn over each window, plunging the interior of the bus into shadow.

On our way to the station, we drive past the children carrying the steaming cans again. Azada explains to us that they contain smoldering aromatic substances whose vapors are supposed to be good for one's health.

The bus station is a place of dust, noise, and constant activity. Travelers, vagrants, beggars, drivers, conductors, and children selling sundry items to the travelers: sodas, cookies, and candy.

We take seats near the back of the bus. Once full, it somehow reminds me of a small movie theater. Finally, we're off. I open the window shades so I can look out at the places we're driving through. But once the sun gets too strong, the driver asks us to close them again. I don't want to travel the entire way without seeing anything, and so I stick my head between the curtain and the glass so I can continue to peek out. We cross a bridge spanning a river. I'm surprised to see two different colors of water: reddish brown and greenish blue. Azada tells me that the waters of two rivers are mixing here. One of them is the Kabul River.

Kabul, Kabul . . . These waters really come from Kabul? Will we actually make it there? I am sure of it. We'll get our visas. It will all work out fine.

As we drive—and just as when our plane came in for a landing the other day—the landscape and its colors begin to change. The dust, dryness, and ochre tones give way to humidity, greenness, and exuberance. Kipling's India, perhaps. Islamabad is the new capital of the new Pakistan. It was designed ten years after the split with India; a city with no history and no past, so as to contradict the two traditional major cities: the center of political power in Lahore, and the center of economic power in Karachi. It's much like Brasília, in these ways. It's designed very geometrically, with wide avenues, modern buildings, embassies, institutions, and offices. Beautiful and cold. Ostentatious and artificial. I'm older than it is. But it sits alongside Rawalpindi—"Pindi," as it's been nicknamed—which is ancient and legendary. We're in Punjab, in the area known as Five Waters.

Azada has taken her shoes off so she can draw her legs up onto her seat. But with the jolting around of the car, they've gotten lost. When we arrive at our destination, some of the businessmen get up and help her look for them. Azada says she's quite embarrassed, but still she smiles.

We get out at what looks like little more than a crossroads. But a short walk brings us to a taxi stand surrounded by a motley assortment of cars for rent. We haggle with a few of the drivers, and manage to find someone to take us to the place we've set up to meet Rustam. Azada meets up with one of her cousins; she'll be staying with an aunt and uncle in Islamabad, since it would be unacceptable under Afghan societal norms for her to stay with Rustam, who is not family. We split up and take separate cars. Rustam's family lives on the top floor of a little house with a garden. There is a sofa and an easy chair in the living room. We greet his aunt, who withdraws immediately. Rustam shows us where we'll be sleeping, and where we can leave our bags. He's given us his bedroom, which is quite spacious, containing two beds and a wall-to-wall bookcase shelved with poetry, novels, essays, philosophy, and history. Both Eastern and Western. We chat for a while about literature, and discover that we have some favorite writers in common. A computer sits on a desk. Another door leads off to the bathroom, complete with a toilet and a shower. We freshen up and head back out into the living room, where Rustam introduces us to his two cousins, all three of whom speak English and attend school. We take advantage of what's left of the morning to set up an appointment in the city, though we're still not sure what sort of things our Afghan friends have in store for us. With our mobile phone, we call the UNHCR office in Islamabad and our RAWA liaison. Both are available to meet tomorrow. Sara calls up the U.S. embassy, but neither the consul nor the ambassador is available to meet with us. It seems that both are out of the country at the moment.

We pass the time over lunch by again discussing traditions with Rustam, and once again the binomial term "East-West" crops up. Many problems seem to stem from the "Westernization" of the rest of the world, like the idealization or the condemnation of things not fully understood. Only from the vantage point of respect can one learn to appreciate the richness that is diversity, the horror that rises up whenever we forget that nobody is in a position of absolute truth, and the fact that ignorance and lack of knowledge lead to fear, intolerance, and—thus—to violence.

The brutal and excessive force that the Taliban and other similar fundamentalists exercise—under the guise of laws, norms, and traditions and with their only objective being the oppression of the people—can only inspire defiance. But, the Taliban aside, Rustam affirms that Afghan traditions that govern the relations between boys and girls, women and men, are much more oppressive than what we can imagine.

The food is ready. We move into a big room and sit on the rug with

Rustam's aunt and cousins. It's a wonderful spread, with a steaming plate of rice and hamburgers made from ground lamb meat adorning the table. Rustam informs us that if people eat or sleep on the floor, it's because they can't afford tables or beds.

We go out after eating. Rustam has borrowed a car from a friend so that we won't have to use taxis. We're in the area of Pir Wadahai, located on the road from Islamabad to Pindi. Shantytown-type dwellings, fashioned out of tarps and boxes, have sprung up on both sides of the road, inhabited by the poorest of Afghan refugees. Nearby there is a popular fruit and vegetable market frequently scavenged by poor children. The streets are narrow, and there's scarcely a breath of space between the different shop stands. But Rustam doesn't want us to get out and try to make our way on foot here. The market is full of life, of the color and hustle-and-bustle of people buying and selling, coming and going. We see more and more children rifling through piles of trash; they move through the back alleys with their giant plastic bags slung over their shoulders, almost as big as they are, and filled with anything edible they could get their hands on. They'll resell what they can, or take it home to their mothers as a way of providing their family with food. We take a few photos from inside the car. Rustam maneuvers us a bit closer. The children laugh: some come running up to the car while others go running off into the crowd. A group of girls shriek at seeing the cameras and start to run off, but a short distance away, they stop and turn back to look at us, smiling. Rustam calls them back over to us to talk with them: yes, they're Afghans; yes, they rummage through trash all day; no, they don't go to school. They're pressed so close up against the windows that it's impossible to get a good picture. One girl of about ten says she collects vegetables with her brothers from noon until six. Her father works in the market as well, offering to carry people's purchases back to their houses for them in exchange for a small fee. The girls continue to be enthralled by us. One takes a deep breath and says something in Dari. Rustam bursts out laughing.

"What did she say?" we demand.

" 'These women are very beautiful!' "

"Tell them that they are very beautiful as well."

Rustam translates. The girls burst out in a new round of laughter, and take off running once again.

Rustam starts up the car and we head out of the market toward Islamabad. We go past a magnificent park set high up on a mountain and filled with Pakistani families enjoying themselves. We decide to get out and walk around a bit ourselves, stopping to sit under the shade of some trees for a while. A vendor comes up to us, and we ask for a round of sodas. Everything is green, as far as the eye can see. It's quite humid, and the park is full of mosquitoes strafing us from all directions. We get up and walk down a path toward the parking lot; by the time we arrive, it's already starting to get dark. Our car is reluctant to start: it coughs, sputters, and protests, but in the end it decides to behave itself, and we aren't left stranded.

From there, we drive to a modern, commercial district, which even includes a few fast-food restaurants. We stop to do a bit of window shopping, and end up going in a bookstore to get a storybook for Najiba's daughter. We wonder if the children will be alright; we wonder how things are back at the house in Peshawar. We buy a few more books. Taking Rustam's advice, I decide on some Eastern stories, some Persian poetry, and a textbook on basic Pashto.

For the first time since we've been in Pakistan, we decide to eat in a Pakistani restaurant, one where the air-conditioning is running on max. The service here is exquisite, and the customers seem so as well: well-dressed families, nicely made-up women, and distinguished gentlemen. A group of Westerners—tourists—are seated at a nearby table. Though we're dining in a Pakistani restaurant, we ask for our food to be very mildly spiced, but by the second bite, my tongue and lips are already on fire. If this is mild, then what could "hot" be like? I light up a cigarette, and Rustam says:

"In the West, it's considered nothing for a man to light a woman's cigarette. But if I had done that for you here, everyone would think there was something shady going on between us."

As they say, *"You won't seem like a stranger if you adapt to what's in front of you,"* or in other words, *"When in Rome, do as the Romans."*

We leave the restaurant and step out into the chilly night air.

We return home, and go to bed early.

Tomorrow will be another day.

I chuckle to myself as I recall a comment Rustam made earlier that afternoon. He'd said something funny, and I turned away, hiding my face from him with a flourish of my chador so that he couldn't see my reaction. Rustam burst out laughing, and exclaimed: "You don't know how much men around here would love it if their women did that! It's a gesture of modesty that drives them crazy."

Such are the weapons of seduction here! In a society apparently without any sexual connotations is there a secret language of the chador, which may be used suggestively, as women's fans were used in the time of Goya? What other concealed messages are passed back and forth in the streets, in the distance, in anonymity? What do Afghan women find attractive in a man? What does an Afghan man look for in a woman?

Islamabad.

Even the steepest and highest mountains have a path leading to the summit.

We eat a hasty breakfast. We have to be in the hotel lobby at ten, where a member of RAWA will come pick us up. And we're pleasantly surprised when it turns out to be the same woman who attended to us in Peshawar. We say good-bye to Rustam, who's escorted us here, and go off with her. Her *muhrram* hails a taxi, and we head off for one of the orphanages that the organization operates.

Just as in Peshawar, nobody knows about this place's existence. Anonymity and secrecy are vital to ensure the safety of the women who work here and provide a safe refuge for nearly thirty orphans. The organization pays for them to all attend Pakistani schools, and during the summer vacation, they all stay with Afghan families.

"Most of them are good students, very intelligent boys and girls with a great desire to learn," one of the women tells us as we chat with her in a large, well-lit room whose walls are adorned with artwork done by the students themselves.

The orphanage teaches each child to live as part of a community: both the boys and the girls take part in all the chores and cooking, though each has his or her particular responsibility. Two women live there permanently, and each day two teachers come and give classes in both Persian and Pashto, two frequently spoken languages in Afghanistan that aren't taught in Pakistani schools.

But this isn't the only orphanage that RAWA runs in the country.

"As a general rule," our liaison tells us, "children come to us because their relatives know about the organization's activities. Some of them show up in pretty bad shape: they've been kicked out of their house, or they suffer from nightmares caused by all the real-life horrors that they've been subject to. That girl there, the one in red, came here when she was four, and she would cry day and night. We learned later that the *yehadis* had broken into her house and murdered her father."

We ask about where the money comes from to take care of the children's food, clothing, and education, and for the organization's general operating costs. They figure about fifteen hundred rupees per person per month, coming mostly from voluntary donations contributed by RAWA sympathizers.

We say good-bye to the students, who do the same in English before continuing on with their language class. Our liaison leads us into another room, where she has set up a series of videos, recorded by different members of the organization. Most of the images were filmed clandestinely in Afghanistan and depict the abuse and human rights violations perpetrated under the Taliban regime.

Another of the organizations' members comes in and sits down with us.

Next we see a recent film, shot earlier this summer, documenting the hardships brought on by the drought in many regions of the country. It's said that this is the worst drought to hit the country in thirty years, and it could have disastrous consequences for the population. Doubtlessly, they are already starting to feel its effects, and some people estimate that up to 1.5 million Afghans could die of starvation in the next several months. There is just no water. The wells are all dry. Irrigation canals hold nothing but dust. Livestock are growing thin and have no place to graze, and entire herds are being sold to ranches in Iran and Pakistan.

Another film comes on, documenting some of RAWA's many activities aimed at reclaiming respect for human rights and democracy in Afghanistan. As I'm taking notes, I learn that one of these most recent activities was realized last December 10, which was celebrated as a day of respect for human rights in Islamabad. Video footage shows men and women brandishing signs and placards calling for a new state of liberty and democracy in Afghanistan, affirming that women's rights are human rights as well, and accusing the Taliban of being fundamentalists. Afghan fundamentalists and Taliban sympathizers attacked the demonstrators, seriously wounding several of them, while the Pakistani authorities made many arrests. The press in our country didn't pick up any of this.

The third clip is even harder to watch: the public execution of a woman in the Kabul stadium.

Her name was Zarmena.

She was the mother of seven children.

She was accused of murdering her husband, but there was no proof.

They say that her husband was a member of the Taliban, they say he abused her, and they say that she killed him in the middle of the night.

All rumors.

But the Taliban arrested her and sentenced her to death.

The stadium is filled to capacity. The Taliban force the population to attend executions and thus witness the punishments handed out publicly. It's the same principle by which they take young boys from their homes and force them to participate in these acts, intending to harden them, break their spirits, and incorporate them into their ranks.

In the center of the field, a mullah reads excerpts from the Koran. Several Taliban take turns reading the charge, conviction, and sentence.

The *sharia*—Islamic law—is very clear on cases of murder: the victim's family is permitted to seek retribution through the execution of the defendant, but there are other options available as well. They can spare her life and demand an indemnity. Here in the stadium, the victim's family chooses this latter option, sparing Zarmena's life. And here everything should end: Zarmena should be released and allowed to return home with her seven children, who are present there in the crowd. But this is not the case. The Taliban representatives—reaffirming their dedication to reading Islamic law (the only valid law, in their eyes) to the letter—hold a brief conference in the center of the field before announcing in loud voices that, nevertheless, the execution will proceed as planned. The stands are packed. The people have come to witness this: punishment as example.

Zarmena is introduced to the crowd, seated in the back of a van and escorted by two other women. Taliban women. All three are covered in blue *burkas*. The van slowly drives over to the place of execution, right there on the grass of the soccer field. Zarmena turns to look behind her and—through the *burka* that enshrouds her entire body at all times—says something to her executioner, who is armed with a long rifle. Then she bows her head one final time, and a single round is fired into the nape of her neck. Her body slumps limply backward. The lower part of her *burka* falls open, exposing her legs clad in loose, printed pants. Quickly, the two Taliban women move to cover up the lifeless body. Zarmena's seven children have seen everything. The video's ambient sound captures the crowd's reaction: one of tears and lamentation.

The woman who came in just a few minutes ago dries her eyes. Our liaison translates her words:

"How much longer will Afghanistan continue to be nothing more than a prison for women? How much longer will we be forced to don a *burka* every time we step out into the street? How much longer will we be denied access to medical attention, education, and jobs? How many intelligent, professional Afghan women—driven here, to Pakistan—are reduced to hawking vegetables in the streets and collecting garbage in order to live? You all are women too . . . You must be able to understand what we feel, how we are suffering."

These words are too much.

The woman can no longer contain her emotions, and—sobbing—goes swiftly from the room.

"Would it be possible to obtain copies of these videos?"

We want to help denounce such iniquities. Broadcast the harsh realities that the Afghan population—and in particular the women—is subject to.

We leave the orphanage accompanied by our liaison, who escorts us as far as a large lot filled with shops and huts fashioned out of plastic tarps and boxes—another of the shantytowns we've become so familiar with. These hovels are occupied by the most recently arrived refugees: the most destitute. This miserable camp—sans water and electricity—is not far from one of the city's most prosperous neighborhoods. Every so often, the Pakistani police will come through here and disperse the camp, at which point they'll pack up and move somewhere else. But for the moment, they are here. They don't have to pay rent on this land. Many of the new houses on the other side of the road were built by these very refugees, as cheap labor is one of the few opportunities available to them. We're reminded of those who work at the brick factories, and other such manual jobs.

To get water, these refugees knock on the doors of their Pakistani neighbors. Some let them fill up buckets or carafes to take home. Others don't; water is scarce in Rawalpindi, and it has to be pumped out of wells that consume incredible amounts of electricity. Men who don't work at construction-related jobs either sell fruits and vegetables, collect paper, or rummage around in the garbage for things of value, such as wooden crates that can be broken up and sold as firewood, which they use also to fire the ovens where they bake their daily bread.

We're invited into of these makeshift huts. A woman is sitting there, fanning herself. Flies buzz everywhere. The heat is unbearable. We can barely fit inside, as several other women carrying babies come in as well.

A newly-born infant of sixteen days cries inconsolably, her naked body covered in scabs.

"It's from the heat. *Garmi!*" says its mother.

Another baby's body is covered in welts.

"The mosquitoes are eating him alive," explains the mother.

Another emaciated child comes in, hanging on to his mother's hand. She shows us her belly, swollen with hunger.

"Have you been to the hospital?"

The mother laughs. No. She'll have to get better on her own.

Another woman proceeds to tell us how five of her children have died of starvation. Her husband rescues boxes and papers from the gutters. It's enough to raise between 100 and 150 rupees every three or four days. They have four surviving children who work as well.

RAWA has managed to convince a few parents and a teacher to come here to give classes to some fifteen children living in these slums. They also provide paying seamstress jobs to a few of the women here: a woman can embroider up to twenty handkerchiefs in a day.

The families who have set up in this camp come, for the most part, from provinces in the north of Afghanistan. Accustomed to the much cooler temperatures of their homeland, they suffer much here in the heat of Pakistan, where they've come fleeing the Taliban, who have burned everything back home: their homes, their fields, their businesses.

Before leaving, we decide to walk around the camp a bit more. The wooden crates used for firewood are piled up outside the huts. A woman is using her oven to boil some water. Walking single file, we make our way up and down the ribbonlike dirt paths that countless foot traffic has worn into the grass. More huts, more hovels. But just down the embankment is the paved road flanked by real houses complete with glass windows.

Then we make our way back to the hotel to meet back up with Rustam and Azada. Our liaison will look into getting us copies of the tapes. We'll be in touch. We say good-bye with three kisses.

We see Azada come in, and hurry over to see her. It's been just twenty-four hours that we've been separated, but it seems like an eternity. I realize then just how much affection and caring I feel for this woman; just how strong the bonds are that we're forging between us. And just for an instant, my heart shrinks as I think about the day when we'll have to bid our fondest farewells and return home to Barcelona. So far!

Rustam has a bit of a surprise for us: he's taken the car to the shop, and now it doesn't protest noisily every time he tries to start the thing.

We have just enough time to make it to our next meeting at the UNHCR offices. We're greeted there by the person whom we were put in touch with before our trip here even began; the same woman who put us in touch with her colleague in Peshawar a couple of days ago. After an affectionate set of introductions, she gives us a brief history of Afghan refugees, and of the work that UNHCR does on their behalf.

Pakistan, despite having no legal obligation to do so, gave asylum to refugees who started to filter into the country after the Soviet invasion began. As the war dragged on, the waves of Afghans washing across the border increased: some were fleeing the purges and reforms of Communism, others from Islamic oppression, but all were seeking to escape the ravages and destruction of war. Now, people are fleeing Afghanistan because of the drought, and a whole new wave of refugees is expected near the end of the year. Pakistan asked for help from UNHCR in order to accommodate these refugees, and today there are roughly 203 new camps, each with its own clinic and school. UNHCR helps to finance these things, in part by paying the salaries of teachers, sanitation workers, and doctors. Medical care is generally provided free, although some clinics charge a small, symbolic fee that is quickly reinvested back into the camp; for example, to establish a new maternity ward. The education refugees receive in the camps is actually better than that received by poor Pakistanis, for the public school system there is highly inadequate. Afghan refugees enjoy some of the best conditions of any refugees on earth, as they may enter and leave the camps as they please, and they are free to seek work and even come and go from Afghanistan without any impediments. Also, with regard to medical attention, you can't forget that Pakistani hospitals have a specific element of their charter dedicating a portion of their services to the poor and indigent, and so Afghans who go to a Pakistani hospital almost always receive treatment. There are also the repatriation programs run by UNHCR. Some refugees who choose to participate in these programs are poor in Pakistan, and will continue to be so in Afghanistan, but they return anyway, just out of their desire to live in their own country. But the reality of the situation is that many decide to stay in Pakistan once they've assimilated, because the economic situation is better there.

Once again, I can't believe my ears. She hasn't said one word about the Taliban. Not a single mention of the systematic violation of human rights that occurs daily in Afghanistan. I have no idea where these marvelous refugee camps of which she speaks are located. I can arrive at no other conclusion other than that this person has never set foot in a camp in her life—that she hasn't even left her office since arriving here in Pakistan—because of her apparent absolute ignorance on these matters. Thus, not being able to speak openly about how things really are, she refers us to her colleague in Peshawar who can.

We pile back into the car.

I feel saturated with images and impressions, almost to the point of bursting. It's not exhaustion, desperation, nor sadness, but I feel the overwhelming need for silence, for a space in which to digest everything. A great need to be alone, so that I might free myself in my own way from this strange sense of grief that's literally crushing me.

Azada announces that we'll be going to meet a man who used to live in the camps and work at a brick factory before going back because he wasn't making enough to support his family. He'll go with us to visit a doctor—also an Afghan refugee and a neighbor of his—who treats refugees in a neighborhood near another brick factory.

I want to scream, "Enough already! Enough with the misery! The horrors!" I'd like to give up and just shut my eyes to it all. But I grit my teeth and bear it. I know that despite the temptation to say "I can't take it anymore" and give in, I really can. I just have to persevere a bit longer to move past this anguish brought on by seeing so many souls laid bare, stripped of all protection and exposed to so much pain. I know that nothing is truly unbearable. I can assimilate the pain, immerse myself in it, refuse to fight it, and thus move a few steps closer to that line which—when crossed—enables one to grow and learn. Turning tail and running away would do nothing. Moving ever toward the threshold of suffering and crossing it without fear enables us to discover new reserves of strength, lifts our burdens, peels away the serpent's old, restrictive skin. It draws us out of our cocoon so that we may become butterflies.

"Are you alright?" Rustam asks as he drives.

"Yes, I'm fine," I answer. "Don't worry."

I may not be fine right now, but I will be soon enough. I will cross the threshold.

In a neighborhood of narrow streets thronged with people, we pick up the doctor's neighbor who guides us through to the outskirts of the city. We pass a bare expanse of land and drive up to a rectangular building the size of a garage built of cinder blocks where the doctor—a tall, thin, middle-aged man—sees his patients: the Tom Joads of this country who live just on the other side of the clearing. I'm taken aback at the sight of their huts, lumped close together in a low depression in the ground; a lump rises in my throat and my eyes blur with tears. I grit my teeth to fight back the tears, and sit down on the doctor's wooden bench to listen and ask.

He was a military doctor in Afghanistan for nearly ten years. Four years ago, he decided to lend his services to the people of this area. He has problems with the Pakistani police from time to time because his dispensary is technically illegal, and they could close him down at any time. It takes him three hours to come from his own meager home to this other pocket of poverty where his patients live. Now, during the summer months, there isn't much work, and he attends to perhaps fifteen patients per day, though this can vary. Just as the maladies vary with the changing of the seasons: winter is marked by bronchitis, the flu, anginas, and pneumonia, while the summer brings bouts of diarrhea, gastroenteritis, dysentery, malaria, and typhus—infectious diseases common to people living in dangerously unsanitary conditions such as here, where there are no latrines or plumbing, and where flies and mosquitoes can breed and spread germs unfettered.

This doctor sees patients for free, charging only when he has to special order a medicine that he doesn't immediately have on hand. Most can be bought at the bazaar. He gets a discount if he buys in bulk, and this break is enough to make ends meet. Here in his office, he has the bench that we're sitting on, a medicine cabinet, desk, and chair. A microscope sits on the desk, which he uses for diagnosing cases of malaria.

"No, there is no infant vaccination program here." He responds to our questions with a smile tinged with sadness, though without a hint of bitterness. He's a brave, spirited, and peaceful man who talks about his job with a sense of hope. He sits there in his rope-strung chair with the aplomb, dignity, and elegance of a prestigious surgeon: a professional well respected by the community he serves.

We say good-bye in the waiting room before taking off. His manners, attitudes, and responses would not have seemed so strange if we had been sitting in the office of a successful private practice with leather chairs, mahogany desks, Persian rugs, and prestigious degrees framed and hung up on the walls.

The neighbor—the man who left the brick factory for more money at the sandal factory—is waiting for us outside. He thanks the doctor for having taken the time to speak with us. The doctor nods and offers his hand before turning around and retreating into the office.

Our guide drives us to the nearby brick factory, where he's set up another meeting for us. The representative of a group of families leads us through the maze of drying bricks while children run up to us from all around: smiling, mobbing us, and competing with each other to be in our photos . . . until the representative sends them off with a sour look. Finally we reach the house where a group of women are waiting for us. Rustam and our liaison will have to wait outside. Purdah.

They're women of the mountains, mostly Pashtun. I'm struck by the number of large gemstones and piercings with which they adorn themselves. Their clothes also show a great profusion of metallic ornaments; one woman in particular is wearing an outfit made of thick red cloth hung with hundreds of tiny, coinlike objects that tinkle like tiny bells every time she moves. Later, Azada tells me that women from the mountains are known for their elaborate styles, and that many will wear silver-plated necklaces or earrings filled with something called *hawang,* an aromatic substance that they use like perfume. I know this smell. Several times, during our women's group meetings, I've detected it: it's a dense odor—somewhere between incense, cardamom, and cloves—that permeates one's clothing.

These families came to Pakistan some eighteen years ago, just after the uprising against the Soviet troops began. These women haven't had to suffer through the horrors of civil war; they weren't subject to the rapes, kidnappings, and abuses that the *yehadis* and Islamic fundamentalists inflicted upon the women of their former town. They didn't have to endure the terror and oppression of the Taliban regime. They've been refugees for almost two decades, living as best they can though sometimes on precious little food, but they have never had to live in fear. You can see this in their sparkling eyes and their self-assured attitude. When they laugh, they do so without a hint of sadness, without that particularly Afghan sadness that leaks from the eyes of other refugees, especially the newly-arrived ones. Being with them is like a breath of fresh air.

An elderly lady approaches us as we're on our way out. She would be very honored if we would come inside and have a cup of tea with her. Azada thanks her warmly on our behalf, but explains that we have people waiting for us and must be on our way.

Once again, we get back in the car, which has been running very smoothly since the tune-up. The four of us women sit in the back, with the two men up front, Rustam behind the wheel. We head to the man's house—which doubles as his shop—where his wife is waiting for us with a considerable group of neighbors. We file inside and sit down on the floor, while Rustam waits outside. They're honored to have us visit, and for refreshments they bring out a soda from the bazaar for each of us. Our host recalls his days of working in the brick factory, and is happy to have moved here to the city. He earns enough by working at the sandal factory to provide for his family.

I scan the premises: the simple shop is relatively large, with walls fashioned out of boards, and a fan hanging from a beam overhead. Cooking utensils are piled up in a dish drainer.

One of the women, upon hearing that Sara is a journalist, asked her where she studied at, adding: "I studied journalism too, in Kabul."

Once again, I feel the lump returning to my throat.

The dark-haired woman sitting across from the Kabuli journalist was once a university professor. Now, both are refugees.

We want to take some pictures. The professor starts fixing up her hair and chador, but the shop owner informs us that we may photograph children and the store, but not the women. At this, they all get up and file out without complaint. Outside, under the glow of a streetlight, the women all admire Sara's deep red chador. Just then, behind me, I hear a voice calling to me: "Madam, madam!"

It's a girl, maybe thirteen or fourteen years old. She speaks an English that, to me, seems impeccable: easy and confident. Three or four other girls of about her age gather around, apparently impressed by her daring. I congratulate her on her English. She studies at home. Her friends don't know much, she says, and besides, they're shy. When she grows up, she really wants to be a journalist herself, so she can write about what's happening in her country. She asks me if will and desire will be enough to make this dream come true. Her parents must be educated as well—perhaps professors or journalists themselves—and she may indeed find a way to realize this goal of hers. Or perhaps not. I want badly for this young woman to achieve her goal. A scholarship would be ideal . . . a system of scholarships for iron-willed girls like her—and like Nasreen's daughter, who wants to be a doctor but without money will probably not be able to study medicine. I wish this girl luck with all my heart, and tell her that I'm sure that one day she will make a fine journalist indeed. She has so much determination in her eyes—so much confidence in both her words and posture—that it simply would not be fair for her to not do so. She's a fighter. Perhaps she will prove the old Persian proverb to be true: *"Even the steepest and highest mountains have a path leading to the summit."* Inshallah!

We exit the walled-in community through a gate that dumps us out onto a side street. Rustam is waiting for us next to the car, which is one block over on a wider, paved road. Our guide for the day walks us out this far. We say good-bye to him, thanking him heartily for all he's done for us. He remains there, standing on the corner, until we're out of sight.

It's already starting to get dark out. We suggest getting something to eat at the restaurant Rustam mentioned to us yesterday: an open-air buffet situated atop one of the mountains that encircle the city. We can see its lights from the road: from below, it looks like a great star set against the shadowy blackness of the mountain and the night sky. At the intersection where the road splits and one fork continues on up the slope, we are stopped by a police patrol. Across the intersection, another car coming the opposite way has been stopped as well. Rustam explains to the officers that we're headed up to the restaurant for a bite to eat. We're tourists. The police shine their flashlights on us, peering closely.

"You can't proceed. It's too dangerous."

Rustam insists.

"It's not possible. Turn around."

Thugs, robbers, bandits, smugglers, and drug traffickers . . . At night, this mountain, not five minutes from the Islamabad city limits, metamorphoses into the secret cave of Ali Baba and his forty thieves.

We find another Afghan restaurant, and go in to eat and talk. Are there other people like the ones we've met today? Other Afghans working at their own little piece of land, fighting to better their lives and to better the lives of others? Indeed there are, though many are exhausted after so many years of dedicating all their efforts to taking care of their families and putting food on the table. First, people have to eat, they have to be able to live with a certain amount of dignity. Then they can embark on more ambitious projects.

What do the Afghan people want more than anything? Rustam puts it in very simple terms:

"That we be allowed to live in peace, that the foreign interference which has been decimating our country for the past century comes to an end, that we be able to do things in our own way, that democracy be established, and that we recover the freedom to exercise our rights as human beings. Afghan intellectuals can't turn their back on the country. Those who have gone away—to the West—and are trying to forget where they're from are committing treason against Afghanistan and her people. We have to work for change, and we have to do it here."

Azada has to be back at her aunt and uncle's house soon. We go with her to the spot where one of her cousins is waiting for her, and then the rest of us go back to Rustam's house. We've barely picked up the threads of the conversation when a sudden downpour strikes us. A monsoon?

"Do you know what I'd like to do right now?" I ask the group.

"Go out in the rain," Rustam answers immediately.

"Yes."

"Go, then," he says naturally.

I climb out through a window and drop onto the terrace, so as not to disturb Rustam's family, who are already asleep. The water is up to my ankles. A minute later, I'm soaked through to my bones. It's exhilarating. I feel completely happy. I've finally crossed the threshold of sadness and, just as I'd thought, peace and a higher state of consciousness have taken its place. I'm shivering with cold, and go back inside through the window.

"Hurry, take a hot shower and get into some dry clothes," Rustam says.

Sara and Meme look at me as if I'm crazy, foolish, eccentric, and just plain nuts all at the same time. I don't care. On the other hand, I like Rustam's reaction. There's nothing I like better than being myself—being accepted just as I am—and I like it when people take the odd with the normal and don't even bat an eye. Before going to bed, I jot down in my notebook: "I danced during a monsoon!"

THURSDAY, AUGUST 10, 2000.

Peshawar.

Trees do not move when the wind does not blow.

We drive back to Peshawar early in the morning, and go straight to the Taliban consulate. Today is the day where we find out whether we've been granted our visas. The driver parks on a side street—just as he did a week ago—and accompanies us into the office. The waiting room is full of people including two Western-looking women dressed in Afghan clothing, and a man bearing a Swiss passport. The same official we met with last time greets us with a nod and makes his way to the main office. The minutes tick by, but nothing happens. Nobody goes in or out. Ten minutes, fifteen, twenty . . . Finally the official returns with a sheaf of papers. When our turn comes up, he tells us that he's very sorry, but the consul has left for the day without signing any visas, and there's nothing we can do but come back tomorrow.

We go back outside to where Azada is waiting with the car.

"We won't know anything until tomorrow."

We take advantage of the extra time to run a couple of errands. On the way, we realize that tomorrow is Friday: the Islamic sacred day. Will the consulate be open? We make a quick U-turn and head back. Our driver goes in to ask; yes, they'll be open tomorrow, but only until noon.

We breathe a collective sigh of relief. The truth is that we were starting to think that this whole thing was a charade, that we'd be given one excuse after another until our trip was over and it was time to return home. They hadn't denied our visa applications, but they hadn't granted us them either. It could be worse; the rationale wasn't as absurd as it could have been, probably because of the Taliban's efforts to improve their image and gain recognition among the international community.

Upon returning home, Najiba greets us, warmly as always. The children are fine and without a trace of fever, and her eyes show not the slightest trace of worry.

Another grand new leaf has opened atop the palm on the patio.

We dedicate the afternoon to household tasks, and to lounging out on the patio to chat.

When Najiba's husband arrives, Azada launches into a lengthy conversation with him about our upcoming trip to Kabul, trying to foresee any possible hitches, tie up any loose ends, and to decide how and in what order to do things. It gets intense.

Rustam won't be able to accompany us, because his beard hasn't grown out sufficiently. Azada will travel under an assumed name, something easy to remember: she looks at me, and selects the name that she actually chose months earlier, when we barely knew each other and when I first asked her if she would be the principal character in a book I wanted to do on Afghanistan.

We'll travel as simple tourists for all intents and purposes, and we'll conduct ourselves as such anytime we go out in public. Our relationship with our interpreter will be strictly professional, to protect her identity and not put her safety at risk. If something should ever come up and she were not able to make it to one of our designated appointments, she'll try and send us a message through one of her confidantes (if that is at all possible) and we'll then continue to conduct ourselves as tourists all the way back to Pakistan.

"Don't worry; everything will be fine."

Then she tells us how to identify a Taliban in public: it's not just by their magnificent turbans, but also their clothes. She also describes the clublike sticks that they usually have in hand, and how they sometimes fill them with coins so as to make their blows more damaging. Indeed, there are people who have died as a result of one of these beatings, which can occur at any time and for the slightest little triviality.

Before we go to bed, Azada draws up a list of the places she wants to show us in Kabul, places that it's important for us to see. We're so sure that we'll be receiving our visas tomorrow that we go ahead and make our plans as if we've already got them in hand. And why wouldn't we get them? Everything is going so smoothly . . .

My mind is ablaze as I try to fall asleep. I don't believe in destiny, luck, fate, or predestination, but I believe in life and I believe in myself, as well as in the choices that we each make out of the infinite number of possibilities presented. Looking back, it's easy to discern a continuous thread of decisions and circumstances—favorable or adverse—that have in some way led us here, to the present. *"Trees do not move when the wind does not blow"* affirms an old proverb, stemming from the region around Kabul. Everything we do has causes and consequences, though we may never even see the majority of them.

FRIDAY, AUGUST 11, 2000.

Peshawar.

There is always a road that leads from one heart to another.

We get up at the break of dawn, eager to have our visas in hand. We tell ourselves that if they weren't going to grant us them, then they would have denied us yesterday. The waiting room is full of people again, including a young, blond Western man who smiles at me.

"Stop staring at people," Meme says.

It's too late. The young man comes up to me. He rattles off something in Spanish—the Spanish of someone who's traveled in Latin America. He wants to know if we're headed to Kabul, yes, and if we've gotten our visas . . . He's going there too; leaving tomorrow, assuming they grant him his visa. The conversation sags, but there's nothing we can do about it. We don't want to get caught in that sort of dialogue about traveling that so often descends into that typical yet annoyingly logical question, "why don't we travel together?" That wouldn't work for us. Better to cut it off now at the risk of seeming rude rather than having to lie or give some convoluted explanations later.

Finally they call us into the office. The consul greets us amicably, with his ever-present smile. He searches and searches through a mountain of

A street in the Peshawar refugee camp.
(All photographs courtesy of Random House Mondadori, S.A., Barcelona, Spain.)

Women in a Peshawar embroidery shop.

Weaving rugs in Peshawar.

Refugees work day and night in a Pakistani brick factory.

Afghan refugees in Peshawar.

A beggar hides her shame beneath her *burka* in a Peshawar bazaar.

An Afghan girl begging outside
a fabric shop in Peshawar.

A Peshawar shop where several young students live.

Young Afghan refugees constructing birdcages in Peshawar.

Children scavenging for discarded onions outside an Islamabad fruit-and-vegetable stand.

Woman baking bread in a
Peshawar refugee camp.

Women in Kabul.

A class at the school in Peshawar.

The ruins of a street in Kabul.

papers until he comes across our applications, which are all clipped together. He asks for our passports, and the sweet Taliban devil rocks lazily
back in his chair before stamping them. We've got our visas.

Let's go! Let's go!

We make our way out of the office doing our best to stifle our excitement and keep calm until we meet up with Azada back at the car.

We're going to Kabul!

The first thing we must do now is go celebrate. Our driver takes us to
a small Afghan spot, and we go in for an ice cream. After that, we drop by
a pharmacy to stock up on some provisions, and then—exhausted—we all
go to an Internet café so Azada can catch up with her e-mail. While she
hacks away at her keyboard, the rest of us run into a big, modern super-
market to pick up some supplies for the road: cookies, gum, candy . . . and
also to get the ingredients for tonight's celebratory dinner: macaroni with
tuna and tomato sauce.

We have lunch within walking distance of the café, because our driver
is starting to feel lightheaded. It's the heat. *Garmi.*

After eating and resting for a bit, he feels well enough again to take
us back to Najiba's house, where she is overjoyed to see us with our visas
in hand.

Unfortunately, we won't be able to visit the refugee camp that Najiba's
husband put us in touch with after all. We'll have to leave before we have
the chance. One more thing to add to our list of people and places that
will have to wait for a second trip. Next year, perhaps?

Next, we do some shopping, having located a secondhand clothing
shop. Sara needs a bag for her tape recorder, camera, and notebooks that
she can more easily fit underneath her *burka.* Azada looks for some sandals. A man selling purses, wallets, and used duffel bags turns out to have
been an engineer when he lived in Afghanistan. We head back to the car,
and Azada goes off with the driver on another errand. We'll wait here inside the car. In the afternoon sun. Basking like lizards. We watch a man
near one of the shops wash the dust from his hands, feet, and face, the water

splattering on the ground. Finally Azada returns, with two books that she's bought for me. One is entirely in Dari, while the other is bilingual (Dari and English), which is a collection of short, fun stories about the character Nasruddin, a cunning and tricky survivor who lives off his own ingenuity and the foibles of others. He reminds me of Spain's own Lazarillo or El Buscón, or the German character Till Eulenspiegal. These kind, shameless characters form part of the popular culture of all cultures, and their tales can make us both laugh and think. Several nations claim to have given birth to Nasruddin: Iran claims him as one of their own, while in Turkey, there is even a much-celebrated holiday named after him. Uzbekistan, however, contends that Nasruddin was born in the famous, ancient city of Bukhara, which was in its day a grand center of culture, poetry, and art. But whatever his country of origin may be, Nasruddin is indeed a much-loved character throughout Central Asia, and everyone knows and laughs over his adventures.

From here, we move on to a park located near the city center. It's usually frequented by Afghan prostitutes, and we're hoping to perhaps interview some of them. But either because of the time or because of our own inexperience in such matters, we don't manage to find any, but we do see—sitting on the ground alongside a pedestrian footpath near the park entrance—an elderly woman, her *burka* lifted up to expose her face, begging for coins. Azada goes up to her and, with her usual affability and charm, strikes up a conversation with her. Respectful and obliging, she calls her "mother"—*maadar*—and asks her about her life and circumstances.

The woman—Afghan, of course—takes care of her daughter and grand-children. Both she and her daughter are widows. Some time ago she was able to get a job doing laundry for a foreign woman, until one day, the woman disappeared. Now, she begs for coins all day, saving up what she can. She opens up her bundle of worldly possessions, revealing a few crusts of bread and a plastic bag containing a few small tomatoes.

"What did you bring us, Grandma?" is the first thing she hears from her grandchildren when she arrives home every night.

The woman breaks down into tears: a disconsolate sadness that has been pent up for far too long, a sadness born of built-up pains with no one to vent them to, of having to put up a facade, day after day and without fail, for her widowed daughter and her hungry children. Meeting someone like Azada, with the grand sense of humanity that she naturally exudes, with her sympathy and sincere interest, has opened up the floodgates of emotion.

A few weeks ago, Azada wrote to me that she was thinking about this woman to fill one of the spots that may open up at the school if they are able to get funding for the HAWCA project that includes a new school kitchen.

I know of yet another proverb that reads, *"There is always a road that leads from one heart to another."* Azada knows how to find this road.

Before heading back to the house, we make photocopies of our passports and our Taliban visas. Najiba's husband will keep copies of these documents here, just in case. It seems a prudent thing to do, though we don't expect anything will happen. We feel safe among our new friends' serenity, sensitivity, and consideration.

At a prepared food shop, we buy two roasted chickens for lunch on the road to Kabul tomorrow, and Azada finds herself a pair of sandals. *Tabrik!*

Once again, it's already getting dark by the time we return to the house. Azada's uncle is there waiting for us; he's come from the refugee camp to accompany us to Afghanistan. He greets us with the same timidity characteristic of most Afghan men, though also with an enchanting smile. Azada contacted him right after we got our visas, and he dropped everything so that he could come with us. I'm not sure how the lines of communication work between them, as there are no phones at the camp, and so I figure that someone must have gone there to bring him the news. Once again, I marvel at the simplicity with which these people evade and overcome obstacles in their path.

Najiba has cooked up some white rice, but she insists on cooking the pasta also, and invites everyone in.

Two plates of pasta with sautéed onions, tomatoes, and tuna make for quite a spread.

Tonight there's no time for our usual evening soiree, as we have bags to pack. Azada's gotten two more *burkas;* one for Sara and one for me (Meme had already gotten another back at the market). Before I try mine on, I spritz the inside of mine with a bit of perfume. They're secondhand *burkas,* and I'm picky when it comes to odors.

We go over our budget for the umpteenth time, making sure we have enough money for the hotel, food, transportation, and all the other expenses that could arise during the trip. Then we give Najiba the copies of our documents for safekeeping. We double-check to make sure we aren't forgetting anything. Once again, it's just us women in the room, with the men gathered outside. Purdah.

I go out onto the porch.

Azada's uncle is smoking. Najiba's husband says something, probably along the lines of "she smokes too," because he immediately offers me a cigarette.

I accept, and we smoke together in silence.

Tomorrow we'll be in Kabul.

SATURDAY, AUGUST 12, 2000.

Afghanistan.

One can appreciate prosperity when he deals in calamity.

We set our alarm clocks for 4:15 in the morning. We move as quietly as we can so as to not wake the children or neighbors. It's still dark out, though the eastern sky is starting to take on a surge of violet. We make our beds, gather our bags, wash up, and get dressed. I go outside to smoke a cigarette. Azada's uncle has slept on the porch; he's still there, stretched out against a wall, and I move to the opposite end of the porch so as to not disturb him. The taxi arrives at 5 A.M. on the dot. We put on our *burkas* before stepping out into the street and readying ourselves for the trip to the border city of Torkham. From this moment onward, Azada will be Palwasha, a Pashtun name meaning "Dawn's Light."

The first thing I feel upon disappearing beneath the *burka* is precisely that: of having disappeared, of having ceased to exist, of being nowhere save for inside this blue sweatbox that reduces my world to a space scarcely bigger than my own body.

We leave the city and reach the first police checkpoint, still on Pakistani soil. A large sign prohibits foreigners from passing. We're about to enter land known as the "tribal zone," which isn't governed by the laws of Pakistan's northwest province. This strip of frontier is something of a no-man's-land, where neither Pakistan nor Afghanistan exert any control. Here, the tribal chiefs are in charge, and it is their laws that must be obeyed. The checkpoints are set up along the side of the road, which continues on through the legendary Khyber Pass. We're stopped at three of them, though we count several more as we go. Each time, our driver has to get out and pay the armed soldiers whatever "tax" they demand, usually fifty or one hundred rupees. The official Pakistani police know of such corruption, but even in the cities traffic police can pull a car over at random and—whether there has been an actual infraction or not—demand a fee. We're wearing our *burkas* during the trip so as to conceal our status as foreigners, which doubtlessly would prompt the police to demand an even greater payment. So whenever we leave a checkpoint behind us, we lift up the front of our *burkas,* but move quickly to cover up our faces whenever Palwasha warns us that another one is coming up.

We climb and climb our way up into the mountains until we can no longer discern the valley where Peshawar sits behind us. Soon, our driver points to a spot up on the slope to our right. There, climbing on foot up an invisible path, is a line of men laden with large bundles on their backs: narcotraffickers. Patently visible. The drugs entering Pakistan from Afghanistan have reached such incredible numbers that now, as I write, the Pakistani government has officially closed the border with Afghanistan so as to both stop the new flood of refugees desperately fleeing their country as well as stop the influx of more drugs. It's not all out of benevolence, though: part of the motivation has to be that it's difficult for homegrown Pakistani drugs to compete in a market with products brought over the border in such a manner.

Part of me keeps watch for anything that might betray or draw attention to us, and for the slightest signal from Palwasha or our *muhrram,* but the other part of me is drifting among the craggy peaks, ecstatic and incredulous: I'm here, crossing the legendary Khyber Pass, made famous by the Mongol empire, which also crossed these mountains so very long ago. Previous dynasties preferred to use the Gumal Pass for their expeditions and for plundering India. It lies farther to the south, to the east of Ghazni, the marvelous and rich capital that—roughly a millennium ago—competed with Baghdad in terms of splendor, and whose armies—mainly Pashtun—carved their own fiefdoms out of India. Ghazni was destroyed a century and a half ago, thus giving rise to the star of the sultanate of Delhi: a Muslim state defined by Persian culture, set in a Hindu land, and ruled by Turks who enjoyed Pashtun support. Could this be the origins of Indian Muslims and—by extension—the cause of the rift that would eventually form Pakistan?

Yet another route provides a northern alternative to Khyber. It's the pass that Alexander the Great used after crossing Afghanistan and the Amu Dar'ya in order to penetrate the Swat Valley, where he conquered the ancient fortresses of Bazira and Ora before turning toward the plains of Peshawar.

Around eight in the morning we reach the border outpost of Torkham, which has been open for only about half an hour now. Still, it's a swarm of people. Food stands are set up along the side of the road, as are rows of taxis for hire, whose drivers are competing for the attention of travelers. On one side of the invisible line that is the border, Pakistani cars are picking up people for the trip down to Peshawar. Across the way, Afghan drivers are picking up people just crossed over from Pakistan. I can see a few Pakistani soldiers out my window, but above all it's just people, people, and more people. Afghan men and women coming and going. The Afghan-Pakistan border is absolutely permeable.

We stop and get out of the taxi, and lift up the front part of our *burkas*. Our versions have a sort of skullcap that secures the *burka* squarely at the crown of the head. There is a gauze mesh in front of the face and the fabric that drapes over the shoulders and torso is smooth and intricately embroidered. The rest of the fabric is pleated and hangs down, covering the entire body. Both pieces are sewn together, as well as stitched into the skullcaps so the *burka* doesn't shift, though the front piece can be thrown back to uncover the face.

Here it's alright for us to look like foreigners.

We present our passports to the Pakistani officials. One is seated behind a great wooden desk, and invites us to sit down as well. He takes some notes by hand, very parsimoniously recording all our information on a blank sheet of paper. We try to project the same sense of calmness as he does. We're about to do it. Patience. When he's finished writing down what he needs to know, he gets up and exits the office. We breathe a sigh of relief. We look around at each other and smile to see us all in this guise, draped in our *burkas* like a monk in his robes. The official pokes his head back in and asks that we wait just a moment. We do so, and a tall, well-mannered, and honest-looking man with penetrating eyes comes in. He greets us by shaking hands, and sits down informally on the edge of the desk. He doesn't introduce himself, but we learn later that he works for the Pakistani Intelligence Services.

First off, he informs us that we've come here illegally, that we needed a special permit to travel through the Khyber Pass—rife as it is with bandits and drug traffickers—and that nobody is authorized to do so without a military escort. This is considered a crime, and he ought to send us back to Peshawar straightaway. We deceived the checkpoints by hiding ourselves under our *burkas,* and he wants to know why.

We are genuinely shocked. When we were granted our visas by the Taliban consulate, nobody told us that we would also need a special traveling permit. We're genuinely and profoundly apologetic and contrite: we had no idea that we were committing a crime.

Perhaps we were trying to enter Afghanistan clandestinely, he insinuates, all the while keeping his penetrating gaze focused directly on us. Perhaps we are journalists?

Journalists? No, we're not journalists, and of course we weren't trying to sneak into the country. After all, why would we, considering that we had our visas?

The intelligence officer continues to focus on the issue of the *burkas:* who told us that we had to wear them? And who got them for us? Obviously, they aren't new, so they must have come from someone else. Whom?

We could have said that we bought them the day before at a second-hand clothing shop, but for some reason we give a litany of other excuses: they prevent people from staring at us, that we're tired of being hounded by children begging for coins in the streets, et cetera. Plus, from what we understand, women really should wear them in Afghanistan.

This man with the eyes and nose of a hawk then returns to the topic of our professions. He wants details: the names of the companies where we work, and the type of work that we do there.

He's alert, hoping to catch us in a bind, but we're alert as well, giving only brief answers to his questions and avoiding the lengthy explanations that inevitably would trip us up and betray us. We're just tourists, nothing else. And not even intelligent, well-informed tourists either, since we've obviously made a terrible mistake. When we're not sure how to answer one of his questions, we feign as if we don't understand him.

Then he changes the subject and asks us about our stay in Pakistan, as if the interrogation were about to end. He's interested in what we've done for the past few days. Well, we went to see the Peshawar art museum, we spent a few days in Islamabad . . .

"What was the name of the hotel you stayed in there?" he immediately asks.

Without hesitating for an instant, we give him the name of the best hotel in the city.

"Can you tell me your room number there?"

We look around at each other, shaking our heads.

"No, I guess we can't remember."

"But you had one room? Or did you get three separate ones?"

"No, it was one room for the three of us."

Here he pauses for a moment, perhaps to unnerve us or trick us into explaining things he hasn't asked us to explain, just for the sake of filling the silence. But we've seen our fair share of spy films, and aren't about to fall into that trap. We keep quiet and wait.

Do we work for our government or some other public institution? No.

So, if we're not journalists, nor do we have any relationship with the world of journalism, then why have we come here? What do we hope to find? What is the purpose of our visit?

All we want to do is a bit of sightseeing, and also visit Kabul.

There's no tourism in Kabul! Everything's been destroyed. Kabul is in ruins, and the country is at war.

I suggest to Sara that she mention her interest in the silk trade, and her fascination with the ancient history and legendary past of Central Asia.

"Stop with the bullshit. I don't want to hear about the silk trade, or anything like that," he says to me in Spanish.

Then our interrogator moves on to the subject of the interpreter who is traveling with us. He wants to know how we hooked up with her; where we know her from.

"The hotel put us in touch. When we got our visas, we asked about interpreters at the reception desk. We needed one to get to Afghanistan, and we preferred that it be a woman."

He looks scrutinizingly at us, and then stands up swiftly. "We'll be talking with her next," he says as he makes his way to the door. He orders our driver to come with him.

Now we're very worried. Have we come this far, to the Afghan border, only to be denied entrance and turned away? We hadn't gone over all these details with Palwasha beforehand, and she'll have no idea what cover stories we've just come up with. Or will she? As soon as Sara sees her come in, covered by her *burka* and led by the Intelligence Service agent, she reacts quickly and exclaims: "We already said that the hotel put us in touch with an interpreter!"

Palwasha understands immediately, and proceeds to confirm our story.

Now it's her turn to answer an endless stream of questions: her name, her parents' names, her address in Peshawar, and the names of any other family members living there. These things were planned out beforehand. Palwasha answers everything calmly and confidently from beneath her *burka* while the agent notes down everything she says, and assures us that he'll be checking up on all of it. There are no smiles for the Afghan interpreter. The agent is fair with her, but kindness is reserved solely for us, the foreigners, the Westerners. Perhaps it's unintentional, or even unconscious: perhaps speaking with a *burka* makes them forget that underneath is a living, breathing human being.

Again, he presses on our desire to visit Afghanistan, a war-torn country without any tourist attractions. But the thing he seems most skeptical about is this issue of our *burkas,* until Meme interjects with her broken English:

"In Pakistan, Pakistani," she says, exposing her Pakistani garb underneath her *burka.* "And in Afghanistan, Afghan," she continues, pointing with both hands to her covered head and shoulders.

The Intelligence agent can't help but laugh. Such an explanation has tipped the scales of his suspicions and convinced him that we really are who we are and appear to be: a group of eccentric, dim-witted, and inoffensive tourists. Shaking his head, he motions for the customs official to stamp our passports. Then he hands them back to us and—in a protective and paternalistic tone of voice—tells us that he's going to make an exception in this case and let us cross the border after all. But he also tells us that we have to come see him without fail upon our return from Afghanistan so that he can provide us with a military escort to take us back to the city and guarantee our safety. After all, he says, we're guests of the Pakistani government, and they feel responsible for us. They can't run the risk of having us travel unescorted through the frontier region, where we could be kidnapped, raped, or killed, never to be heard from again. We assure him that we will indeed do so, repeating that never did we intend to do anything illegal; it was just that nobody had told us about the need for any special permits or passes. He bids us farewell, and before exiting the office he tells us to take off our *burkas,* which won't be of any help anyway.

And we oblige him.

Once we leave the building, we say good-bye to our driver, who has been present throughout the ordeal, sitting there calmly in the office. We learn that he had to pay a fine of a thousand rupees to the agent who interrogated us for them to allow him to return home.

We cross the border on foot, our heads covered only by our chadors and with our *burkas* tucked under our arms like jackets, trying to discern our companion's turban among the mob of people. We move back and forth, crossing over between Pakistan and Afghanistan, until we manage to find him, quite troubled by our delay. He's already gotten us a car and loaded our bags into it, but before driving off we have to check in with the Taliban border post, and have them stamp our passports as well.

The Taliban official who receives us smiles upon seeing our *burkas,* and I figure our good disposition has made a good impression on him. But when we ask him if we are required to wear them, he tells us no. He leads us under a bit of thatched roofing proffering shade, asks us to sit down, and offers us a cup of tea that we decline. He also asks us about the purpose of our trip and about our occupations, and then he wants to know if we'd like to interview an Afghan woman right now. I don't know if this is an offer to help us out or a ploy to uncover our true intentions. It could prove to be our only chance to interview a Taliban woman, but accepting such an offer would belie us and—in any case—what honest statements could a Taliban woman possible make under the threatening, watchful gaze of her oppressor? And so we assure him that our interest in Afghanistan and Kabul is solely tourism.

And that's that.

Compared with the inquisition we faced on the Pakistani side of the border, this has been a piece of cake.

Then the Taliban official turns his attention to our interpreter. He wants to know why she is traveling with us. She responds humbly, her head and body covered by her *burka* and bowed slightly: these foreigners need an interpreter, they insisted that it be a woman, and they were put in touch through the hotel where they were staying. But she adds if there is any problem with the arrangement at all, she'll turn around and head straight home.

The official reminds her that no Afghan woman is permitted to work for a nongovernmental organization. She replies that she isn't working for any organization; she's merely accompanying these women to serve as their translator. The official is satisfied.

Our passports are stamped and we pile into the car that our companion arranged for us while we were going through all the customs procedures. Complete with a Taliban driver, of course. Taliban men are easy to recognize by their appearance: a long, thick beard, grand turbans (while the rest of the male population covers their heads with either a small, circular cap or a turban improvised out of the large, square, traditional Afghan kerchief that has many other uses as well), their pants are cut a bit shorter and their long shirts are cut squarely and not rounded like the rest of the population, they wear loose-fitting vests, and many paint dark lines under their eyes and chew *naswar,* a strain of green tobacco that they place either under the tongue or between the lower lip and gums.

The driver doesn't permit us to talk for the entire trip, to say nothing of listening to the radio. Listening to music is prohibited in Afghanistan.

It's almost nine in the morning by the time we're finally on the road in our driver's brand-new Toyota. The drive to Kabul will take about eight hours, but Palwasha tells us that it used to be little more than an hour and a half. The Afghan capital lies just some two hundred kilometers from the border, but now—after so many years of civil war—the road connecting the two is almost nonexistent. The pavement has been blown away in places by bombs and land mines, and the resulting potholes are indeed impressive.

Leaving a few orange groves behind, the road now winds its way into the desert, flanked in spots by shady tunnels of tamarind trees. A short while later, the road turns and begins to follow the Kabul River.

We cross the valley where the violent battles that made up the third Anglo-Afghan war took place. British forces tried three times to invade Afghanistan from their foothold in India, and three times they were repulsed, suffering catastrophic losses.

The fighting among foreign powers for control of Afghanistan didn't begin with the Cold War or the armed conflict between the Soviet Union and the United States. Afghanistan had already been the stage where various forces vied for control of Central Asia, including the Russian czars, the British Empire, and the shahs of Persia. Agreements and broken treaties, pacts and strategies, territories and various Afghan cities, were lost and reclaimed: Herat, to the west; Peshawar and Kandahar or Quetta to the east; and the Uzbeki and Turkish territories to the north, along the banks of the Amu Dar'ya. An Anglo-Russian commission established Afghanistan's northern border; an agreement between Britain and Persia fixed the Afghan-Persian border that divides Baluchistan; and the British sketched out the Durand Line, which is still in effect today and which divides Pashtunistan and marks the border between unconquerable Afghanistan and colonized India. This was ratified by India but never recognized by Afghanistan, and this resulted in the appearance of a new state, Pakistan, in 1947.

The landscape is a harsh and beautiful mix: a rocky desert, almost white in places; vast stretches bleached by sun and solitude, barren and brownish gray; a river—the Kabul—more blue than the sky; and bits of green fringe, there where the rocky soil is interrupted by patches of fertile earth. In the distance are the White Mountains, called Safed Koh, in Dari, and Spin Ghar in Pashto. Imposing and impressive. To the right are the unexpectedly verdant Nuristan Mountains.

At various points along the road are Taliban outposts, distinguished by the white flag they fly atop a tall pole. The white flag—the international symbol of peace, truces, surrenders, and cease-fires—has, in the Taliban's hands, been converted into a symbol of violence, oppression, and terror. Only the highest Taliban officials and most respected men are allowed to wear white turbans. It's even prohibited for people—especially women—to wear socks of this sacred color.

We jolt our way ahead over the rough terrain, our bodies bouncing off the car's seats and windows. Palwasha's uncle is sitting up front, next to the driver, while the four of us occupy the backseat. Palwasha is still covered by her *burka*. We switch seats every so often to relieve cramps. We're drenched in sweat. It's so hot that even bottled water tastes like it's been freshly boiled.

To the right lies a recently harvested field. When poppies are in full bloom, all of Afghanistan becomes a giant red carpet. During the harvest season, thousands of migrant laborers are hired to do the work, just as fruit pickers or tuna fishermen would do in other countries. Opium is, after all, the Taliban's principal source of income.

We're approaching the capital of the Ningrahar province: Jalalabad, "where splendor resides." On the outskirts of this city—founded some five centuries ago by a Mongol emperor from India—the road is not as bad, and even becomes something of a boulevard, shaded by the dense foliage of the great, thick, hundred-year-old trees that grow along both sides of the road, their top branches interlocked to form a canopy. To our left is a military air base. A bit farther ahead and to the right lies the garrison post where, on January 13, 1842, the British sergeant Brydon came. According to legend, he was the last survivor of the entire British force, which numbered some 17,500 men and was decimated by the Afghans in seven days as they retreated through the canyons, gorges, and ravines between Kabul and Jalalabad.

This city, situated in an oasis ringed by mountains, always served as the kings' winter capital, and before war changed the face of the country forever, many Afghan families spent their winter vacations here as well. The famous blossoming orange trees were the inspiration for an annual poetry contest.

During the first few centuries of this millennium, the Jalalabad valley was an important center of Buddhist pilgrimage, and three separate and distinct written accounts describe how Buddha himself visited the valley to face the dragon Gopala, a tormented spirit whom Buddha pacified with his shadow. It also formed part of the trade route that linked China and India, traveled by caravans loaded with silk, spices, ivory, rubies, lapis lazuli, and turquoise.

But none of this matters now. Not archaeology, art, or the preservation of cultural vestiges from Afghanistan's past . . . there's room for none of these things under the Taliban's regime, save for destroying them forever.

We enter Jalalabad. For years, the only people to do so were either refugees or soldiers. We pass the medical school, and I feel a flash of affection for the doctor at the refugee camp who studied here, before war had decimated the place. It seems impossible that just a few of years ago—the Taliban occupied the city on September 11, 1996—young men and women could attend classes in this very building, dress however they wanted, and go out and have fun together. After the Soviet troops were expelled—and up until 1992—the capital, like so many other urban centers, was controlled by the Najibullah government, which was still receiving aid from the Soviet Union. Meanwhile, Islamic groups occupied the rural areas and launched attacks on government positions and the capital itself.

We stop briefly to buy bread and fruit (an Afghan melon) to eat. Scattered among the various stands at the bazaar are an assortment of money-changing stations, each with bills stacked nearly a foot high on top of wooden fruit crates turned upside down. We stay inside the car; our companion will do the shopping for us.

And we're back on our way.

The craters and potholes are back. We grab on to whatever handholds we can, all our muscles flexed to soften the jolting ride, My entire body is sore. Our driver accelerates a bit on the smooth stretches. During one of these stretches—and before anybody can react—we actually bump into the car ahead of us on the road. Palwasha is thrown forward into the back of the seat in front of her . . . but it's not serious.

Our driver stops the car and gets out.

The other driver stops and gets out as well.

They argue, yelling at each other for a short while, and then each returns to his respective car. And that's it: whoever screamed the loudest was right. Our driver doesn't even ask if we're alright; he simply shuts the door, spits out the window, and we're on our way again.

At various spots on the road, we see little piles of potato-sized stones. I've been watching them for several miles now; they seem to be everywhere, and I can't figure out any discernible pattern to them. So I ask. It just so happens that they mark places where land mines still rest. This way, drivers can weave in and out of the danger zones. Many of the craters and potholes along the way are the result of exploded mines such as these. Some of them may even have been built in a Spanish factory. Spain has sold arms to this country in the past, and continues to do so, as well as to Saudi Arabia (which supports the Taliban) and Iran.

There are no population centers along this stretch of road. But every so often we see—as if fallen from the sky—boys and men who, as soon as they see a vehicle approaching, toss spadefuls of dirt, gravel, or dust into the potholes and signal to the drivers which is the best route to take. In exchange for this service, drivers or travelers may offer them a tip . . . without stopping. They simply toss a few rupees out the window as they go on by. By now, I've gotten somewhat accustomed to the bouncing and swerving, the dust kicked up by other cars on the road, and the heat that, in other circumstances, would be unbearable.

The road seems well traveled enough: cars, vans, the occasional bus, and above all trucks. One of the things that I've noticed most about this road linking Afghanistan and Pakistan—besides its deplorable condition—is the steady stream of big trucks heading in both directions. Most of those heading to Pakistan seem to be carrying tires, melons, and logs. But others—especially those heading into the interior of Afghanistan—carry covered loads. There are a lot of these. Too many, it seems to me, for a country that's been at war for twenty years, subjected to economic sanctions, and maintains no diplomatic nor commercial relations with anyone. I can't imagine what the loads of tires are for. The enormous logs are the products of the logging being carried out in Afghanistan's remaining forests, and are on their way to be sold as lumber to Pakistan. The covered trucks must be transporting drugs or some other form of contraband. As Meme says: "I know Afghanistan produces a lot of melons, but not that many!"

In fact, Afghanistan produces more pounds of opium annually than melons. Under Taliban supervision, it has become the world's largest single producer of opium, shipping it out of the country by the truckload. There are no trains in this country, and the national airline, under sanction by the U.N., isn't authorized to conduct flights. So the drug filters out in truck beds, destined for Pakistan. The hermetically covered trucks coming from Pakistan are doubtlessly transporting arms to their Taliban allies. What other explanation could there be for the massive amount of truck traffic along this road, comparable, it seems, to highways leading into one of our major Western cities during rush hour?

The landscape here is indescribably beautiful—particularly for me, who adores harsh, inhospitable lands where any life at all seems a miracle. Sara thought it looked desolate, but I saw a certain grandeur in it, a sense of strength and dignity similar to its inhabitants. Solid fighters and survivors. The pale ochre of the desert mountains, the brilliant black of exposed rock in the gorges and ravines, the river's radiant blue, the changing tonalities, the nomads' encampments dotting the horizon, and the sudden and irrational explosions of green in the middle of the desert . . . All these things seem to parallel the people's resolve, their capacity for stoic resistance, the strength of their affections, and their disposition to smile. Between bends and bumps in the road, I feel myself falling in love with this country and her people. An irrational and unjustified love, perhaps, but one full of feeling nonetheless. A sense of nostalgia for this place will stay with me forever.

We stop for lunch around 12:30, parking the car near the river and the Sarobi gorge, which was known in ancient times as the "silken throat." After taking Jalalabad, the Taliban ran guns through this very spot, however impractical the location may have seemed. After several days of fierce fighting on the eastern side of Kabul, they finally managed to break through and take control on September 26, 1996. This is after they soundly defeated Hekmatyar's forces the winter before, who had invaded from their base in Sarobi, and—without interrupting their assault on the capital, which was controlled by Massoud—they subjected Kabul to a withering blockade, stopping even shipments of humanitarian aid while the population suffered through a winter on dwindling food and firewood. Littering both sides of the road here are the rusting, abandoned carcasses of tanks and other vehicles: vestiges of this very recent war.

Before heading off on his own, our driver parks the car alongside a small, one-story building that functions as something of a snack bar catering to travelers. They serve food and drinks, but you can also bring your own food and picnic there. The rest of us sit down on an embankment that drops down to the large, smooth stones of the river's edge. We take off our sandals and splash our feet in the water. But when I make a move to roll up the cuffs of my pants so they won't get wet, Palwasha immediately catches my attention. Facing the river and with her back to the road, she's lifted up the front of her *burka* so she can wash her face. It doesn't look easy: standing in the river, draped in literally meters of fabric, and trying to splash a little water on you face without letting your chador fall in. I decide to dip mine in the water and moisten it, and the damp cotton feels wonderful in the breeze. I also manage to wet my hair a bit by cupping water in the palm of one hand while holding on to my chador with the other. A few meters downstream, our *muhrram* dives right in, without inhibition, shirt, or turban, and I'm more than a bit jealous. When the other picnickers leave and we're the only ones left by the river, we take a few photos, and go over our story one more time, just in case we're questioned again, get separated, or whatever: Palwasha is just an interpreter whom we hired through the hotel, and we are simple tourists, nothing more. We'll have to remember to act as such. Palwasha's uncle catches back up with us. Time for lunch.

We break out the covered saucepan wrapped in a cloth, which contains the two roasted chickens we bought yesterday afternoon. We also slice up the melon and the bread we bought back in Jalalabad, and carry everything into a large and completely empty cafeteria-like area. The rug on the floor is abrasive and prickly, even through our clothes. Several plastic jugs filled with water are lined up on a wide strip of oilcloth, and we wash our hands. Our beloved *muhrram* brings a round of sodas over to us. Lunch is wonderful. Palwasha mentions that when she left Kabul with her family, they had to spend a night in a place much like this. There was no electricity, and the large dining area was packed with other people fleeing the city and country. Everyone was concerned about making it through the checkpoints, as well as being very afraid of how close the armed mujahideen were to them. She laughs and recalls that during the night she had a nightmare and woke up screaming, much to the dismay of those trying to sleep around her.

Palwasha then packs up the leftover bread and chicken in the saucepan, and carefully wraps the saucepan back up in the cloth so it can be easily carried with just one hand, using the knot like a handle.

"It's what we usually do when we go on picnics."

Then she tells us that this very stretch of river was a favorite place for residents of Kabul to come when they wanted to get out of the city, especially on holidays, when they would arrive very early in the morning and not return home until the wee hours of the night. It wasn't this long of a drive when the road was in better condition, and there were trees, grass, and flowers along the riverbank . . .

But now, almost nobody comes here. It's prohibited.

We get back in the car and drive off.

We pass another burnt-out husk of a tank, draped in a thick, tangled, shiny web of destroyed cassette and film magnetic tape. This isn't the first time we've seen this. Destroyed tapes can be found everywhere, caught on scrap metal or telephone poles, or blowing through ditches like tumbleweeds. After taking control of a city, the Taliban would march through the streets and proclaim their orders and decrees over a megaphone or, sometimes, via the only radio station that they spared and now control. One of these decrees was that people had fifteen days to destroy all televisions and recording devices, and throw them into the streets. They even hung the broken TVs from trees like ugly decorations, and if someone was discovered to have a working television in their home, the punishment was severe and public.

The landscape is changing; we're heading into a more mountainous region. I can no longer see the stripe of the river. The craggy slopes rise so steeply that they occasionally blot out the sun. We stop for a moment; the men get out and pray. We get out of the car also, and snap a few photos without even trying to conceal our actions. Nobody ever told us not to. After all, aren't we tourists?

Our stop is brief, and soon we're on our way again. Down to our right we see a hydroelectric plant that once supplied power to Kabul and Jalalabad. Now, however, it lies abandoned. A bit farther up, we pass the dam itself and the little village where the plant's employees once lived. Now, though, it's long since been deserted, and fallen into ruins.

Here the road conditions seem to improve a bit—the asphalt isn't as shattered as it has been—and we continue on up past the rocky canyon Tangi Gharu, which many guidebooks claim to be the most spectacular vista in all of Afghanistan. Entering a tunnel, we find our path is blocked by a flock of goats. Later, going around a bend, I look down and marvel at how much altitude we've gained in only a few kilometers. Our driver stops near the top so we can get out of the car and gaze in awe out at the canyon and the road winding its way up the steep slopes. He mentions something to Palwasha's uncle, who repeats it to Palwasha, who in turn translates it for us: "He stopped here in case you want to take a photo."

We're all a bit surprised, as this is the first time our driver has even looked at us (to say nothing of speaking to us). Thus far, it's as if he's been transporting boxes. But we recover quickly and thank him.

The climb comes to an end when we finally reach the Kabul Plateau. Our driver stops at a fruit stand and pays a boy a few rupees to hose down the car. We have to roll up the windows. From here on, the road is still somewhat less than perfect, but the potholes are fewer and farther between. We're nearing Kabul. Heat and fatigue are taking their toll on us, but being this close to our destination fills me with a new sense of determination. My traveling companions are starting to nod off one by one, but the bumping and jolting keep me awake. I can't sleep now! I want to complete this last leg of the journey with my eyes open, my mind clear, and my senses alert.

One of Central Asia's largest prisons is on our left: Pul-e-Charji. Immediately after passing it, we find ourselves in Kabul's industrial region, which experienced a huge boom in growth during the sixties and seventies. Factories produced textiles, plastics, chemicals, bicycles, paints, and enamels . . . but now it's completely deserted. Even the buildings that managed to survive the attacks by Hekmatyar, Massoud, and other Islamic military leaders have now fallen into ruin, their walls crumbling and their roofs caving in. It's been almost a decade since the destruction began, and nothing has been rebuilt in the past few years since the Taliban occupied the city and subjected it to their fierce control, which included no plans whatsoever for rebuilding the economy or infrastructure. We drive deeper into the city and its terrifying desolation. Buildings that still manage to stand are scarred by windows either broken or boarded up. We drive through a residential area, pass a military school, a library, a theater, a secondary school, the Ministry of Sanitation . . . everything is closed down and paralyzed; buildings are all deserted, and show the scars of bombs and bullets on their blackened facades. We drive down a wide avenue. A local proverb advises that *"One can appreciate prosperity when he deals in calamity,"* and here it is as tangible as stone: nothing remains of yesterday's prosperity, save for the memories.

Kabul the Beautiful has become Kabul the Silent.

Our driver turns up one of the many little hills that dot the northeastern quadrant of the city. As we near the top, we see the Hotel Intercontinental, where we'll be staying. The driver loops around, so he can drop us off in front of the door. At one end of the building I see a sign that fills me with joy: "Bookshop." Perfect. It's nearly five o'clock in the evening.

The five of us go in the hotel's enormous lobby, which extends off to both the left and right. The front desk is right near the door, and so we go up to the receptionist and ask for a room for three. Unfortunately, that won't be possible; the best they can offer is two adjoining rooms, one a double and the other a single. We decide to take it . . . after all, it's more space, and two bathrooms instead of just one.

A hotel employee hands us our keys and carries our bags over to the elevator so he can take us to our rooms. We ask Palwasha and her uncle to come up with us, but the receptionist says something to her, and Palwasha tells us they can't go up with us. They say good-bye to us here, and we'll reconvene in the lobby at 8 A.M. tomorrow morning.

We're not sure what's going on, and Palwasha can't explain it to us in front of the receptionist, who speaks English. Her *burka* precludes any knowing winks or looks. We shake her hand good-bye. No hugs or kisses this time; after all, she's just our interpreter. We barely even know her. We get in the elevator with the bellhop and watch as the doors close, feeling just a bit uncomfortable. Just before they shut, Palwasha's uncle comes running up: we've forgotten the leftover chicken from lunch. We smile and laugh, and then the doors close again.

Our rooms are spacious, clean, and well lit. The balconies extend out the back of the building, and offer an impressive view of the city, which spreads out across the plateau below us and up the sides of the hills. The mountains ringing the city rise off in the distance.

Until we meet up with Palwasha tomorrow morning, we won't know for sure what happened down in the lobby. Later, we'll find out that the receptionist had not only stopped her from going up to the rooms with us, but she had also asked her a series of questions about what she was doing there and where she worked. The receptionist had also told her not to say anything about the interview to us. Palwasha feigned ignorance about much of Afghanistan's situation, claiming that she was just a poor girl who attended school in Peshawar and who took advantage of her language skills to make a little extra money acting as an interpreter for foreigners. She was then "asked" to leave the hotel, unless she wanted trouble. They told her that things had deteriorated here over the past couple of days, and that several women had been arrested for doing clandestine social work. Palwasha simply repeated that she was just an interpreter for a group of tourists, and then walked away with her *muhrram*.

While all this was going on unbeknownst to us in the lobby, we were exploring our rooms. There are no televisions, of course, but the bathrooms are spectacular. We all take hot showers, and wash our clothes in an orgy of soap and water. We all laugh uproariously at having turned every conceivable surface into a washboard. The single room has a sofa bed and a trundle bed in addition to the regular one. So we could have all fit into one room after all and saved ourselves some money. Had we been duped? Apparently so.

There's a knock at the door. A hotel employee hands us a little vase filled with flowers, and asks if everything is alright. Yes, everything's great. But we soon discover that every time we leave the room for whatever reason, one hotel employee or another pops up. They're all men, and very attentive, but they seem to be coming out of the woodwork. It's a bit bothersome. Are we being watched?

I go down to the lobby to try to find that bookshop that I'd seen as we drove up. It's closed. I check the posted hours, and peer in through the front window: it's packed with books and postcards. A story collection and a cookbook are set up on display. I make a mental note not to leave Kabul before I've had a chance to stop in and pick up a few volumes. As I turn to head back to the hotel, I see a group of Taliban men standing outside the library.

We all head down to the hotel restaurant just as it's starting to get dark out.

The feeling of not being able to take a step without being followed by one hotel employee or another is disconcerting, to say the least.

"Remember how I bet you all a dinner that they weren't going to grant us our visas? Well here we are! And what better place to repay my debt than in Kabul?" Meme exclaims.

She and Sara order Spanish omelets, which they have on the menu here. I ask for *qabalee palau*. Two Western-looking men are sitting a few tables away. As we're eating, a group of three other men come in and sit down at yet another table. We ignore them all. What surprises us is that they pay no attention to us as well. Isn't it odd that they don't even come up to say hello?

No more customers come in. This enormous building is practically deserted; it's like the ghost hotel from the Stanley Kubrick movie *The Shining*. The lights in the main lobby have been turned off, while those in the dining room cast an eerie, spectral glow. The number of employees greatly outnumbers the number of guests. We're attended to by three or four different waiters over the course of our dinner, while others hang back, waiting for their chance to offer an increasingly stifling bit of service. We just have to smile. Spanish omelets here are round, cooked in small frying pans, garnished with tomatoes and onions and served with hash browns. One of the waiters, upon seeing us fanning ourselves with our napkins, draws up a set of curtains and opens a window. Kabul's cool night air sweeps in, and things freshen up almost immediately. We order coffee and chat for a while after dinner, like any good tourist would do. The hotel concierge comes up to us to let us know that he's taken the liberty of hiring a car to pick us up first thing in the morning and take us to the Ministry of Tourism so we can obtain some sort of cards, "so that you won't have any problems," he says. Bureaucracy.

Back up in the room, we go over our list of places that our Afghan friends think we should visit. We hope that dealing with whatever it is that we have to deal with at the Ministry of Tourism won't end up making us late to our first meeting of the day.

The room gradually falls silent, as each of us writes down our impressions of the day in our notebooks. Meme drifts off to sleep, while Sara and I compare notes to see if either of us has forgotten anything.

Then I go out on the balcony, where I can see the waxing moon ride high in the crown of night over Kabul, looking like a giant slice of white watermelon. Only a few points of light describe its profile.

Afghanistan.

Kabul will be left without gold before it is left without snow.

At breakfast, we're attended to by so many waiters that if someone were to enter the restaurant just at that moment, he or she might think that we were queens from some exotic kingdom. Meme goes back up to the room, while Sara and I go sit in the lobby near the reception desk to wait for our interpreter, Palwasha. We see the three men from the restaurant last night—surrounded by bags and suitcases and with cameras hanging from each of their necks—bid an effusive good-bye to the concierge. Might they be journalists with some special permit? Since February of 1999, journalists have been forbidden from entering Afghanistan. Tourists, then? But who (save, perhaps, for a journalist) would think of touring a war-torn country?

The clock strikes eight, and our companion, Palwasha's uncle, walks in. He's come to pick us up and take us to the first of our preestablished clandestine appointments.

Meme still hasn't come back down yet, and so I go up to let her know that we're ready. I don't want to wait while she finishes getting ready, though, and so I go back down to the lobby. The concierge has taken a seat next to Sara, and I can hear the two of them conversing in English.

It looks like it began innocently enough. The concierge seems interested in our plans, and Sara simply mentions that we're here to look around Kabul. He reminds her that we need to get our passports stamped at the Ministry of Tourism, and adds that we really ought to hire an official driver and interpreter. Sara reassures him that our first stop of the day will indeed be the Ministry of Tourism, but with regards to the car and the interpreter, we've been very happy with the one we've had since Pakistan, and she's waiting out front right now with a taxi.

But the concierge is adamant: he won't let us leave the hotel in anything other than an official car, and with an official interpreter to accompany and protect us. Sara is getting exasperated; we already have one, and we're not interested in paying more money for yet another one. But the concierge has an answer for everything; he understands our dilemma, and he'll go outside right now to talk with this woman and get our money back. Sara insists that our interpreter be a woman, to which the man replies that women are not allowed to work in Afghanistan, and therefore there are no female interpreters. This particular woman just can't go with us. And he goes on to grill Sara with more questions about Palwasha: Who is she? What's her real name? Where did we pick her up? How do we know her? Where does she live? He offers to throw her off the premises, and make sure that she never comes back. Sara gets up: no, she'll go outside and speak with the interpreter herself.

Parked outside in front of the door is a white car with a blue logo painted on the door that reads "Afghan Tours." A group of Taliban men are loitering in the shade nearby. Sara goes up to the car, and Palwasha opens the door and gets out to greet her. But before she can say a thing, Sara explains the situation to her: they won't let us go with her, won't let us go out in the city unless it's with an "official"—and male—translator. She breaks down into tears: this hotel is like a prison. Palwasha quickly replies, much as she always does: *"Don't worry."*

She thinks we should just comply for the day so as not to arouse any more suspicion, which is what we'd agreed to do if any unforeseen problems (such as this) were to arise. She'll come back to meet us tomorrow morning at seven, and will fix everything then so that—despite this setback—we'll still be able to do most of what we'd planned on, like speaking with the people, and visiting the literacy classes for women and the clandestine schools for children that are scattered across this country. We resignedly agree, clenching our teeth, and say good-bye to Palwasha out there in front of the hotel.

The concierge offers to act as an interpreter himself—though he quotes a relatively high fee—but first he'll have to check and see if he's needed here at the hotel. This is driving us up the walls: not only are these people interfering with our plans, but we're being forced to absorb unforeseen expenses as well. So we're at least somewhat less disappointed when he returns and says that yes, he can accompany us today, and for slightly less than he'd initially quoted. Thus it is that we get into the Afghan Tours car along with our new male interpreter, and drive off toward the Ministry of Tourism.

We walk up a flight of dilapidated stairs and pass by several empty homes until we reach something of an office: a man sitting behind a desk, a group of Taliban officials, and a wooden bench where we're invited to sit. They ask for our passports, examine them, examine us, and one of the officials says something to the concierge. They don't stamp our passports; don't give us any sort of card or document at all. Nothing. They simply return our documents to us and we head back out to the car.

Before we set out on our tour for the day, we discuss payment with our driver and interpreter. Since we've already made our annoyance quite clear, the concierge-interpreter adopts a more conciliatory attitude, and convinces the driver to give us a bit of a rebate in addition to having lowered his fee by a few rupees.

And so our tour begins.

Our first stop is atop a hill at the opposite edge of the city. The place is called Tapa Maranjan, and from there we can see the remains of the once-grand mausoleums, since reduced to mere rubble by the bombings. One of them was the resting place of the king Nadir Shah. After checking a few facts with the driver, the concierge tells us a bit about the monument's history. A few weeks later, back in Barcelona, I consult a few reference books, and discover that the facts we'd been given didn't correspond to the places that we visited, and that these "histories" are probably better described as a hodgepodge of names and places scraped together and splashed with a healthy dose of improvisation. Our tour guides had turned out to be nothing but frauds. But, at the time, we had no idea that we were being conned, and so we listened intently to everything they told us.

Standing at the top of Tapa Maranjan does offer us a grand view of the city. At the foot of the promontory is a vast expanse of green that—at the start of the twentieth century, during the reign of Amir Habibullah—was a golf course. Farther down is the space where equestrian competitions were once held, though now it serves as the soccer field for the young men of Kabul who head out every afternoon to play under the watchful eyes of Taliban officials, as we will see later this afternoon. Facing this field is the great stadium of Kabul—the Ghazi—where the executions are carried out. And next to the stadium lies the giant Id Gah Mosque and its interminable facade that overlooks the main street where the major Islamic holidays are celebrated, especially the festival that ends Ramadan, the month of fasting. We snap some photos. No one has yet to tell us we can't do so, and since we've been forced to dedicate the day to tourism, we don't see any reason not to.

Our interpreter points out two men and a dog that seem to be looking for something on the hillside. He tells us they're searching for land mines so they can deactivate them.

From our vantage point here we can also see—in the city center—the enormous communications tower that was converted into an office building after the Taliban rose to power. It's a tall, impressive, monolithic structure, situated atop the mountain Koh-i-Asmai, "the Great Goddess Mother of Nature," whose name dates back to ancient times when Kabul was a Hindu city. Until recently—at least, until the wars started—Kabul's Hindu community continued paying homage to this goddess in an ancient temple near the Mosque of the King of the Two Swords, whose name refers to a legend dating from Islam's beginnings, when it was imposed through strength of arms. The legendary warrior-king who fought with a sword in each hand was one of the first promoters of the new religion, and he died while defending Kabul's sacred Hindu temple. If Islam hadn't ended up taking hold, nobody today would remember him.

We want to visit the stadium. Our driver stops the car in front of the entrance gate, and our concierge-interpreter gets out to speak with a group of men posted there. They decide to allow us to drive out onto the field. I recognize this as the same way that Zarmena, the woman executed a few months ago, entered the stadium as well. The driver stops just long enough for us to snap a couple of photos. The stadium is practically empty, with just a single, lone man sitting in the stands. We ask what sorts of activities are carried out here.

"They hold soccer matches here on Sunday afternoons."

Our guides make no mention of the executions that continue to be held regularly here, on this very playing field, once considered to be the best in all Afghanistan. Executions, amputations of hands and feet, impalings . . . and the people are forced to attend these atrocities. The Taliban close off streets with yellow barricades and drive the people here.

Next, we ask to visit the Kabul Museum, but on arriving the Taliban guards inform us that the museum is closed, and that we'd need to obtain authorization from the Ministry of Culture in order to see the exhibits. It's alright; anyway, we already know that there's little left inside, that the magnificent collections and artifacts that were once housed within have long since been stolen and plundered. Again, I'm reminded of Shelley's "Ozymandias": nothing remains of Afghanistan's prehistory. Nothing of the small, exuberant mother goddesses who controlled both life and fertility as well as death and all the horrors of darkness. And the frescoes from the Valley of Bamiyan . . . will they still be there? I wonder also what will have happened to the delicate collection of kafir statues, the Nuristan infidels, the coins from the Greco-Bactrian period, and the most recent pieces un-earthed in the past twenty, thirty, and forty years?

The ruins of an enormous palace lie near the museum; we visit them next. We're told that this was the royal palace. But more likely, this structure—situated at one end of Darulaman Avenue—was actually the building where the Parliament was housed and which was designed by a French architect during the reign of King Amanullah, whose attempts at modernizing the country scandalized the population. Our driver can't find the right street that leads up to the palace, and he has to stop and ask a group of boys who are harvesting grasses and piling up the bales on the ground.

"What are they doing?"

"Drying out grasses to be used for kindling."

In a second-floor room of the purported royal palace, we bump into a group of Taliban, lounging among the ruins, their weapons stacked on a nearby pallet. They're drinking tea, and invite us to join them. Meme is steadfastly against it. Sara and I look at each other: we're used to deferring to Azada's judgment in such cases, but here make the (apparently unforgivable) mistake of asking our interpreter. He ushers us out in all haste, while apologizing and excusing himself profusely to the Taliban men, whom he seems to fear more than we do.

We go up one more floor, but it's in vain, as there is little of import left inside the palace or out, at least in terms of art, monuments, or emblematic structures. Our concierge takes advantage of the moment to tell us that whenever there are Taliban around, we must hide our cameras and not take any pictures. Outside the palace (where magnificent gardens once stood), we snack on a melon that we'd bought a bit earlier, sharing it with our driver and interpreter. They tell us that Afghan melons are excellent for replenishing the energy sapped away by the heat and sun. Our interpreter then offers to take a photo of the three of us women, and we accept. Our earlier annoyance is waning. He seems like a good enough man.

Back in the city center we go past a supposed queen's palace, though it's closed off and guarded by a group of Taliban men so young that one of them hasn't been able to grow his full beard out yet. Our concierge speaks to them, and they drop the chain gate and let us drive on in. We make our way up a hill at whose crest rises an enormous building that doesn't in the least look like a queen's place of diversion. Our interpreter-concierge is nervous: they've only allowed us a few minutes to take pictures, and we turn right around and descend the hill. At the bottom, the young Taliban officers clear us before letting us proceed on our way.

Meme wants to change a few dollars, so we have some extra money on hand for the day's expenses, and so we drive back across the city. We'll spend the rest of the day doing just this: circling through the same sites, plazas, streets, and avenues. Once there, our driver is the one who gets out. Whereas in Peshawar it was nice to have our driver or male companion always ready to run this or that errand, here it's become a frustration: we're never allowed to set foot outside the car to poke around the streets or look at people. Only from inside the car. If our hotel is a prison, then our car is just an extension of it. I try to imagine what it must be like to spend every day like this, and forced to do so beneath a *burka* as well. Without so much as the freedom to go out shopping, or for a breath of fresh air. While we wait in the car for him to return, we take some pictures of women in *burkas* walking by. Blue shapes drifting amid a sea of men; men who come and go, either on bicycle or on foot, and smile with curiosity at us whenever they near our car. Perhaps they're remembering the days when Western women routinely came to visit Kabul. They're all sporting beards and the traditional small cap as prescribed by the Taliban regime. We don't have the slightest idea of where we are, nor do we have a map of the city. Finally our driver comes back. The five dollars that Meme changed come back in a wad of Afghan bills that she can scarcely fit in her purse.

Then we head for the zoo, and pay the entrance fee. The place is full of boys and young men. Today, we're the principal attraction, surrounded by the few animals who reside here in deplorable conditions, including a sad-eyed lion and a monkey who still responds to the provocations of the youngsters. There's little else to see. When it first opened its gates in August of 1967, the facilities respected the prevailing concepts of what a modern zoo should be like: the enclosures were large and spacious, and they displayed a large number of Afghanistan's indigenous birds and mammals, as well as several species that migrate across the country every spring and fall from southern Siberia, eastern Africa, India, or Saudi Arabia. In the following years, an aquarium and museum were added. But now, we see none of this: only a few cages, mostly empty, a crowd of children splashing around in a pool, and another crowd who follow us around and beg us to take their picture. And thanks to our woeful guide whom we've had the misfortune of linking up with, we don't get to see the two great monuments within the zoo that commemorate important events in Afghanistan's history: at the eastern edge of the premises is the Column of Knowledge and Ignorance, erected by King Amanullah and inscribed with the names of all those who died defending the country's modernization from traditionalist forces; at the western edge of the site stands another column erected in honor of one of Nadir Shah's Nuristani generals. Still, it's unlikely that either is still standing today.

Our driver doesn't seem to want to do anything but drive in and out of the city center in such a way that we spend most of our time on the outskirts where there aren't very many people. And every time we do reenter the city center, we do so along the same route, through the same streets and plazas every time.

On one of these trips—along the same road that leads in and out of the city—we see, to our left, rising up along the full length of the mountains' slope, a line of what looks like stones lined up one next to the other like spines on the back of some dragon of lore. These are the remains of the ancient city's walls. And they have their own legend, as we will discover later in one of the books we'll buy in Kabul: there was a king who wanted to construct a great wall so as to protect the city. He ordered all ablebodied men to work on constructing it, driving them to exhaustion and even death, but nobody dared to disobey him for fear of punishment and repression by his guards. Such was the king's cruelty that those who dropped from exhaustion were buried inside the very wall they were building. Among the workers was the fiancée of a young man who refused to accept the abuse that the men were subject to with any sort of docility and submission. Such was her conviction that one day she showed up to work alongside the men. The king would occasionally walk among the workers to inspect his project's progress, and soon came upon this woman who, surprised, swiftly covered her face with her chador.

"Why do you cover up now that I have already discovered you working alongside the men?" the king asked.

"These are not men. If they were, then they wouldn't permit anyone to treat them as slaves and not rebel against him. And I am a woman who refuses to subject herself to the cruelty of your laws."

The woman then bent down, picked up a stone, and slung it at the king, hitting him in the chest. The king fell dead from his horse. Upon seeing what this young woman had done, the men then rose up against his guards and defeated them. Thus, the wall was never completed.

Afghan traditions and legends are full of similar stories of women rallying the troops and returning valor and dignity to soldiers on the verge of losing these things. Here in Kabul, for example, along Maiwand Avenue sits the eponymous Maiwand monument, which commemorates the Afghan victory over the invading British troops. We drove past its crumbling remains, situated in the center of a traffic circle, several times today. The inscription at the base of the monument describes how, when the Afghans were on the verge of surrendering, a young woman named Malalai rallied them, saying, "If you all do not fall today at the battle of Maiwand, who will protect you from the memory of this shame?" They say that these words filled the spent and weary men with such courage that they won a great victory.

Afghan women are valiant women. I now know a few of them myself, and am proud to have spent time here with them.

We return to the streets of Kabul, and see a sizable convoy of four-wheel-drive Toyotas laden with Taliban soldiers, armed to the teeth and smiling. They don't seem to be doing anything other than generally patrolling the city. They're everywhere. Arrogant and sinister. Doing whatever they feel like doing. In fact, this same day, while we were out driving circles around the city in our official car, our interpreter Palwasha witnessed an atrocity they committed, when a squad of armed Taliban stopped a bus on which she was traveling. They demanded to search each woman's bag, discovered that three of the passengers were carrying books, and dragged them off the bus to arrest them. The Taliban realize that—despite their prohibitions—there are underground schools where women meet clandestinely to learn to read and write, and they spare no expenses in trying to discover these networks. Sometimes, they succeed.

The other vehicles circulating through the streets of Kabul are either taxis or buses. Most people get around the city on foot, though a few have bicycles. On buses, women in their *burkas* have to stand, crowded together in the back of the bus and separated from the rest of the passengers by a curtain. Men get to sit in seats up front.

We want to go see the famous Lake Kabul. We stop on the bridge leading across the river to photograph a pair of women in *burkas,* one of whom is carrying a baby in her arms. An older man is accompanying them. Because of the drought, Lake Kabul has completely dried up, bringing me to finally understand the Kabul saying, *"Kabul will be left without gold before it is left without snow."* If the mountains surrounding the city were to ever lose their snow, the ensuing drought would envelop not only the central plateau but the entire country as well, and death would soon follow. Gold is worth nothing if the rivers run dry and if there is no water to irrigate the fields. In Afghanistan, a serious drought is a death sentence: for crops, livestock, and people.

Around noon, our driver and our interpreter want to call it a day. But we're not about to accept that. They're sadly mistaken if they think they can drive us around in circles for half a day and then just drop us off back at the hotel. We didn't come to Kabul to spend our time veritably locked up in the room. So we ask to go out to a restaurant for lunch. Resignedly, they take us to a spot next to one of Kabul's old theaters, its façade blackened and scarred by war.

Inside, we're escorted to a booth, and draw the curtains that cut us off from the rest of the dining room. We eat alone—lamb kebabs and a bit of salad—while our driver and interpreter set up out in the larger, male dining room. Our interpreter pokes his head in from time to time "to make sure everything is alright," but we get the feeling we're being rushed. We're starting to feel fed up with it all.

Upon exiting the restaurant, we walk past the car to snap a few photos of the old theater. A mass of children surrounds us, smiling and chattering. Our concierge starts to yell at them, then gets out of the car and starts beating and kicking them until they flee, some in tears. Back in the car, he tells us that they're taking us straight back to the hotel so we can rest. He won't take no for an answer, but he does promise that we'll go back out later in the afternoon. As we're pulling up to the hotel, he asks us not to tell anyone that we went out for lunch.

Once there, we take advantage of the chance to visit the bookshop, which is open now. A young man is working the counter; he speaks English and chats with us while we browse through the books and postcards. Many of the books have postcards depicting various landscapes stuck to the cover or title page. The shopkeeper tells us that the Taliban have done this, using the postcards to cover up any images of people or animals. If he were found to be in violation of this law, the punishment could be a beating, closing the shop for a ten-day period, or destroying it completely. I buy the cookbook that I saw yesterday in the window; the picture of a lamb and a child on the cover has been blotted out. I also decide to get an old, beat-up copy of a book summarizing customs, traditions, and characteristics of the Afghan people, as well as the book of Afghan legends where we learn the story of Kabul's unfinished wall.

We go up to our room to lie down and read for a bit. After a while, I decide to head back downstairs, as I figure I have a few dollars left I can spend on books. It'll be my last chance. I just wish I had more to spend, as there are so many different things I'd like to buy: a book on Persian grammar, a German-Persian dictionary, books of poetry, and more postcards. The shopkeeper is a very charming and cultured man, though he seems so young. He seems surprised at my love of books, and I explain to him that everywhere I travel I buy books to take home with me, especially collections of stories and traditional legends characteristic of the countries that I've visited. I decide to also get a book on Afghan rugs and leaf through several others, including some on *buzkashi,* the national sport of Afghanistan and stemming from the northern regions of Uzbekistan and Turkmenistan, where the art of horsemanship is an integral part of life on the steppe. In times of peace, there were three great festivals per year, each on a different date and in a different city: the regional and national championships, and then the winter tournament. The major cities in the north of Afghanistan had their own teams and champions—distinct from the games played in the stadiums—and they played on the plains outside the cities and towns to celebrate occasions such as a wedding or the birth of a male child. The game consists of this: the decapitated body of a goat is slung across the back of a horse, which starts out inside a circle in the middle of the field. One team has to drive the horse to a predetermined point—usually a kilometer or two away—and then return to the original circle. The horsemen of the opposing team (each team has anywhere from twenty to thirty horsemen) tries to stop the horse and snatch away the dead goat so that they can carry it to their end of the field. A fall during this competition can sometimes prove fatal. The fighting for the goat is fierce, and sometimes the riders end up in a free-for-all, trying to grab the goat from whichever rider has control of it, whether they are on the same team or not. The shopkeeper tells me that the body of the goat is soaked in water overnight before the competition to make it even heavier, and that the riders are colossal men, with incredible strength and skill. He says that they will eat up to five kilos of meat a day, as well as large numbers of eggs and other such foods, but they are never fat.

"They're all muscle," he says.

Around three o'clock, we gather up our driver and interpreter because we're ready to go out again. As in the morning, we circle time and again through the same streets, plazas, and places that we now know by heart. But we don't give in. We put up a true fight: he's annoyed us all day, so now we annoy him into taking us out for a walk. We head for the university neighborhood, situated at the base of Mount Asmai—named for the Hindu goddess—and near our hotel. This modern university extends over quite some area, and the newest buildings were built as recently as 1976, when this main campus was created to consolidate the separate schools, which were until then scattered throughout the city. The oldest is the College of Medicine, which started up under the reign of King Nadir Shah in 1932. Near the university's campus is the Aliabad Hospital, which also shows scars of the war: windows blown out, walls shredded by shrapnel and blackened by fire. We don't see a single person—not a single sign of any activity—but our guide claims that everything is fully functional, that students still attend classes here, and that the hospital still admits patients. I'm positive he's lying. If the Taliban are in the process of closing down schools for boys, if girls are not permitted to attend school, and if the Taliban are themselves mostly illiterate enemies of culture and education who send men of college age to fight on the front lines, then who is left to sit in these classrooms?

We ask to see the neighborhood that sprung up during the days of the pro-Soviet government, which is on the list drawn up by our Afghan friends of places we ought to see, and which our own concierge had mentioned earlier this morning. Again, ridiculously, we cross the width of the city. For the umpteenth time, we pass the Id Gah Mosque and the old bus station that shuttled travelers between Kabul and Jalalabad, arriving finally at a group of square, gray, charred, and scarred buildings, each perhaps five or six stories high, informally known as Microrayon. I don't know why.

Nearby sits a bread factory that, according to our guides, is also fully functional. Who knows how, or in what condition it is.

We often drive by a group of Taliban men, and see the quick and furious look in their eyes as they notice a car full of three women, their faces uncovered. But as soon as they realize that we're foreigners, they relax and calm down.

At one particular moment, our interpreter says that we'll soon be passing by what was formerly the Russian embassy, and looks fixedly at us.

We show no reaction.

Later we find out that the Taliban have converted the place into a hellish prison, holding a large number of mostly female refugees who have fled here, to Kabul, from the northern, war-torn regions. The men, on the other hand, are locked away at Pul-i-Charji prison. RAWA has written several impressive, caustic reports on conditions at both sites, drawn from eyewitness testimonies.

We want to see the downtown area—the old city center—and see the hustle and bustle there, see people, leaving these empty streets behind us. They take us there along a different route—including some quite narrow streets marked by a certain amount of activity—before turning back onto a main avenue and passing Pul-e-Khishti Mosque, situated next to one of the oldest bridges in the city. We've been by here countless times already. Our patience is wearing thin. Our concierge must be noticing this, because he directs us to a street laced with shops proffering handmade festival dresses, jewelry, and antiques. This must be the famous "Chicken Street," a veritable baited hook that used to attract tourists in droves back during Kabul's more prosperous days. We insist on getting out of the car. Nearly nobody here remembers past times of splendor, and although the shops are all open, most of the artisans look listless and idle. I try and picture the street as it must have been long ago: shops packed together, their owners lying in wait for potential buyers, competing with their neighbors for their business, throwing amicability to the wind, inviting passersby to stop in and have a cup of tea, and tourists poking through their wares, choosing, haggling, and buying. Now, silence has taken hold of this street, as it has everywhere in this city. There are no more silversmiths working metal, no artists working on paintings or engravings. Shopkeepers display their wares and invite us to look around, though they harbor little hope of selling anything. We look around in a few of the shops, but everything is sad in Kabul. Even more so in these old places of art and commerce, where today, bright and marvelous works seem acutely out of place in the midst of so much destruction and oppression. We even feel ashamed and embarrassed to be browsing around here, to say nothing of the overwhelming sense of claustrophobia we're feeling at having our concierge ever with us, his talons gripping us tightly, barely letting us breathe. We're on the verge of taking off running, just to lose him.

Lining the other side of the street are a number of clothing shops representing each one's respective culture: Pashtun, Hazara, Uzbeki, Tayiko. The dresses are ornately decorated with embroidery and ornaments covering nearly every square inch of cloth. They each must weigh a ton, and cost an arm and a leg as well. One of these shops is reached by a short passageway that opens out onto a patio where a group of men are weaving rugs: a typically female occupation, until recently. I greet these men with a nod of the head. Since we're in Afghanistan, we try not to use Dari or Pashto words, in order that we appear more like simple tourists and so nobody asks us where we learned to speak like that. Instead, we use English in all cases. From the patio, we take pictures of the shop and the dresses hanging there. The men mutter something among themselves, and one of them stammers out a bit of English, asking us in a calm tone of voice to be very careful and not let any Taliban see us taking pictures, as this is forbidden and we'll be in a lot of trouble if we're caught. We thank him, and stow our cameras away. The men seem relieved that we've understood them and heeded their warning, and break out into smiles.

We head back to the car, after offering an excuse to the shop owner for not buying any dresses: they are very beautiful indeed, but we wouldn't be able to wear them in our country.

Then we drive down a wide street full of shops and a surprising number of people, including even some Afghan women—more than we've seen all day. They're all draped in *burkas,* most streaked with blue over an asphalt gray. The car stops and our interpreter—perhaps offering something of an olive branch—surprises us by asking us to get out, not to poke around at our leisure but rather to go inside a nearby restaurant and have an ice cream. We go inside and head straight for a booth where—upon seeing us coming—the waiter asks a group of women already there before us to leave.

The truth is that we're fed up, and in an almost furious mood. We try taking a few haphazard photos of the restaurant by poking the camera out through the curtain. Right in front of our disgusted waiter, I smoke a cigarette without a care or my chador. And we leave the booth before our concierge comes to look for us. We don't want to be cooped up there any longer than we have to. Outside, we show up at the car so unexpectedly that our driver and interpreter have to come running out after us. What a hassle.

Next we pass by the stadium and the old golf course-turned-soccer field where dozens of boys are knocking a ball around, watched over by a group of Taliban lounging on the grass next to their Toyotas. Our driver takes us to the top of the hill where we began our morning, where he and our concierge ask us to take a few pictures of them—even though it's prohibited—so we can send them to them. But how could we, if there is no postal system in Afghanistan? We don't actually bring this up, but neither do they. Then they change their minds and decide that they'll buy a roll of film, so they can develop it themselves and therefore we won't have to try the mail. In the end, this doesn't happen either. Still, both our driver and our interpreter pose, smiling, for our cameras. We walk along the promenade in the changing light of dusk.

"On the other side of those mountains is the front, where the war is still being fought."

We feign surprise instead of interest. This man is hopeless as a source of information, and a complete bore of a tour guide. Then, a Toyota pulls up to the promenade, stopping in front of a mausoleum. Two Taliban men spread a white piece of cloth on the ground and begin praying.

We don't dare to photograph them, and the sense of apprehension we're all feeling is contagious. Earlier this morning, I would have had no qualms about quickly snapping a picture of them behind their backs, but after seeing evidence of their crushing oppression all day, I am afraid to. If I had to live here, in Kabul, under the constant Taliban menace—harassed by their patrols and laws—what other things would I no longer dare to do? When would I give in to it all? When would I decide—as I do now—that something just isn't worth the risk?

We go. Our "official" tour through Kabul has been a disaster. Finally, the day is at an end, and we can call this pantomime to a close. It's about time.

"To the hotel!" we order our driver.

Our concierge—perhaps excited by the idea of being rid of us and getting his money—suddenly becomes chatty. We do as well. Until, that is, he blindsides us with an announcement:

"Everything is set up for tomorrow." (Apparently, at some point during the day, he asked us what time we were thinking about leaving the hotel the next morning, and we carelessly answered.) "A car will be there at 7 A.M. sharp with a new interpreter, ready to take you to the border."

We look quickly at one another, and answer that we're very appreciative of all the trouble he's gone through, but that we'll be returning to Pakistan with the car and interpreter that we originally hired. He insists that there is no other option; that we just can't leave the hotel without an official escort. We're dumbstruck. Could it be possible that we've come all this way for nothing? Is there no way humanly possible of freeing ourselves from this iron control? After an intense silence that seems to last an eternity, his hard countenance softens and admits that he can arrange things so that we can go out in our own car and with our own interpreter—our friend, he says—but that it will cost us ten dollars, five each to him and the driver. We agree to the terms, but add the stipulation that we'll only pay them after we're safely in our car with Palwasha.

"Then there's no deal."

"Fine, no deal then."

We feign that either way it's just the same to us, but we are starting to feel a certain tinge of uneasiness. The concierge adds that he is just trying to help us and that if we have any problems when it comes time to leave tomorrow morning, he won't intervene or do anything else for us.

A group of Taliban is gathered at the hotel entrance. We pay the driver and concierge the fee—in dollars—that we'd agreed upon that morning. They look unhappy, and try to convince us that we'd agreed on a higher price. We refuse to play their game and get out, leaving the two of them to work things out there, inside the car.

Back up in our room, we count out our remaining money. There isn't much left after having paid for our unexpected and undesired driver and interpreter and—since we're still not sure what is going to happen tomorrow morning—we decide to skip dinner. Seated on our beds, we polish off the cookies and other snacks that we bought back in Peshawar. Sara and I can't forgive ourselves for having missed the opportunity to speak with a group of Taliban this morning, back at the palace ruins when we were invited to join them for tea.

"We were foolish; that was a once-in-a-lifetime opportunity."

But there was that group of Taliban downstairs in the lobby. If we go down and let ourselves be seen, perhaps we'll have a second chance. Maybe they'll be sociable and chatty as well. Meme thinks our desire to strike up a conversation with them is ludicrous, and refuses to go down with us, preferring instead to stay here in the room. But Sara and I head down to the hotel restaurant. Sure enough, a group of eight to ten of them is there, eating at a table at the far end of the room. We sit down at our own table—not too far away but not too close either—and order coffee. They're obviously talking about us, as they frequently steal glances at us and laugh. The two Westerners from the other night—and whom we saw earlier this morning—are now nowhere to be found. Who could they have been? What were they doing here in Kabul? We order a second cup of coffee each. No, we're not having dinner, we say to the waiter. The group of Taliban has finished. They get up and leave without coming up to us.

It's getting late, and we go back up to the room. Meme tells us that the front desk called up to ask if we would like a wake-up call at a particular time. She told them that no, we have our own alarm clock. This subtle inquiry seems a bit odd, but we don't pay it much mind. We set up in Meme's room to chat for a bit before going to sleep, and a short while later someone comes knocking at our door. It's late, but we're not very surprised. This isn't the first time that someone's come up to make sure that everything's alright, or to give us a vase of flowers for the room.

Sara covers her face with her chador and goes to see who it is. Meme is lying in her bed, and I'm on the couch in her room. I can only make out the word "interpreter." It's a man's voice, coming from outside in the hall.

"What a hassle this has become," I mutter to Meme. From where we're at, we can't see the door, which is situated at the other end of a short corridor, near the bathroom. We hear Sara close the door. She walks slowly back into our room, looking distraught.

"What happened?"

Sara swallows hard in an effort to maintain her composure. It was a young man whom she'd never seen before. He started off by saying that he had something very important to tell her, but first she'd have to promise that she wouldn't betray his confidence; that she wouldn't tell a soul that he had warned them. He was sweating, and kept glancing left and right down the hall, as if on the lookout for a hotel employee or some other person. He was either very nervous or very frightened. Sara promised that he could trust us, though she had no idea of what could be so important. But she froze—petrified—when the young man told her that he'd overheard that at 7 A.M. tomorrow morning, a group of Taliban officials would be lying in wait to arrest our interpreter, and whoever came to meet her. He then asked if there was a phone number or address where she could be reached and warned not to come.

Sara replied truthfully: no, we have no number where she could be reached. Then she added, "We don't know anything about her, not even where she lives."

The young man reiterated how important it was to warn her, and told Sara to check with us, to see if we could think of anything between the three of us. She told him to wait in the hall and shut the door.

We blanch with panic upon hearing all this. Still, we decide the best course of action would be to feign disinterest, even indignation at being bothered at such a late hour with ridiculous stories.

Sara goes back to the door to convey this, but the man is no longer there. He's gone.

But a few moments later, there's a soft tapping at the door again, and there he is again, more nervous than ever, but still insisting on the dire need to keep this meeting secret. Telling anyone would trigger an avalanche of problems.

Sara stays in character with the skill of a master actress.

"Look, your problems don't matter to us one bit. We're guests in this hotel; we're paying good money to stay here, and we're not going to tolerate worthless disturbances in the middle of the night when all we want is to get some sleep." Then she slams the door shut.

What can we do?

First of all, stay calm and think.

Much easier said than done.

But we manage to do it, though for a while I, at least, feel incapable of rational thought, my mind wiped completely blank and with fear threatening to win the battle. My throat has gone completely dry. Never in my life have I felt so afraid. Not for myself, but rather for what may happen tomorrow morning at seven o'clock sharp, when our interpreter comes to pick us up, completely unaware that she and her uncle—that charming and cheerful man—may not be meeting us but rather meeting horror and, possibly, death.

We really have no way of warning her about this news, as we honestly have no phone number or address of where she's staying. And even if we did, we couldn't call from the hotel—what with all these Taliban around— and we certainly couldn't ask a stranger to make the call for us.

Nor could we leave the hotel and call from some other place; that is, if there is any other place whose telephone system hasn't been destroyed. We have no one to turn to. There are no embassies, no consulates, and no representatives of anyone or anything in this country, where suspects are convicted with all impunity but without witnesses. The police are Taliban, the authorities are Taliban, and tomorrow they are going to arrest our interpreter because she is a woman and allegedly working for us.

What if tomorrow morning, two of us distract the hotel employees while the third runs outside to meet Palwasha's taxi, yelling for them to take off without looking back? Ridiculous. No matter what we do, when she comes, it will already be too late.

It won't do any good to try to intervene: to try to rush them or protect Palwasha with our own bodies. They'll shoot her all the same, and forcibly put us in a car and expel us from the country. Though in all likelihood, they won't arrest her in front of a group of Western tourists, who could later describe any atrocities in detail. No, there isn't anything we can do, save to wait with the Taliban officers for the taxi to climb up the hill to our hotel. We may never see Palwasha or her uncle again, and nobody will ever know what became of them.

We're horrified that our desire to visit Afghanistan may very well end up costing the lives of our interpreter and her *muhrram*. We're horrified also by our complete inability to warn them about the dangers awaiting them.

We imagine the scene a thousand and one times: Palwasha arriving in a taxi, while the Taliban await her, sitting in a Toyota parked in the driveway that circles up to the hotel doors. We're confident that nothing will happen to us, since we're foreigners who've entered the country legally, with visas conferred by the Taliban consulate, and also because an international scandal could be troublesome for them, as they are right in the middle of trying to clean up their image in the eyes of the international community. No, nothing will happen to us; we'll just get into a car and head for the Pakistani border. But our Afghan friends won't be so lucky.

The feeling of helplessness is overwhelming.

"This is all because we wouldn't give the concierge the ten dollars he asked for. Let's just go downstairs, give him the money, and that will be it," Meme suddenly says.

Neither Sara nor I think it will be that easy. Even if she's right, and the concierge is getting revenge by reporting Palwasha to the authorities, there's no clear-cut way back now. He couldn't call off the sting if he's already alerted them. Plus, going down to offer him money at this hour of the night would blow our cover and the last bit of protection we might be able to offer Palwasha; that is, to continue with our story: we're just tourists, we got in touch with this woman at our hotel in Peshawar, and arresting her seems abusive and insulting to us. They shouldn't want us to feel afraid . . . not for our lives or even for Palwasha's. We have to act as arrogant and Western as possible.

Finally, we come to the conclusion that we have to preempt things. Once they've arrested her, there will be nothing we can do. We can't wait and see what happens; we'll have to move first if we want to stop the arrest before it happens. We'll stick to this premise, and hash out a clear and logical line of thought: we've entered the country legally, complete with visas. During our questioning at the border, we specifically stated that we were traveling with an interpreter. In other words, she came here with us and with the Taliban's full knowledge and approval.

We decide to demand that a representative of the Taliban "government" listen to both sides of the situation before any arrests are made. If we can get a higher level of authority involved, there is a chance that—hoping to avoid a scandal—they'll let our interpreter and her companion go. Waiting for something bad to happen won't do any good; if anything, they'll lie to us and send us on our way with a few mollifying words, after which Palwasha and her uncle will be whisked off to who knows where, where they'll be punished, tortured, and perhaps executed, just like so many other thousands of Afghan citizens.

We'll go down first thing tomorrow morning and demand that they send for a government representative, to whom we'll indignantly explain the situation. Sara will have to take charge of the negotiations, owing to her superior command of the language, while Meme and I will be able to offer little more than moral support. We can do this, we will do this, and we'll have to do it well, as it's our only chance to save our friends.

Sitting on the floor and in the fan's breeze, we speak in low voices, just in case someone is out in the hall, listening for our reactions.

"We've taken this all too far. We should never have come to Afghanistan," says Sara.

But what's done is done.

The thing that pains me the most is the fact that the fate of two lives—that of Palwasha and her uncle—will be with me for the rest of my life. I'm positive that if things go wrong tomorrow morning, the Taliban officers won't have to think twice about shooting the both of them, right there in front of the hotel doors. I just can't bear to think about having to return to Pakistan without them, about having to tell Najiba, Rustam, and all our other Afghan friends what happened, about returning to Europe and living each day until the end of my life with the knowledge that our Afghan adventure was responsible for the deaths of two people.

To calm myself down, I tell myself that there's no logical reason for such a young, capable woman to die or disappear so arbitrarily, so gratuitously. But I'm also keenly aware of the fact that, according to this world's absurd logic, it would be completely normal if Palwasha were to die. Here, death comes for those who dare to shine light on the dark vacuums of power and destruction.

We also consider the possibility that we've overanalyzed everything, and that they won't be arresting our interpreter and her *muhrram;* that the Taliban patrol coming at 7 A.M. tomorrow morning won't know much about the situation, save for the orders from their superiors to deal with the foreigners justly and amicably. Ultimately, however, we have to recognize that these patrols operate with total autonomy and impunity. We recall that in July, a bit before we embarked on this voyage, seven men and nine women—including one American—were arrested for providing medical aid to residents. The men were freed after a couple hours, the American woman was expelled from the country after a couple of days, but the rest of the women were lost without a trace. So, just in case they keep us detained before sending us home, we ought to destroy any compromising evidence we have on hand. Luckily, we've left most of our notes back in Peshawar, but our day planners and notebooks do contain the phone numbers of several Afghan aid organizations such as RAWA and UNHCR . . . proof that we're not quite tourists, after all.

So we begin to tear out any incriminating pages and burn them in the ashtray in Meme's room. But barely two are gone before the room is so full of smoke that we have to throw open the windows before we suffocate.

"We're such idiots!" someone (I'm not sure if it was Sara or Meme) exclaims. "What are we burning papers for if we have two toilets we can flush them down instead?"

We set about tearing the pages into tiny bits and tossing them into the toilet by the handful, followed by the flush.

"Watch that it doesn't clog!" warns Meme. "Let's do it a sheet at a time."

We also change the rolls of film in our cameras, in case they want to confiscate them.

We are veritably terrified by what could very well happen in the morning, but we try not to let ourselves disintegrate into a state of panic. I think all three of us are conscious of the need to keep our heads about us right now. Each individual's ability to stay calm will help the other two do so as well.

"I just want this all to be over, and for us to be back at Najiba's house tomorrow night, laughing about everything that happened," says Sara.

Yes. It would be wonderful to already be there, at home, reminiscing, dying of laughter at what we did. But for this to come to pass, first we must get through the anxiety of not knowing what is going to happen during the uncertain yet ominous morning that awaits us.

"Maybe Palwasha won't even come."

That's a fatuous hope. Of course, we've already discussed the possibility that something could come up and that Palwasha wouldn't be able to make it to one of our appointments, but the chance that this will happen tomorrow morning is all but nonexistent.

"I hope she doesn't!"

But we all know she will.

We also know that nothing and nobody can alleviate our agony.

We turn out the lights.

We've already packed our bags for the morning, and set the alarm clock for 5 A.M.

We'll be down in the lobby by six, ready to put on our poker faces, make our bluffs, and meet with whatever we might meet. Everything that happens before seven will be of vital importance.

MONDAY, AUGUST 14, 2000.

Afghanistan.

It's better to see things coming than to wait and be told about them later.

We sleep fitfully, if at all.

In the darkness, Sara gets up to go to the bathroom. I feel so nauseous that all I want to do is vomit.

"I had a dream where Palwasha didn't come."

I can't even bring myself to answer.

We all shower and get dressed, trying not to lose our collective, relative cool.

We go down to the lobby. I have a huge knot in my stomach.

We go up to the reception desk, but nobody is there. We call, annoyed, until an employee comes out.

"Get our bill ready while we're having breakfast, and get a representative from the Taliban government here immediately."

The young employee is dumbstruck, but we don't wait around to see what he does next. We turn around and march straight off to the restaurant.

The waiters are gathered by the restaurant doors, and make no move to attend to us, though their eyes are constantly on us. Finally, feigning impatience and anger, we rap our knuckles on the tabletop to grab their attention, and ask for breakfast. This prompts a swift deployment, and we're brought toast, butter, and coffee. We also order three bottles of water for the trip.

Six-thirty comes and goes.

Our concierge (and yesterday's interpreter) comes over to our table. He's heard that we've asked to speak to a government official, and wants to know if there is some problem.

"That's just it; we don't want any problems leaving the country today. That's why we've asked to speak with a government official: so he can tell us exactly what procedures to follow."

The concierge spouts off a list of explanations: we can leave whenever we want and with whomever we want. He's just gotten off the phone with the minister and confirmed it.

Sara builds herself up.

"We want to speak personally with a competent government official which—after all—you are not. Plus, you haven't given us much reason to trust you. You said one thing yesterday, but something different today. Frankly, we can't believe anything you tell us. We entered this country legally—as did our interpreter—so please do us the favor of making sure that once we're done with breakfast, a representative of the government is here to guarantee our safety."

The concierge tries to talk us out of this, but we are adamant.

"We're not leaving unless a Taliban authority is here with us."

The concierge walks away with a concerned look on his face, and this improves our spirits a bit. The waiters are waiting for something to happen.

We finish breakfast and head over to the reception desk with bags in hand, ready to go. But our bill isn't ready. The concierge insists that we can go without any problems, and that our interpreter will be going with us in the car we arrived in. The more anxious he seems, the more secure we feel. Still, we demand our bill, and to speak with a government official.

Then, the hotel manager appears.

"Forgive me; I understand that someone was harassing you last night . . ."

"We've been harassed ever since we got here. We were forced to relinquish the services of the interpreter we hired ourselves, we were told that we couldn't leave either the hotel or the country if it wasn't in an official car, and the Taliban consulate didn't inform us of any of these things. We want guarantees that nothing is going to happen to us. All our documents are in order, and we just want to confirm this fact with the authorities, who are the Taliban, not you."

The concierge moves to return the money we paid him yesterday.

"We don't want the money! We want to go peacefully, so please contact the authorities."

In the midst of all of this, Palwasha's uncle enters the lobby and tells us that she is waiting for us outside. We feel relieved and worried at the same time. He looks at us, clearly surprised at the scandal we're causing. He speaks no English, and so we can't convey to him the trouble that's brewing or the need for him and Palwasha to get out of here as soon as possible. Last night, we searched the Dari dictionary I bought for a word to mean "problems," but now there's no time. With every passing moment we grow bolder, giving more and more rein to our indignation. Several more employees have gathered behind the counter to assist in the discussion. The man who warned us of the trouble last night is there as well. We demand that they give us our bill, and finally it's given to us for our signature.

But the performance goes on. Sara continues to vent her anger at the treatment we've received from the hotel.

"It's a crime how you treat tourists here."

Out of the corner of my eye, I see Palwasha's uncle speaking with the concierge. Later we learn that he's explaining that he's come for the money that we owe his niece.

"Let's get out of here," Meme mutters.

We feign a bit of satisfaction, though as one final measure we tell them to write down the phone number of the Ministry of Tourism on our bill. Just in case. But this provokes another heated debate:

"We don't have that particular number, madam."

"Impossible! Did you not just tell us in the dining room that you'd just gotten off the phone with the minister himself?"

The hotel employees don't seem to know how to respond to this. Now, they're the ones who look truly shocked. Again, we demand to speak with a government official.

The young man from last night grabs our bill and hastily jots down a number. We pretend to be satisfied with this, though we suspect it's merely a made-up number. Now it's time to get out of here, without pressing our luck any further. But just before we're out the door, Sara turns around and—with Oscar-caliber bravado—she stuns the crowd with one more admonition: "We all know that the trip to the border is a long one, but if we have even the slightest of problems along the way—believe you me—you are going to have far worse."

Then we exit the lobby and walk quickly to our waiting taxi. Palwasha opens the door and is about to get out to greet us, but we push her back inside.

"No, let's get out of here, it's too dangerous."

Palwasha still doesn't seem at all concerned. We beg her to listen, as the situation is serious and there's no time to lose. Sara gives a quick summary of all that's happened. The danger isn't over yet. The concierge could still report her or us to the authorities. If we stick together—if she stays with us—she's running an unacceptable risk. We suggest we split up and beg her and her uncle to make their way back to Pakistan along some different route: if the Taliban want to arrest them, the first place they would look would be the main road. A car loaded with three foreigners—perhaps the only three in the entire country—would be even more conspicuous.

Sara breaks down and cries. There's so much tension that she's had to endure.

Palwasha speaks for a while with her uncle. Then she turns to us with a smile.

We have no idea what's going on.

"I highly doubt that there's any real danger; they just wanted to scare you into renting one of their own cars so they could get some more money out of you all. If you want to go ahead with the plans we've already laid out for today, we'll do so, but if you want to head straight back to Pakistan, just say the word."

We assure her that we're only afraid for their safety—for her life and for the life of her uncle—and that we'll do whatever they think is best. Just don't take any unnecessary risks on our behalf.

"Right. Let's go then. But first, where are your *burkas*?"

Over the next two days, we'll visit five underground schools scattered across Afghanistan. We'll change cars and drivers several times. We make our way via car, rickshaw, and on foot, draped in our *burkas* whenever we pass through a little-traveled region after passing through Taliban checkpoints, inside a car whose driver exudes an absolute confidence.

The underground schools are for women and girls who have been denied an education under the Taliban regime. The population is responding and reacting to the abuse. Those who blindly flee the country become destitute, and lose control over their future. Among those who stay, there are some who discover they can't bear it there, especially the women who until recently enjoyed a life defined by freedom to move, work outside the home, study at universities, get together, dance, and sing. Many of these women (and some men as well) find themselves unable to cope with the loss of these liberties, and flee as well—though they seek their freedom in suicide. Others choose subversion, choose conscious and clandestine disobedience toward their oppressors, who stop at nothing to break the people's will and stop the country's path to recovery. This is how these clandestine networks came into being, along with the support conferred by various humanitarian organizations. Women who once worked freely and openly at any of the country's institutions of learning now give classes in their own homes or other small locales. Women who worked in the fields of health and medicine also work now underground, making secret house calls to provide basic medical care and a general knowledge of personal hygiene to groups of women.

Before we crossed the border, we had been put in contact with representatives of several of these organizations who were more than willing to meet with us. Shrouded in our *burkas,* we visit a literacy teacher in her home, who explains her work to us:

Women's health and literacy classes were first started by the women themselves. It's important to remember that the level of literacy in Afghanistan was already extremely low—especially in the expansive rural areas—before the wars even broke out. Now, whenever women from the same street, neighborhood, or town want to learn to read and write, they form groups of ten or twelve students. They choose one of their homes as the place for holding classes, based on security and convenience of location. The various humanitarian organizations that support these initiatives provide teachers and materials. Underground schools for young girls are formed in much the same way, and—whenever possible—they try to follow a regular schedule and program of study.

The Taliban know about these classes, and therefore everyone who participates in them is extremely conscientious about precautionary measures. Students come and go from the "school" at staggered intervals and never as a group, and they conceal their textbooks beneath their *burkas* in many ingenious ways. Even the youngest of children know that under no circumstances whatsoever should they show one of their books to a Taliban if they're ever stopped in the street. They also know that if they suspect that they're being followed, they should backtrack or walk in circles to avoid leading them to the school—and the teacher and other students. It's even better to skip a day of class, just for security's sake. However strange this concept may seem, here it's a natural part of life.

The teachers are professionals complete with degrees who worked in the teaching profession before the Taliban prohibited them from working for a salary. In school—and so that the penalties if they were ever to be discovered would be less severe—they use books authorized by the regime for the youth classes. We're told that these schools aren't always very good, and that the Taliban are slowly converting them into schools for studying the Koran.

Other classes that we visit use a different text, one complete with illustrations of people dressed in Western clothes. It's something of a pilot program, which was put into effect barely a month ago, but they will likely drop the textbook because it's just too risky. I ask why they don't simply keep the books hidden at the house where the classes are taught; if the risk is so great, then why the need to carry their books through the streets with them every day?

"The students need to keep their books with them, so they can do their homework," they explain, simply enough.

Among all this, it's important to mention that men have had an integral part in all this too. Every girl who goes to school—every woman who dedicates two hours of her day to class, each teacher and professor—has the support and complicity of her entire family, men and women. It would be unthinkable—impossible—for it to work any other way. Some Westerners have the impression that in Afghanistan, all the men are Taliban and all the women are subject to their rule. This is simply not the case: the Taliban are an armed oligarchy who get their support from external sources, while the rest of the Afghan population—men, women, and children alike—all are denied basic human rights (though it is the women, however, who bear the brunt of the oppression).

We're also told that, despite all the precautions, they have had to close down some of the schools, though fortunately none of the students have been arrested or harassed. Once, the Taliban arrested one of the teachers and charged her with giving classes out of her home. But a subsequent search turned up neither students nor any proof to sustain the accusations. The group then chose a new house in which to hold class, and the school started back up as if nothing had happened.

The main problem that the humanitarian organizations that support these schools have is a common one: there is simply more demand than there are available resources. The number of women who want to learn to read and write and the number of parents who want to send their children to one of these underground schools are always on the rise. Some prospective students are teenagers born during the war under the fundamentalist regime and never having had the opportunity to attend school. The demand is handled according to a strict application procedure. The humanitarian organizations contact the teachers they have rapport with, and they in turn contact their old colleagues. Women who take literacy classes are also happy to spread the word, telling their friends and neighbors about them, thus creating ever more extensive networks. Another major problem is the availability of funds. Classes are free to attend, but the teachers must receive a salary that they can live on. Books and other school supplies cost money too. Without the influx of outside funds, this work would not get done.

The regional coordinator with whom we're meeting takes us to visit one of the local classes. We meet with the teacher and a few of her students, and ask them why they are willing to risk so much.

"Because in the future it will be important to have an education," they reply.

We put on our *burkas* when we go from place to place. Two of the classes we visit are relatively close by, and we can go on foot. Also, we travel in separate, small groups so as not to attract any attention. I go with Sara and an Afghan woman. Before leaving the house, they tell Sara to tug down on her pants a bit, as her ankles are showing, and this could give us away.

It's not easy to walk around wearing a *burka*. It's hard to see through the gauze mask that is the only window to the outside world. You don't know when to duck your head, nor can you see the ground, stairs, or any changes in terrain. The threat of stumbling is constant. The gauze mask forces you to concentrate your vision, and the pressure the skullcap exerts on your forehead produces headaches after a while. You can't see what's going on to your left or right unless you turn your entire head around.

Without realizing it, I've left my group behind, concentrating so hard on my path ahead that I fail to notice that they've fallen behind me. They can't call out to me either, as the street is thronged with people, and any loud calls would betray us as foreigners. On our second venture outside, the woman accompanying us speaks in her own language the entire way, as if all three of us were Afghans. Sara and I have to keep silent, or limit ourselves to simple grunts, but listening to her voice allows us to stay oriented and keep heading in the same direction.

The *burka* doesn't weigh much—the fabric is fine and smooth—but it's like looking through the lens of a camera, and I still don't think being shrouded in lead could be any more stifling. It's not a question of claustrophobia, but rather one of loss of identity: you're no longer a person; you are nobody under that *burka*. You can hear things, you have an albeit limited field of vision through the gauze mask, you can feel the heat and perceive smells, but still you've been cut off from the rest of the world and the life that exists outside there, on the other side of the *burka*. I think about the strange love-hate relationship that Afghan women have with this piece of clothing: they hate the fact that they are forced to don this personal cell every time they leave the house, but at the same time it's an object highly desired by those who can't afford to buy one, because without it, they are confined to the four square walls of their houses.

A member of RAWA is waiting for us at another of the schools. She's a friend of one of the HAWCA professors, and we all get together at her house. This Afghan organization—in addition to the humanitarian activities that it's taken on during the past twenty years of war—has organized discussion groups and classes on politics across the country, led by highly educated women and focusing on women's rights, the current political situation, and possible options and solutions, although everyone realizes that the clandestine movement toward democracy has yet to be sufficiently consolidated. On the other hand, for Afghanistan's problems to be solved, it is imperative that the world outside her borders be conscious of the harsh realities of life in this country, and that the United Nations take practical and clear actions. If it wants to, the U.N. could even establish sites where the *Loya Jirga*—the Great Assembly—could convene, prevent fundamentalist groups from participating, and thus finally give the people the opportunity to manifest their collective will. For this to happen, the U.N. must act independently, without attending to the interests of individual powers.

This woman tells us that they have to change sites every two months to evade the local Taliban authorities, who are currently conducting "search and seizure" measures against members of RAWA. They are also using their official radio station—The Voice of the Sharia—to urge the population to turn in any suspected members.

She also tells us that the public executions held in the stadiums continue to be routine: on Fridays—the Muslim holy day—men are sentenced to death or amputation, while the women receive their sentences on Tuesdays, because they are not considered important enough to be judged on a holy day. A few days ago, in Kabul, the radio was advertising the execution of three women—two for adultery—though a specific date has not been set yet.

The situation has grown steadily worse over the past few weeks as the raids conducted by the most violent of the Taliban's squads—those who operate under the Ministry of the Preservation of Virtue and the Prevention of Vice—are becoming more and more brutal. Whenever someone sees them coming down the street, he or she takes off running for their life. Luckily, they only patrol on Tuesdays and Wednesdays, and although women are their principal victims—persecuting and torturing them into submission and stripping them of their identities—men and boys are also harassed: some men are thrown in jail for not wearing their beards at just the right length or for not dressing in exactly the prescribed manner, and boys are often beaten in the streets for letting their hair grow too long. Men are also required to visit their mosque five times a day to pray. It doesn't matter whether he is fortunate enough to have a business, a job, or a shop at the local bazaar: whenever the mullah makes the call, he must drop whatever he's doing and head to the mosque. Those who don't obey are arrested in their own homes and face punishments ranging from economic sanctions to corporal punishment.

Once again, the women reiterate the importance and necessity that external voices cry out on their behalf and put an end to the silence surrounding the Afghan people's suffering. The "A Flower for the Women of

Afghanistan" campaign was able to call the world's attention to them, but it wasn't sustained, and today these women ask, "Where is Emma Bonino now?"

They bring fruit and drinks for us. The grape seeds are green and hard like tiny pearls, and the thick, acidic skin contrasts sharply with the sweet, refreshing flavor of the pulp. They alleviate both our thirst and the heat.

Before we go, the teachers present each one of us with a set of earrings fashioned out of blue enamel and silver. Meme's are etched with stars, Sara's with hearts, and mine are inscribed with the image of a lotus flower. These women's affection—their genuine joy in having been able to share this time with three unimportant strangers—moves me so much that I have to choke back the tears welling up in my eyes.

Through the window and partially hidden by its dark curtains, we see a man accompanied by a group of children come knocking at the house across the way: he's begging for alms. Many of the male beggars in Afghanistan today are former teachers or government employees.

"Poverty—especially among women—has become common in Afghanistan, forcing people to go begging and to live with a sense of humiliation and shame," the women explain.

The law against women obtaining paying jobs presents a very serious problem indeed, because so many of them are responsible for their entire families after their husbands have been either killed or thrown in jail.

A country of widows. A country of devastation. A country held in the grip of a few powerful criminals who oppress the population and deny the single largest demographic group—women—their basic human rights, as well as the right to participate in their country's reconstruction, which certainly won't be possible without them. But this is also because the Taliban aren't concerned about their country's future: not with rebuilding it, nor with economic, social, or cultural reconstruction. The Taliban are not a political group; they have no governmental plans, no projects, and no ideology. They aren't even a true religious group; they're motivated by their zeal for their supposed faith, in whose name they impose a particular and false interpretation of Islam and Islamic law. Their rejection of the West and all things Western—which they condemn as a perversion of the purity of their beliefs—is another example of their nonsense. After all, where do their weapons come from? Why do they have an official Web page? Why would they maintain a New York office? Everything is false to them, save for brutality and strength through arms. Not even their fundamentalism is authentic. They forbid the use of drugs, and yet the cultivation and distribution of opium is their principal source of funding. They prohibit prostitution, but engage in rape and take pleasure in torturing women.

Prostitution has grown quite a bit in Afghanistan under their rule. The women are usually young widows with children to take care of. First, they start out by begging in the streets, though this is also expressly forbidden. Then, when charity runs dry owing to general and pervasive poverty, they resort to prostitution. In August of 1999, RAWA published an extensive report on the subject, full of testimonials by actual women.

We move on to another school. The teacher's eleven-year-old son wants to see us. She tells us that he's waited here just to be able to meet us when we arrive. We say hello, and he shakes our hands, beaming with joy. For him, our visit is a huge event. But we've scarcely just removed our *burkas* and sat down to talk with the women when we hear a knock at the door. The lady who lives in this house goes to see who it is; when she returns, she apologizes, but tells us that we'll have to leave right away. One of her neighbors saw us go in and came over to see why so many women were gathering there. She said it was nothing—just some friends who came over for tea—but it's best that we leave now.

We do so, taking off down a different street than by which we came.

Upon exiting the house, the first thing I see is our *muhrram* waiting for us. He's packed our bags in the giant kerchief that he also sometimes uses as a turban. When he sees us come out, he slings the bundle across his back and starts walking away, but not before signaling with a tilt of his head

that we should follow him. This brings a lump to my throat. I start off after him and—my eyes focused on his back through the gauze mask of my
burka—I start to cry. I let myself cry as much as I want. Nobody can see
me. All I have to do is make sure nobody can hear my sobs. I don't know
why I'm crying so; all I can do is think about how much these people are
risking just to meet with three irrelevant women—women who have neither power, influence, nor contacts—and tell them about what is happening
in Afghanistan, show them firsthand the suffering that is their daily life
here in a country shunned by the rest of the world. If anything, they've
proven to us that—despite it all—men and women here continue to fight
to survive and preserve their dignity. *"It's better to see things coming than to
wait and be told about them later"* advises another Afghan proverb. And only
those who have seen these things can fully know just how real they are.

I walk on, my eyes fixed on the bouncing bundle carried by our
muhrram. This man has dropped everything to accompany us, so that we
might be able to truly see these things: his family at the refugee camp, his
young daughters, and his modest home that will stay closed up until his return. When we do go back, we learn that a rat somehow got inside his
chicken coop, killing three hens. I continue to walk, blinded by the tears
hidden by my *burka*. When I first decided to come to Pakistan and
Afghanistan, one of the things that I promised myself was that I wouldn't
cry, out of respect for these unflagging men and women.

"When all this is over and the horror has passed, perhaps then I'll permit myself to cry a little and remember all the things that have happened,"
Azada told me once.

My tears—the tears I feel while watching a bullfight from the stands—
seem like an affront to her pain, an egoistical outlet, almost a mawkish act
of self-compassion that in all likelihood would worry her, move her to
console me, to alleviate a pain that does not belong to me, a sadness that
only she and her people have any right to.

One of the school coordinators expresses it thus:

"Unfortunately, we've grown used to the fact that most Westerners

manifest their support simply through crying and talking about the oppression women are subjected to here, when what we really need is help
and compassion."

A car is waiting for us down the street. Again, once we're in a less popu-
lated area, we remove our *burkas* in favor of our chadors and our status as
simple tourists. The friendly driver takes us to the next exchange, where
we'll switch cars again and continue on with the second leg of our trip.
Our new driver is a young man with an easy smile who can't stop looking
at us in the rearview mirror. We have no idea whether we can confide in
him or not, of whether he is a member of the Taliban or just one of the
many citizens who engages in a bit of civil disobedience toward the laws
imposed by terror. This isn't a Toyota, though, which is the Taliban's vehicle of choice. We have to stop several times along the way, for the engine
tends to overheat and send a thick cloud of steam up through the hood,
obscuring all visibility. The driver never loses either his cool or his good
nature, and we all end up laughing every time we have to stop to let the
engine cool off and refill the coolant tank with water.

After passing through a Taliban checkpoint, the driver takes a cassette
tape out of a little hiding place under the dashboard, slips it into the car
stereo, and we continue on our way with music blasting at full volume.
This dispels any remaining suspicions we might have been harboring about
this young man, and we feel safe and relaxed enough that I even light up a
cigarette right there in the car, much to the delight of our driver, who
seems more focused on his rearview mirror than on the road ahead. Despite the potholes and the otherwise generally poor condition of the road,
he stomps down on the accelerator from time to time as if he were a stock
car driver, and we hold on for dear life and laugh like mad. He asks us if
we know how to drive. Yes, all three of us have driver's licenses. But when
he asks if we want to try driving on this particular road, all three of us say
no. Then he smiles contentedly, and lays on the gas yet again.

We're nearing our next meeting place.

"The only thing that we ask—for reasons of security—is that you don't mention the names of the towns where you've visited schools," is the standard request made by our Afghan contacts.

Once again we have to don our *burkas,* which we've stowed away inside one of our bags. Our driver can't believe his eyes: he seems at once surprised, amused, and complicitous. Having reconverted into Afghan women, we get out of the car and step into the street. From here, we walk to the apartment of the family waiting to meet us. Once there, we have to enter the building secretly and silently so that nobody—especially the neighbors—realizes that a group of foreigners are gathering here. We mustn't forget that another thing prohibited under the Taliban regime is any dealing with foreigners, especially Westerners. The family's apartment is on one of the top floors, while the building's common bathroom is located downstairs, off the patio. Therefore, if one of us needs to use it, we'll have to cover up well and go with one of the women who live there, so as to avoid any awkward encounters. Once we've all gathered there, we file into one of the bedrooms, where we're offered ice water. Despite the heat and our thirst, we don't dare drink the water; we can't afford any intestinal distress on our tear across Afghanistan. No water, no ice, no ice cream, and no unpeeled fruit: these were the doctor's orders when we went to get vaccinated and prepped for this trip just over a month ago. So we refuse as politely as we can, for neither do we want to offend these people who generously offer us whatever they have.

A short while later, one of the women tells us that now it's safe to go to the bathroom. The apartment has neither running water nor electricity, as we'll find out as soon as it starts to get dark. We bathe with a bucket of water that they've brought upstairs for us, and emerge feeling like new. The children ask for our clothes so they can wash them, but we assure them that this is not necessary. We've brought a change of clothes. Then we're invited out onto the terrace, though they ask that we cover ourselves with our chadors and sit in the most secluded corner, protected from view by the cloths hanging from the railing. Nobody must be able to see or hear us. Before night falls, other women come calling: teachers, collaborators, and project workers.

The regional coordinator tells us about the difficulties they're having. Arbitrariness and the lack of real legal and judicial systems make for different levels of oppression in different regions of the country, depending on the rigor and violence of each local Taliban patrol. This woman is in charge of eight classes, and she visits each once a week to stay up-to-date with any problems or issues that arise, and to deliver supplies and materials. Also, her visits serve as an opportunity to exchange thoughts, impressions, and news with the other women and teachers so everyone can cheer each other up and help dissipate the sense of solitude and isolation that so often comes with this line of work. The coordinators' visits are often the teachers' only link with the outside world; they can't even send letters to one another, since the Taliban continue to run such things as if the war had just broken out yesterday. Nothing works. Not even the mail. If someone wants to communicate with friends or family who have fled the country, they have no other choice but to travel to Pakistan and see them in person.

We eat dinner out on the terrace. Isn't this an unnecessary risk, if we must avoid at all costs that the neighbors know we're here? No, it won't be a problem as long as we keep our voices down, don't peek out over the edge of the railing, keep covered up with our chadors, and go down to the bathroom with an escort. Once again I have to marvel at their ability to remain calm and discerning in the face of danger, and to not let themselves be overcome by fear.

The woman who lives here is relatively young, though with several young children. She's scarcely had a chance to meet us, as busy as she is cooking and attending to all the guests. Finally she sits down, sweaty and exhausted, next to her husband, though still checking to make sure that everything is set and that nothing is missing. The banquet-quality spread is made up of multicolored vegetables, meats, rice, and salad . . . It's all delicious. When we can't possibly eat another bite, she puts away the leftovers and brings out the tea.

The women talk excitedly about the general health and first aid programs. One of the women here works at just this thing: she goes from house to house, her kit hidden beneath her *burka,* attending to sick women. If the country's economic woes—which give rise to begging, prostitution, or starvation—are grave, then its health issues are no less serious. Women are not only denied the rights to education, work, and freedom of movement, they are also prohibited from seeing a doctor. Relations between men and women not of the same family are strictly forbidden: women can't meet with shopkeepers, with tailors, not with anybody—doctors included. A sick woman has no recourses through which to seek attention. The women tell us that the number of deaths from childbirth and sickness have skyrocketed, even though the vast majority of these cases could have been easily treated and cured.

We ask about what tools most doctors have at their disposal.

Our resident doctor gets up to find her kit, which she always carries with her. It's a small, leather case that instantly reminds me of the ones that traveling family doctors used to carry and that I've only seen in movies. She shows us the tools of her trade with a certain pride: a device for measuring blood pressure, a stethoscope, a pair of tweezers, and a small vial of iodine. Nothing more.

We're dumbstruck. Evidently she notices our surprise, because she tells us that "we don't have the means to treat the most serious of cases."

It's getting dark now, and they bring out a big kerosene lamp. Our hostess tells us that only the Taliban have electricity in their homes here. There are several hydroelectric dams in the region, but most have either been shut down or have fallen into disrepair. The generators were replaced by ones of Pakistani manufacture, but they quickly broke down, and now the water just flows straight through. From our vantage point on the balcony, we can see that most of the buildings are completely dark, but the Taliban homes are there too, like illuminated islands in a black sea. We're told that they live in quite a state of luxury, and that—despite the ban that they themselves have imposed on the population—the light from their television sets can be seen flickering in their windows.

One of the men tells us how the people are tired, run-down by so many years of war, and left with little strength with which to fight the Taliban regime.

I disagree. I think that they are indeed fighting, that they are at the cusp of a great revolution, the only possible one and the only constructive one: one of culture and education. These networks of underground schools, coupled with these efforts to bring women the medical attention they need, prove that the Afghan people have not surrendered; have not relinquished the fight.

The man sighs and shakes his head. The women say nothing.

We sleep there on the terrace, everyone together: teachers, coordinators, doctors, and Palwasha, who explains that the women are reticent because they don't know us well, and they're shy.

A cat picks its way among the sleeping bodies.

A splendid full moon contemplates the city.

I cover myself with my chador.

TUESDAY, AUGUST 15, 2000.

Afghanistan.

A true friend is one who takes your hand in times of affliction and worry.

We get up early, wash up, and eat breakfast before donning our *burkas* and heading out into the streets to visit other clandestine schools. Today our *muhrram* is a nine-year-old boy, and he stops a rickshaw in the street for us. He sits up front with the driver while the rest of us pile into the backseat, which is scarcely a hand's width wide. Getting in while wearing a *burka* and laden with all our bags proves quite an exploit. Fitting three women on the seat is another.

We make the trip in silence, letting our *muhrram* give the driver directions. Again, I feel that my *burka* has turned me into an invisible creature, one that can see without being seen, completely excluded from the world unfolding itself before my eyes. We stop and get out in a small, mostly empty alley and follow our young guide through the twists and turns toward the next underground school, where we'll meet up with the rest of the group, who've taken a separate rickshaw. It turns out to be the house of an elderly woman who taught in a school in Kabul for over twenty years. She's an affable, caring woman. We spend awhile with her and her students, who have temporarily put aside their studies in order to talk with us.

We also visit another class of young girls; their teacher is a tall woman with a sad yet elegant aspect about her and whose only hope is that someday this senseless horror will pass, that it won't become a permanent state of affairs. From this hope she draws the strength to teach her students, convincing them that what they're living through—for these girls have known no other way of life—isn't the way things ought or have to be, that the mere fact that they are girls is no reason for them to accept the oppression they are being subjected to, and that the only weapons they have with which to fight this oppression are knowledge, understanding, and culture.

I congratulate her. *Tabrik!*

And now we must head for the border. Time to return to Pakistan. Later today, back in Peshawar, the inauguration of a new HAWCA school will be celebrated. Yesterday, Palwasha sent someone over to Najiba's house to let her know that we'd be returning soon—that there was nothing to worry about—and also to see if she could delay the festivities until later in the afternoon, so that we might have a chance of making it there in time.

We meet back up with our *muhrram,* who seems to appear out of thin air, and disappear just as easily once he's gotten us safely to our destinations. I have no idea where he spent the night last night, because he wasn't at dinner, nor did we see him in the apartment. He leads us to a car and, once inside, we remove our *burkas.* Again, we seem to have a friendly driver. And there's more: a young man will be traveling with us today, as there's been a slight change in plans. For now, he'll be Palwasha's younger brother.

"I'll cross the border on foot with him. You all will stay in the car with my uncle. It's better that the man from the intelligence agency doesn't see us together."

We stop at one of the checkpoints. There's not much we have to worry about here: Rolls of film? The books I bought in Kabul? Several Taliban officials peer in through the windows. They seem to be enjoying themselves. Palwasha's brother jokes around with them, because they think he's a foreigner as well. Then they wave us on our way, and we drive up toward the customs check. We stop and let Palwasha and her brother get out a bit before we arrive, and wait a moment to watch them walk off: just an Afghan boy accompanied by a sky-blue *burka* carrying a pot wrapped in a cloth. When they're finally out of sight, we get out and make our way to the customs check as well. They don't pay us the least bit of attention. They stamp our passports; we get back in the car, and head toward the Pakistani side, and the last checkpoint that we'll have to pass through on this long, intense, emotional journey.

There at the post, the officer on duty offers us a seat. Palwasha's uncle is still with us. Just then, the same member of Pakistani Intelligence who interrogated us four days ago walks in: we haven't forgotten his eagle eyes and nose. He greets us amicably enough, says he's happy to see us, and then begins with the questions. He asks us how everything went, what we thought of Kabul, if the journey has been difficult, if they treated us well at the Intercontinental, and if we'll be staying at the same hotel as before back in Peshawar.

No, we'll be staying in a different hotel tonight. We answer all questions succinctly, using only a word or two when that's all that's required of us. He offers us a drink, and even asks if we'd like him to prepare a room here at the office where we can rest for a while before continuing on to Peshawar. We thank him, but explain that we've been traveling all day and are just anxious to get to the hotel. Then, without so much as batting an eye, he asks about our interpreter.

"We had to let her go in Kabul. They told us at the hotel that women can't work there, and we haven't seen her since," we answer indifferently.

Then the Intelligence officer asks about the man who was traveling with us, and we tell him that the hotel in Kabul assigned him to accompany us to the border. He then informs us that we will no longer need our *muhrram,* and that we should send him back. From here on in, he'll take care of our security, and assign us an escort to travel with us to Peshawar. The eagle-eyed man then bids us farewell, leaving us in the hands of a Pakistani soldier. The three of us, the soldier, and our *muhrram* (who of course doesn't have the slightest intention of splitting up with us) rent a pickup truck and make our way back through the Khyber Pass toward Peshawar. But before we leave, a mountain of people rush to pile in the bed of the truck, whom I suppose want to make the trip with us. Women in *burkas,* men, and children. Truthfully, it doesn't matter to us. We drift off to sleep, lulled peacefully by the heat and the drone of the engine. We pass the last checkpoint of the tribal zone and head into the city toward the hotel where we'll supposedly be staying. Our stowaways drop off the back of the truck at various points along the way, while our armed escort stays with us. He doesn't seem to have the slightest intention of ever leaving, until he suddenly jumps out at an intersection. Our *muhrram* hands him a few rupees, and he says good-bye. We're not sure if we paid him to get out of the car, or whether we paid him for escorting us all the way from the border. Our *muhrram* drops us off at the hotel's front door.

Dirty, sweaty, covered in dust and stains, we go in one of Peshawar's most luxurious hotels. As soon as the concierge sees us enter the lobby, he comes up and greets us ceremonially. I don't know if such a reception is simply a routine part of his job given to all hotel guests, or if it's because we're patently Westerners and therefore somehow deserving of some sort of reverence. Politely playing the role of tourists, we tell him that we'd just like to sit down for a while and have a cup of coffee. Obligingly, he leads us over to a bench at the far end of the lobby, and shoos away the few men already sitting there. There's space left over, but no Pakistani takes it. Sometimes, this whole business of the purdah has its advantages.

We have our coffee . . . one, two, and then three cups. We take turns in the hotel rest room to freshen ourselves up a bit. The concierge is getting a bit antsy: are these women going to be staying in the hotel? We aren't sure just yet; we've just returned from a trip, and we're waiting for the rest of our group to arrive. He assures us that the rooms are large and quite comfortable. If we'd like, he'd be happy to book us in a three-bed suite complete with two separate bathrooms, so that we can rest up from our travels. Thanks, but we won't be able to decide until the rest of our party arrives.

THE SILENCED CRY | 225

Could you bring us another cup of coffee, though? We're not sure what to do about yet another concierge stifling us with his attentiveness. Meanwhile, all shapes and sizes of tourists make their way through the hotel lobby, though all are impeccably dressed: a Pakistani family, a Hindu couple, and a Japanese group. We're starting to feel more self-conscious about our disheveled appearance. Finally Azada enters through the big, revolving doors and we all embrace like crazy. We gather up our bags and head outside, where our neighborly driver is there, emotional and affectionate and very happy to see us. Once we're all in the car, he tells us that yesterday he went all the way to Torkham to pick us up, and he waited there until they closed the border. So he went home empty-handed, and nobody knew what to make of the situation. They were all quite worried. He repeats over and over again that we are true heroines. We laugh, unable to accept such a title. We stop at a fast food shop just long enough to pick up a few sandwiches; if we make good time, we'll be able to make it to the school's party in time. Apparently, Najiba got the message in time. We eat our sandwiches there in the car, stopping back at the house just long enough to wash up and throw on a change of clothes before piling back into the taxi and heading for the school. We make it there just in time. Najiba and all the other teachers look beautiful. Najiba's mother is also there, as well as a pair of other people whom we haven't met yet. They've moved the table out onto the porch, which they've set up like a stage. The rugs from the classrooms have been spread out on the patio in front of this setup, and perhaps a hundred children are sitting there on them. We recognize a few of them from when we visited their families earlier, and today they've dressed up in full regalia as well. Finally, strung up from the front door and across the porch and patio are long strips of multicolored bunting, which only add to the festive atmosphere.

It begins with an introduction by Najiba, and then the teachers speak, followed by readings by the students themselves. Azada is also asked to say a few words, and when they ask us to address the group as well, Meme and I nominate Sara to do the speaking in English while Azada translates:

"Back in our country, we heard that there was a group of Afghan children in Pakistan who loved learning and going to school so much, and at first we didn't believe them, and so we had to come and see for ourselves. But now you've proven it to us, and so when we return home, we'll be able to tell the rest of the world about you."

The party is just winding down when we are pleasantly surprised to see Rustam appear, accompanied by Mikel, a photographer and colleague of Sara's who only just yesterday arrived in Pakistan after having suffered through every type of vicissitude possible: canceled flights, lost luggage . . . Although the festivities are mostly over, he still has time to snap a few photos. Sara and I buy a few small birdcages that the children have made for us, and end up buying one from each of them. Meme takes down some notes and vital information with which to start a medical file on the child whom she wants to fly to Barcelona for treatment.

Suddenly, one of the girls runs up to us, awash in tears. It's little Rahima; she's twelve. She was supposed to be part of the presentation today, but this morning her father told her that she's too old to be going to school, and forbid her from attending tonight's festivities. Besides, there would be boys there—purdah! And now that her father's left the house and she was able to sneak out, the party is over! The teachers try and console her; they'll speak with her father about it. Then we tell her we'd love to hear her recite the piece that she's memorized for the occasion. We form a circle around her, ask for silence, take a few pictures, and listen attentively. After she's finished, she gives Sara, Meme, and I each a pair of wool cloths that she knitted herself. Najiba subtly explains to us that they're washcloths, to be used in the shower. We thank her—*tashakor*—and cover her in kisses.

The adults sip their sweetened tea while the boys and girls play out on the patio. Mikel is taking some more pictures. A short while later we say good night, though we'll be back in the morning when class starts.

Dusk is falling by the time we're all gathered back at the house. Lala comes as well. While Najiba is preparing dinner, her husband arrives, happy and relieved to see us once again safe and sound. Last night—they hadn't gotten word that we'd be a day late—everyone had been worried sick.

In the end, after dinner and over cup after cup of tea, we tell everyone about our odyssey, and finally Sara's wish comes true: we're all together, back home, laughing about how much trouble we thought we were in.

Najiba's husband laughs along with us, but when it all dies down, he wants to know what we would have done had there been a phone number or an address where we could have reached our Afghan friends.

"Nothing," we reply. We were acutely aware that we couldn't do anything that might give someone away, and that any such error could have proven fatal.

He nods approvingly. And what might we have done had we been able to call our families at home in Spain on that one terrible night in Kabul? For my part, I would have had my husband call anyone and everyone he could, to try to alert the authorities as to what was about to happen in Kabul, and to raise as much hell as possible, because there was no way that we would be leaving Afghanistan without our Palwasha.

We go on talking about the impressions that Afghanistan has left on us. I reiterate just how beautiful I found the country to be, and add that its landscape is just like its people: strong, stern, and ready to face difficulties with a sense of defiance.

Then Najiba's husband speaks, softly and slowly, in a measured, muted voice. He is honored and happy to have us here in his home; what we've done for him is nothing short of heroic. Here we protest: they are the true heroes, they are the ones who accompanied us everywhere, who took care of us and risked so much by doing so. They are the ones who defy danger and oppression in order that they might confer a better future to their children and grandchildren. But he won't accept our protests.

"What you three have done is proof of true friendship. To me—to all of us—you three will always be sisters."

Once again, I feel the lump rising in my throat. An old Persian proverb states that *"A true friend is one who takes your hand in times of affliction and worry."* I hope with all my heart that I can do this for them, and I am infinitely touched and honored that this man thinks of me like a sister. Perhaps someday I will be worthy of such a title. *Inshallah!* We can do nothing save for give them our heartfelt thanks.

"*Tashakor.*"

"*Tashakor* to you as well."

The Refugee Camp.

Every rose has its thorn.

After picking up Mikel at the hotel, we head back to the school for our promised visit. Class has already begun, and each teacher is working with her particular group of students. Najiba is taking down the names of the new ones. At the moment, there are thirty-eight students seated there on the porch.

We're surprised to see little Rahima. Were they able to convince her father to let her attend? No, but he leaves the house very early and works all day, so what he doesn't know won't hurt him. Plus, her mother supports the idea of Rahima going to school.

We stop in on each of the classes to chat for a bit with the students. Seeing them sitting there on the rug in that poorly ventilated room, their faces shining, proves to us that they truly do enjoy going to school. They tell us they don't want to grow up without knowing how to read and write. Many of them work as well—and not just at home making birdcages. Two brothers—one six and the other ten—head straight to the rug-weaving shop after school. Others work for a seamstress. One seven-year-old boy helps his father, a mechanic, by welding pipes. Another works in a bakery, while still another works in an ice cream shop. Little Zakia is eight years old and—every day from 4:30 to 6:30 in the morning—goes to a Pakistani family's home to clean it. They pay her a hundred rupees a month.

"Sometimes they give me a scoop of ice cream too."

Mikel needs a break from snapping photos, and we decide to sit down and rest in the shade.

Only now, as we take advantage of a peaceful moment out on the school patio, do I finally understand this unique Afghan form of sadness, as profound and serene as the water at the bottom of a well. It has taken hold of me. I recognize it and desire it. I accept that it has imbued me, that it is now a part of me and will be a part of everything that I do from now on. Because this particular sadness is not paralyzing, nor disheartening, nor despairing, nor debilitating.

Rustam has hired a new car sans driver that will fit all of us, now that Mikel is here. We drive around to various places so he can photograph the beggars, the drug addicts, the women, and the children rummaging through the garbage.

The majority of drug addicts in Pakistan are Afghans. Even after having fled their broken country, they seek refuge in drugs from the horrible memories of what life was like there. They drift through the streets like lost souls, dressed in rags, dragging their feet, the tips of their fingers blackened from smoking heroin (they will cook a small amount on a scrap of tin foil and inhale the fumes with a cloth draped over their heads). They beg for money with which to buy more drugs.

We're now in the waning days of our journey. Soon we'll have to return to Europe, and there's still so much we haven't done here.

Before stopping to eat, we visit the Pakistani government's High Commission for Refugees, where we've set up a written interview. It is this office that decides if organizations like RAWA are allowed to become officially registered or not. This afternoon, we'll be returning to the refugee camp so that Mikel can take some more photos, and tomorrow we'll spend the entire day there before getting picked back up on Friday, our last day in Peshawar.

On the way home, we suddenly realize that we didn't speak with any official Taliban members during our entire swing through Afghanistan. At the very least, we could try to speak to the head of a Koran school. The Taliban were created, formed, and molded in the *madrasas* of Pakistan, and so interviewing their teachers ought to be interesting as well. If the *sharia*—the Islamic law applied by the Taliban—really was good for Afghanistan, why wouldn't it be implemented in Pakistan as well? We pull up in front of a mosque to ask if we could ask a few questions and get a bit of information; they don't exactly say no, but they say we'll have to come back at another time.

We won't be able to visit the *madrasa*. This interview will have to be added to our list of pending things to be attended to on a return trip.

Islam. Religion. Fanaticism. Fundamentalism. These are important themes; themes that must be distinguished and not confounded. Nor can we allow public opinion to be manipulated, because in reality, the West—which always needs a demon to face and knows how to create one out of diffuse, generalized fears and common threats that justify any sort of action on its part—has now done so with Islam, and people now fear the threat posed by Islamic fundamentalism in much the same way that they once feared and demonized the red threat of Communism. Islam—like Christianity, Judaism, Buddhism, or any other religion on earth—is nothing but a set of behavioral guidelines and rules for life whose original objective was to heighten human dignity and contribute to the creation of a better society. In Islam, as in Christianity, many of the original principles have been perverted by dint of interpretations and interests, as well as through petty complicities and alliances with power. The greatest crimes in history—as well as the greatest manipulations of humanity—have been perpetrated in the name of religion. The Inquisition took place in Spain, and the Taliban are conducting a similar operation in Afghanistan, but the real, common objective is power: the ability to use religion to justify oppression. Power and religious zeal feed the executioner's ability to ply his trade. The real puppet masters have nothing to do with the Koran, the

Bible, the Prophet, or the Master; they have nothing to do with God or with Allah.

The oppression suffered by the people of Afghanistan has nothing to do with Islam or with high-and-mighty Islamic law, which not even the Taliban themselves respect. The violation of human rights has nothing to do with the Koran, which itself commands "that women reap the benefits of what they sow" and that "men and women are obligated to educate themselves."

That afternoon, at the prescribed time, they come to pick us up at the refugee camp so we can once again visit the brick factory. Sara has asked him to bring equipment for taking photographs in the dark. We want physical proof of what the Afghan refugees are doing in Pakistan.

Afterward, we're elated to go back to Azada's house. Her family receives us warmly, and they have a splendid dinner ready for us. Rustam and Mikel will have to sleep in another house tonight. *Purdah*. This comes as something of a shock to Mikel, who is still rather freshly arrived from Europe. It's still all new to him: the food, the customs, the relationships, what is considered proper and what is not.

A phenomenal surprise is waiting for us at the dinner table: the doctor will be joining us. Plus, as a member of the council, he'll also be joining us on the nocturnal adventure that has been scheduled for 3 A.M. During dinner and the subsequent discussion that lasts until it's time for us to leave, the conversation flows pleasantly and nimbly. The topics range from the transcendental to the mundane and from the serious to the fun, and we express our opinions freely and honestly, even playing the devil's advocate at times. The best part of it all is that nobody has to be right. All the different contributions and points of view are met with respect.

We've brought some instant coffee with us, and break out a pair of cups.

At three o'clock sharp we file out into the dark street to find the camp ambulance and a pickup truck complete with armed escorts waiting for us. We've explained to Mikel that the area we'll be traveling through isn't safe at night, and now he sees that we weren't joking. But we make it to the factories without any problems, park the vehicles, and set out walking through the night. The moon ducks behind a cloud. The only sounds are the echoes of our footsteps and the rhythmic sounds of molds being emptied. Much of the camp is here, working invisibly through the night.

One family receives the scare of their lives when they see us emerge from the darkness, accompanied by all these armed men. They'd initially thought we were bandits.

We walk through the night, moving up and down the embankments, trying not to tread on the rows of drying bricks, stopping to talk with various workers, and asking their permission to take some pictures of them at their work. Men, women, and children. We recognize a few whom we'd met on our earlier daytime visit: the deaf woman, the man who used to own a ranch in Afghanistan . . .

Children of no more than six or seven work here without complaint. A woman apologizes that she doesn't have a cup of tea to offer us. A man tells us how he used to live in the city, where he and his sons would gather paper and crates from the trash, but the police there were always making trouble for them: his sons were even arrested on a couple of occasions, and bail wasn't cheap. Brick making might be much more exhausting work, but at least he doesn't have to worry about avoiding the police.

They work at night to take advantage of the cooler temperatures, but they continue to work well after the sun comes up, bringing its suffocating heat with it. The only rotating shifts are for the men who keep the furnaces fed with fuel. I bend down and place my hand on the ground: even at night, the earth covering the furnaces is burning hot.

Up ahead, a woman apologizes for not shaking hands, as hers are caked with clay. I continue on my new descent into hell. Into silence. Full of a deep respect for these life sentences. Why them and not me? Why their children and not mine? I feel so much pain for their lives that anything I could say seems trite and even offensive when compared with the reality of their situation and the dignity with which they endure it. I see Rustam wandering around, also in silence, immersed in his own sadness. I hear

Azada translating our questions and the people's resulting answers, always with her characteristic, exquisite sense of respect and affectionate familiarity for each and every one of these people: slaves of the twenty-first century, each one with a face, a name, a past, and a history. Do they have any dreams left?

We make our way back to the car and depart.

"We ought to interview the people who own these factories."

We jot down the names and phone numbers of those factories whose information is posted on signs along the road. Despite our best intentions, we won't be able to get in touch with any of them.

Outside the truck, silence reigns.

"What do you think, having visited all this?" the doctor asks me from the front seat.

I can't answer. I don't have the words.

"There are no words that could express what I feel. Not in any language."

In the dark, the doctor nods.

He still hasn't found the words either.

It's nearly dawn by the time we arrive home. Everyone goes to bed except for Sara and I. We sit out on the porch. She takes down a few notes in the lamplight. A pair of lizards with bulging eyes are basking next to the glowing bulb. I lie down on the wooden cot, searching for the protection of darkness. As I rest here, the brick makers are still out there toiling away. Dawn's first light breaks over the horizon. More than thinking, I worry—freely and knowingly—until reaching the last drop of this strange gift that I've been given, this sense of sadness that has been conferred unto me like an undeserved honor. Indeed it's true: *"Every rose has its thorn."* And I wrap my palm tightly around the stem of my new Afghan rose.

THURSDAY, AUGUST 17, 2000.

The Refugee Camp.

———————

A good perfume is known by its essence, not by the claims of the perfumist.

———————

I wake up gradually. Unbeknownst to me, Azada's grandmother aimed the fan out on the porch to blow on me during the night. Through the patio door, I can just make out the shape of our beloved *muhrram,* who's come to say hello. They told him that we were all still asleep, and he's on his way home. Bit by bit, the others all start to wake up as well. We have breakfast. Mikel and Rustam are late, and Azada sends her cousin off to check on them. Rustam appears a bit later. Mikel isn't feeling well; he's lying down in what had been our bedroom, with no appetite and a general feeling of malaise. He's scarcely eaten a thing since arriving in Afghanistan. Meme makes him a cup of tea, doing what she can to take care of him. Hopefully, he'll feel better in time to make the day's rounds with us. We'd like to have his photos of the health clinic, the shop, the literacy classes, the streets, and the installations of the camp.

While we're waiting for the truck to arrive, Azada tells me that she knows a woman who is going to be baking some bread. We make our way over to the oven. All of my desires have been realized on this trip, and now I'm going to witness the baking process. The woman there, under the thatched roof, is the dark-haired widow I met at the embroidery shop, the one who owns the skinny old cow. We greet each other warmly, and I ask if I can take a few pictures of her making bread. She nods, smiling. Then she kneels down next to a hole in the ground, perhaps a foot in diameter: the oven. Wood is burning down at the bottom, heating the cylindrical walls. Then the woman smothers the flames and—after wrapping her chador around her face to filter out the smoke—she wipes down the walls of the hole with a damp cloth, cleaning them. Then she uncovers a pan of fresh dough, already formed into individual spheres. One by one, she takes the spheres and skillfully tamps them into circles of the same diameter as the mouth of the oven itself. As they cook, the dough rises and takes on a golden brown color. She periodically loosens the edges that come in touch with the oven walls, and in order to bake the top of the bread, she flips it upside down like a pancake onto the smoldering embers. When the first loaf comes out, she dusts off the ashes and offers it to me. I break off a piece and savor its warm, chewy flavor.

"*Tashakor.*"

Just then, our *muhrram* comes over to say good-bye, inviting us to stop by for a drink before we go. We accept, and thus get to meet his two daughters. We bid him an affectionate farewell, thanking him profusely for all that he's done for us.

We owe him a lot.

A bit earlier, at the clinic, while Mikel was photographing the installations, we said good-bye to the doctor.

Back at the house, we say good-bye to Azada's grandmother, who gives each of us a large, square pillowcase made of golden cloth. Sara's and Meme's are embroidered with blue; mine in deep red. She made them herself, many years ago, when she was still young and could see well enough to do intricate needlework. She hopes that we'll think of her every time we lie back on a pillow. She also hopes that we'll come back and visit again, although she knows we do live very far away, and it could be quite some time before we're able to return. She may not be here when we do.

We exchange sad, affectionate kisses, and we thank her for the gifts.

The first thing we do upon reaching Peshawar is to go to the airport and confirm our flights. Surprise! Our tickets have been canceled. The man behind the counter tells us that we needed to confirm them at least ninety-six hours before our scheduled departure, and there won't be another flight until the fourth or fifteenth of September.

Meme and Sara react with the proper sense of concern: they have to be back at work on Monday. I, on the other hand, can scarcely contain my joy: I'm going to stay! I'm going to stay for a few more weeks! My heart starts pounding out of pure excitement and emotion. I can't restrain my delight. It seems almost expected—inevitable, even—that my plans would change. Azada has an old computer at her house. I'm sure she would loan it to me, and I could write my book right there in the refugee camp itself. No, I really don't want to leave this country. I don't know what I would give to find my place in the world here. But I do know that I really should return to Europe, because it's there—from my own world—where I have to fight on Afghanistan's behalf. Still, these few extra weeks that the canceled tickets are presenting seem like a gift from heaven.

The airline representative is full of sympathetic gestures. We have just one option: pay an extra fifty dollars per ticket and get bumped up to first class, where there are still a few seats available.

Meme and Sara look seriously at me.

"Don't you understand that we have to be back at the office in Barcelona on Monday morning? I'm ready to pay whatever it takes to get me on tomorrow's flight," asserts Meme.

"Would you stop laughing? You're acting like an idiot. This is serious," scolds Sara.

They're right, of course, but I can't quite accept it.

The first-class seats aren't guaranteed; the airline representative will have to send a fax to Paris right now, and we'll have to wait here for confirmation. And because of the differences in the two time zones, the Paris office won't be open yet. We wouldn't have an answer for several hours.

We go out to eat, and then come back.

No, they still haven't heard anything.

We sit down in the airport lobby.

The representative's shift ends before any word arrives from Paris. He suggests we stop by the company's main office first thing in the morning.

We had an appointment scheduled with a RAWA representative who was going to bring us the publications and tapes that we'd asked for copies of. We tried to send word to let her know that we would be late, but by the time we got there from the airport, she had already come and gone.

Between coming and going, in one of the parking lots, I finally have a chance to see and smell the mysterious steaming cans carried by children and offered to passersby and cars stopped at intersections. Azada calls one of the children over to us. A few small embers smolder in the bottom of the can. The idea is to sprinkle a pinch of either *ispand* or *maro* over the coals, and inhale the aromatic fumes. *Ispand* resembles fresh ground pepper, while *maro* is a type of elongated seed. Our young purveyor has *ispand*. Azada takes a pinch and sprinkles it over the embers, producing a white cloud that she tries to breathe in, though most of it is carried away by the breeze. We give the boy a few rupees and get back in the car.

It's already getting dark by the time we return home. Our Afghan friends want to celebrate with a farewell dinner. Everyone will be coming: our taxi driver and his family, Nasreen and her family, Najiba's mother, and two of her relatives recently arrived from Kabul. We decide to make a fruit salad as our contribution. The patio is like a mob scene: the women are finishing up with the cooking, Nasreen is putting the final touches on the salads, and not a single other person will fit in the kitchen. Our driver's younger son good-naturedly offers to lend a hand to anyone who needs one. The men are all sitting out on the porch, chatting. The three of us pile into the bathroom—at once—to wash up as fast as possible. Then we move out onto the patio to peel and slice fruit, and realize that we're out of serving trays. Nasreen sends her youngest son to the driver's house to bring back a large bowl. Rustam has sat himself down with the rest of the men.

Once everything is ready, the women also sit down to chat, but on the opposite end of the porch. I ask Azada if it's going to be like this all night: with the men and women eating separately. But no, when the moment arrives and the giant tablecloth is spread out on the ground and piled high with food, everyone grabs a seat, though the men take two adjoining sides of the square for themselves, while the women occupy the other two sides. One of the coed corners is made up by Najiba and her husband; the other is Rustam and one of us.

The taxi driver has brought a video with him of a similar party from a few years ago, where several of tonight's guests are present and dancing, chatting, and generally having fun. The women—almost unrecognizable— are wearing makeup and elegant dresses, not at all in accordance with their traditionally intended use.

We watch the tape after dinner. After it's over, and it looks like the nightly fete is about to begin, something unexpected happens: the women split off by themselves, huddling together like a bunch of American football players. Only Azada and the three of us are left out; we're caught up in an intriguing conversation with one of Najiba's relatives from Kabul. We're talking about the future of Afghanistan, the international community, the role of the United Nations, and the West's attitude toward Afghanistan and her problems. We admit our perpetual shame: in our country, Afghanistan is rarely if ever mentioned, the people are generally ignorant about what is going on here, the government refuses to intervene, nobody tries to call attention to the reality of life here, because nobody really knows. Once again we accept the thinly veiled reproach that one of our own sayings illustrates to perfection: *"He who keeps quiet is rewarded."* A few other men join in the conversation. We talk for quite a while. Not one woman enters into the conversation; not one woman offers her opinion. Not even Najiba, whom we know for a fact has definite thoughts on the matter, since we've heard her espouse them passionately before. I can't believe it when I realize that, hours later, with the guests gone and most of the house fast asleep, the women are in Najiba's room while the men, including her husband, are in another. Meme and I mention this to Azada.

"You all are educated women, women who are working hard at great things with the schools; you have made definitive choices about your lives and about what you want for yourselves, your children, and your country. Why must there be such a gulf between the sexes when it comes to conversation?"

It's something that she doesn't understand either, since they are the ones excluding themselves. None of the men who were present tonight had done anything to make the women feel unwelcome to join their conversation. I remember the last night in Afghanistan, when we were with the teachers and coordinators, who were also very courageous women with worthy enough goals to risk their lives and safety in order to attain them. They also deferred to the man of the house, allowing him to direct the conversation and intervening scarcely if at all.

We talk with Azada until very late, stretched out together on the rug, our heads supported by those red velvet pillows. We tell each other about highly personal and intimate things with complete honesty, as if we've been friends all our lives. Confessions, longings, angers, emotions, secrets, complicities.

We finally decide to go to sleep when Azada's face starts to look a little pale: the unequivocal sign of mortal fatigue that we've come to recognize well over the past few days, especially in this woman who has expended so much energy so that we might come to know her reality.

"I'll miss you guys."

We'll miss her too. Painfully. Inevitably. Joyfully.

"A good perfume is known by its essence, not by the claims of the perfumist" says a Kabuli proverb. The same is true of Azada.

I know I've met an exceptional woman. I've lived with that rare person who shines with her own individual light and doesn't even realize it, so simply and naturally does it come to her. It's not a dazzling light, but it is warm, and it makes you want to make things better.

Peshawar.

Nobody can carry two melons in just one hand.

Our time is up.

Instead of being whittled down, our list of unfinished business—now physically impossible to complete—has grown. Why hadn't it occurred to us to visit a *madrasa* until now? And too bad we didn't think to get in touch with the brick factory owners during our first visit there, at the beginning of our time in Pakistan. And why didn't we accept the invitation to join the group of Taliban in the ruined palace for tea? It would have been interesting to speak to a Taliban woman. But could we have taken any better advantage of our time? No. Absolutely not.

"Nobody can carry two melons in just one hand." But the proverb is somewhat misleading: neither can you carry one melon in just one hand. We were forced to choose between the urgent and the important, two terms often confounded.

There's a lot left to do, but I think that this frenzy of the final day is more an attempt on our part to forget that we're actually leaving; that with this heightened sense of activity, we're simply trying to dull the pain that our impending departure would otherwise cause; that we're putting up protective adobe walls to try to keep out the longings encircling us like a pack of wild animals.

Today is our appointment with the Pakistani government's High Council on Refugees, which we set up a couple of days ago. We head to their offices accompanied by Azada and Rustam. The man we'd spoken to earlier either isn't there or wants us to speak with someone else. His replacement shows us a thick dossier containing descriptions of all the aid and procedures geared to help the Afghan refugees. We mention that the primary purpose of our visit is to learn how HAWCA can gain legal recognition. There is a growing interest in our country in making economic contributions to the organization.

"If you want to help the Afghan refugees, send your donations to us and we will take care of distributing them. As for ratifying a new organization, they have to go through an extensive application procedure, which can be a time-consuming process."

We leave rather disappointed. What if we were to legalize HAWCA back in Spain? A similar such humanitarian organization is registered in Germany; perhaps we could do the same. Azada and Rustam think this is a fine idea. We'll have to look into it upon our return.

There's just no way we can visit the refugee camp with Najiba's husband today, as we still have to solve the problem of our return tickets, and so we next make our way to the airline company's offices. Once there, we hand our tickets to the person in charge. To Sara's and Meme's delight—and my disappointment—we've been cleared. Apparently there never was a problem: we're on the same flight, in our original, tourist-class seats. So what happened yesterday? The representative has no idea. Everything seems to be in order. Why had the attendant told us differently yesterday? He shrugs his shoulders. We don't understand a thing.

But now it's settled: this afternoon, we'll leave for Islamabad with Rustam. Our flight to Western Europe leaves tomorrow morning at 5 A.M.

We eat together—the five of us—for the last time, fully aware of how much we are going to miss each other. Will we ever see each other again?

Inshallah! But we don't know for sure. Rustam proposes a bet: if I can teach myself Dari with the book I bought in Kabul, he'll buy my ticket. But if he can teach himself Spanish first, I'll buy his. In the meantime, we'll write to each other. Of course. We'll be in touch via E-mail. We draw up a sort of balance sheet, a personal balance sheet of the time we spent together, detailing the best and worst things each of us experienced. The nighttime talks take the cake, but I'm deeply moved that, for Rustam, the best moment took place before we even arrived:

"It was when I first learned that you were coming; that three Western women were coming here to learn more about our situation."

We pack our bags.

We exchange gifts in the midst of the now-routine chaos.

"If we were in Spain, I'd kiss you," I tell Rustam as I extend my hand.

"Well kiss him then!" Azada exclaims with delight.

Najiba brings over the bag containing the RAWA tapes. Yesterday, when we were trying to speak with them, they suggested they leave the tapes with Najiba at the school in the morning. Najiba's husband also got us a copy of the historical documentary that we saw a couple of days ago.

Time is flying.

We say our final farewells. A lengthy embrace. Thousands of kisses.

The bus won't wait for us, and we take off in two taxis for the station.

Rustam will meet us there. First he has to swing by the hotel to pick up Mikel. He'll travel with us as far as Islamabad, where he's arranged to stay and work for a few more days.

The bus station is its usual, hustle-and-bustle self: the same children selling snacks and refreshments to the travelers, the same grunts of the porters loading and securing baggage, the transactions of travelers purchasing tickets and receiving their change. The same beggars, the same strange . . .

We have to say good-bye.

To the taxi drivers.

To Azada, that free woman. To Palwasha, and her dawnlike light.

We embrace.

Time is running short.

The bus driver starts his engine.

It's getting dark by the time we reach Islamabad.

We drop Mikel off at his hotel. We'll see him in Barcelona.

We hold on until the last possible moment. Again, with Rustam, we picture the historical documentary with which to annotate these images. Many successive kisses and hugs, and we cast off the mooring lines and finally bring ourselves to face the work that will begin upon our return. Conferences must be scripted, and a video illustrating the situation in Afghanistan and the situation of her refugees must be spliced together. I have to start thinking about my book, about my diary of a journey to Afghanistan.

"Write about what you've seen."

It's the first thing that I'm going to do. That's why I've come. That was the deal that was struck in Barcelona last march with that woman—an Afghan refugee—who had never met me before and whose name I didn't even know.

We get up at 3 A.M.

Rustam drives us to the airport in a friend's car.

We speak little, if at all.

The airport lobby is a mash of travelers trying to get to different airline counters so they can check their luggage. We should get in line.

"Good-bye, Rustam. Thank you for everything."

And there we go, off into the crowd, passing through the security checkpoint and taking our place at the end of the line. We don't check the birdcages that the students made for us. We'll carry those with us. We board the plane. An hour goes by, then another. We're still on the ground. The delay is due to a passenger who didn't get on the plane, and now they have to locate and remove his luggage. The heat is becoming unbearable. The wait is becoming interminable. At this rate, we'll miss our connecting flight in Paris. But finally, we're taxing down the runway.

After we're airborne, I get up and make my way back into the tail of the plane for a cigarette. There's an empty space near the bathrooms with a window but no seats. I go over and peer out at the ground below. Mountains. Ochre land. Under the sparkling, sunny blue sky that we're cleaving through like a bird. I ask a flight attendant where we are.

"We're over Afghanistan, madam."

The spell cast by these words, the nostalgia hidden away in my most recondite place, fills me up to the brim, threatening to burst through like a broken dam.

I lean my head against the window.

Afghanistan.

I've only just now left, and all I can think about is coming back.

Vallirana.

A trumpet player's work consists of blowing into his instrument.

I tried to do it. And I did.

I'm just a trumpet player blowing into her instrument.

Those who hear the music may be moved to dance, cover their ears, leave the room, or pick up their own instrument and form a duo, trio, chamber set, or an entire orchestra. Strings, brass, woodwinds, and percussion all playing one single musical piece.

Since we've returned to Barcelona, Meme, Sara, and I have continued to work on behalf of Afghanistan and her refugees in Peshawar, each of us in the field we're best attuned to. We've held conferences all over the Iberian Peninsula, and helped found a HAWCA branch in Catalonia, raising funds to support its humanitarian projects. We've rallied politicians, journalists, and professionals in all fields, drumming up support and awareness so that the situation in Afghanistan can be better understood and therefore denounced. We've worked to reestablish a democratic government in Afghanistan and undermine the Taliban regime's recognition and legitimacy in the eyes of the international community. And we've tried to create a network that unites and channels the efforts of the people, institutions, and organizations on behalf of Afghan men and women.

I light my last cigarette.

I insert a 3.5 floppy disk, and click SAVE. *The Silenced Cry.*

Quit.

And I switch off my computer.

Chronology

- Amanullah is deposed by a rebellion supported by religious and tribal leaders from the country's south.

THE REIGN OF HABIBULLAH II, KNOWN AS BACHA-I SAQAO (SON OF THE WATERER): 1929

- His nine-month reign is plagued by anarchy and clashes between various segments of the population.
- Victory comes to Mohammad Nadir, who has the support of British-controlled India.

THE REIGN OF MOHAMMAD NADIR SHAH: 1929–1933

- Sees a return to a harsh Islamic conservatism.
- Soviet influence is replaced by a greater British presence.
- A massive repression of Amanullah supporters is carried out, and many intellectuals and members of the Constitutional Movement are either murdered or imprisoned.
- Nadir Shah is assassinated by a student.

THE REIGN OF MUHAMMAD ZAHIR SHAH: 1933–1973

- Muhammad Zahir is very young when he rises to the throne, and rules under the tutelage of his family, especially the prince Muhammad Daoud Shah.
- In 1934, Afghanistan joins the League of Nations.
- Afghanistan establishes commercial relations with Germany, Italy, and Japan.
- Afghanistan remains neutral during WWII.

- In 1942, Afghanistan establishes diplomatic relations with the United States.
- When the British withdraw from India, Afghanistan demands the re-unification of Pashtunistan, divided since 1893 by the Durand Line, drawn by the British to demarcate their colonies. India opposes the claim.
- In November of 1946, Afghanistan joins the United Nations.
- The creation of Pakistan in 1947 confirms the Durand Line as a definitive border. Afghanistan refuses to recognize the partitioning of India, and opposes Pakistan's bid to join the U.N. Relations with Pakistan grow strained.
- Baluchi independence movements begin to spring up, clamoring for the reunification of Baluchistan, split by borders drawn by Britain and Persia.
- A time of foreign aid begins, devoted to developing the country's infrastructure.
- In 1953, Muhammad Daoud, King Zahir Shah's cousin, becomes the prime minister.
- Daoud forms a powerful army, trained by the Soviet Union, and gives them rein to take up the reformist cause.
- In 1955, Afghanistan becomes the founding member of the Movement of Non-Aligned Countries.
- As part of the Cold War, the United States and the Soviet Union compete for Afghanistan through economic and military support policies. The USSR comes out on top.
- In 1961, the border conflicts with Pakistan intensify, owing to Pashtunistan's demands and claims.
- This decade is characterized by social reforms and economic development, but also by political repression.
- During the 1950s, women in Kabul slowly gain entrance to the workforce in such capacities as secretaries, nurses, receptionists, hostesses, etc. A small minority attend university where they study medicine,

law, engineering, and journalism, despite the opposition and condemnation of the *ulemas*—religious leaders who interpret the *sharia,* or Islamic law.

- In 1963, Daud is forced to step down.
- In 1964, Zahir Shah endows Afghanistan with a modern constitution, approved and ratified in a *Loya Jirga*—a Grand Assembly for the resolving of conflicts and the making of important decisions.
- The constitution broaches the subject of equal rights for men and women. It establishes a secular legal system that exists independently of the *sharia,* or Islamic law. It also stipulates a secular government, complete with an elected Parliament and twenty-eight provincial councils. Freedom of the press and freedom of political activity facilitate the appearance of political parties, though of very limited influence, that participate in the general elections of 1965 (which results in the first ever Parliament, comprised of 216 representatives, four of whom are women) and 1969.
- During the 1960s, the University of Kabul was the stage on which rose radical political movements that opposed the government's reformist policies. In 1965, those who wanted more drastic changes founded the PDPA (the People's Democratic Party of Afghanistan: a Soviet-leaning Communist Party) while the Islamic movement opposing such changes was gaining influence among university students and professors.
- The PDPA would never be a true people's party and, in 1969, split into two factions: the *Jalq* (the People)—led by Nur Muhammad Taraki and Hafizullah Amin—and the *Parcham* (the Banner) led by Babrak Karmal.
- During this time, the People's Republic of China became the fourth largest source of foreign aid, behind the Soviet Union, the United States, and West Germany.
- The instability of subsequent reigns, coupled with the effects of the drought that devastated the country between 1971 and 1972, resulted

in the coup of 1973, bringing the constitutional monarchy to an end, and with it, the incipient democracy.

THE REPUBLIC OF AFGHANISTAN: 1973–1978

- In July of 1973, Daoud—the king's former prime minister—acting with the support of the army, the PDPA, and the Soviet Union, put an end to the monarchy with a coup d'etat and proclaimed himself president of the recently created Republic of Afghanistan. King Zahir Shah goes into a self-imposed exile in Italy.

- In 1977, a new constitution is introduced, though it differs little from the first.

- For the first time in the history of Afghanistan, the army functions as a legal, active part of the country's political life, and the civil authorities establish special police forces. The president reaches new heights in terms of autonomy, power, and control over the military, while the *Loya Jirga,* technically the supreme decisive power in the country, is reduced to an instrument of legitimization for those in power.

- In 1973, the first true Islamic party is born: the Jamiat-e-Islami, or the Islamic Society. Burhanuddin Rabbani, a professor of *sharia,* is elected president. The vice president is another professor, Abdul Rasul Sayyaf, the principal student leader is Gulbudin Hekmatyar, who was an engineering student, as was another prominent member, Ahmen Shah Massoud.

- Daoud comes under pressure to suppress the Islamic movement. The leaders are either arrested or flee the country, taking refuge in the Pakistani city of Peshawar, where they are granted asylum by the government of Zulfikar Ali Bhutto. Ali Bhutto does not subscribe to their ideology, but he attempts to use their movement to pressure Daoud on the Pashtunistan issue and undermine his government through armed insurrections at various points throughout Afghanistan.

- The lack of an efficient commercial system, the excessive centralization, and a dearth of qualified personnel put the country's economy in danger of collapse. In order to shrug off some of the political, economic, and military dependence on the Soviet Union, Daoud attempts to forge contacts with other countries, but it is already too late.

THE DEMOCRATIC REPUBLIC OF AFGHANISTAN: APRIL 1978–
DECEMBER 1979

- On April 27, 1978, the PDPA—newly reformed at the behest of Soviet authorities—stages a coup d'etat with massive Soviet support.
- Daoud and his entire family are assassinated.
- Nur Muhammad Taraki, a member of the *Jalq* party, becomes president of the Democratic Republic of Afghanistan.
- The new government introduces radical reforms—such as the redistribution of land, the secularization of schools, the emancipation of women—following the models of the industrialized nations of Europe and the Soviet Union, without taking into account the social and political structure of the Afghan population.
- Discontent grows among an increasingly displeased population, resulting in conflicts, riots, and armed uprisings. The constitution is suspended. Brutal oppression, imprisonments, betrayals, torture, radicalism, and purges force many professionals to flee the country, resulting in the first major wave of refugees.
- The leaders of the principal groups opposing the Communist regime—the traditional and Islamic parties centered in Peshawar—attempt to unite and present a common front, but are unable to reach an agreement.
- Splinter factions of Rabbani's Jamiat-e-Islami (the Islamic Society) form the Hizb-e-Islami (the Islamic Party) led by Gulbuddin

Hekmatyar, as well as a similar party led by Younis Jalis, and where Mullah Muhammad Omar, the current leader of the Taliban, would cut his political teeth. The regional leaders of this party have also been assimilated into the modern Taliban party.

- The fourth Islamic party was the Ittihad-i-Islami (the Islamic Unity), founded by Abdul Rasul Sayyaf, who was incarcerated during the PDPA purges. Several of his old bosses also now play important roles within the Taliban.

- Discrepancies between the PDPA factions intensify. Babrak Karmal and Mohammed Najibullah flee from Parcham to the Soviet Union.

- President Taraki is assassinated in September of 1979.

- He is succeeded by Hafizullah Amin, also of the *Jalq* party. He orders the arrests and executions that are intended to put an end to the continuing armed uprisings in the rural areas of the country and which the army has been unable to quell.

- Hafizullah Amin is also assassinated.

- The Soviet Union is afraid of losing its grip on Afghanistan, and— on December 24, 1979—Russian troops cross the border and begin their invasion.

- The people take up arms against the invaders and against the army defending the pro-Soviet government. They are collectively known as mujahideen: warriors of faith.

- Babrak Karmal returns to the country and assumes the office of prime minister.

- A second wave of refugees begins.

_____

THE SOVIET OCCUPATION: DECEMBER 24, 1979–FEBRUARY 1989

- During the ten years of Soviet occupation, the country suffers total devastation: the invading troops plant tens of thousands of land mines across the country that—coupled with their bombings of

homes, towns, irrigation systems, crop fields, and infrastructure—
raze most of the country.

- Human rights violations abound, with no regard for the international rules governing armed conflicts. Among the worst offenders is the government's secret police, the KhAD, directed by Mohammed Najibullah, who imprisons and tortures his opponents, prompting a new, massive wave of refugees to flee to Iran and Pakistan.

- Youths are obligated to enlist in the army as of their sixteenth birthday, and are subsequenty sent to the front to fight against the mujahideen.

- Thousands of children are sent to the Soviet Union.

- Besides the Islamic parties, the traditionalists fight against the invading Soviet troops. The traditionalist parties include the Afghan National Liberation Front, led by Sibghatullah Mojididi, who had already been imprisoned by Daoud; the Harakat-e-Inqilab-e-Islami (the Islamic Revolutionary Movement), led by Nabi Muhammadi, which espoused a strict application of Islamic law and whose leaders and commaders would go on to become current Taliban directors; and the Mahaz-e-Milli-e-Islami (the National Islamic Front) led by Pir Gailani.

- The Pakistani government, seeking to keep the rising refugee population under control, encourages the parties to establish headquarters in the camps, which quickly become recruitment centers and bases for launching incursions into Afghanistan.

- In May of 1985, the Alliance of the Seven Islamic Parties is formed.

- In May of 1986, the Soviet Union moves Babrak Karmal into the position of chief of the secret police, replacing Mohammed Najibullah, who is named president. The Karmal and Najibullah administrations are nothing more than Soviet puppet governments. "Soviet advisors" intervene in everything: military decisions, the educational system, public and social services, means of communication, and public and cultural activities such as movies and the theater.

- In 1988, Iran manages to unite eight Shiite parties under the banner of Hizb-e-Wahdat (the Unity Party).
- The beginnings of perestroika and the internal problems facing Gorbachev prompt Soviet troops to begin withdrawing from the country, and the Geneva Accords are signed on April 14, 1988.
- The last Russian troops abandon Afghanistan on February 15, 1989.
- The intervention costs the Soviet Union some $5 billion a year, while the aid invested in development totaled just $250,000 over the previous twenty-five years combined.
- The amount of aid the United States had invested in development was roughly $20 million a year. Its contribution to the anti-Soviet Islamic resistance began in 1980 with some $30 million annually. Saudi Arabia and other Arab sources met the U.S. contributions, which reached $50 million in 1981 and 1982. This amount increased every year under the Reagan administration: $80 million in 1983, $120 million in 1984, and $250 million in 1985. The amount the U.S. budgeted for mujahideen support—which was always met by Saudi contributions—reached $470 million in 1986 and $630 million in 1987, 1988, and 1989.

THE END OF THE PRO-SOVIET GOVERNMENTS: 1989–1992

- After the withdrawal of the Soviet troops, the United States and Pakistan take steps to ensure that the Najibullah government will not endure, and pressure the Alliance of the Seven to form an interim government.
- The Najibullah government refuses to fall, and calls on Uzbeki militias in the north, led by Abdul Rashid Dostum, to protect the highway linking Kabul with the Soviet Union, which serves as a lifeline bringing in support. The Islamic interim government ratifies itself, with Rabbani as the president and Jalalabad as the new capital.

- The war drags on.
- In late 1991, the United States and the Soviet Union agree to put an end to their support, and endorse the efforts of the U.N. to propitiate a transitional regime.

THE *YEHADIS:* 1992–1994

- The halt in foreign aid does not stop the internal conflicts; rather, it prompts further fragmentation of the various bands and increased fighting among themselves.
- Massoud, the interim government's Minister of Defense, aligns himself with the Shiite troops under Abdul Rashid Dostum, chief of the Uzbeki militias in the north, and on April 25, 1992, he enters Kabul and occupies the city without a fight.
- Najibullah, after a failed attempt to flee the country, seeks refuge at the United Nations headquarters in Kabul.
- Several factions, including those led by Sayyad, control different Kabul neighborhoods, fighting in the streets.
- Gulbuddin Hekmatyar disagrees with the composition of the interim government, and launches a brutal attack on the capital.
- The fighting for power among the differing factions destroys Kabul. The alliances between troops change as a function of the interests of their leaders.
- In 1993, a new set of positions are laid out: Rabbani continues on as president, but Hekmatyar becomes the prime minister. Massoud sides with Sayyaf's forces against the Shiites occupying eastern Kabul. In January of 1994, Dostum and the Shiites will unite with Hekmatyar to face Massoud's troops together, in an ultimately unsuccessful attempt to depose Rabbani.

THE TALIBAN: 1994–TODAY

- The Taliban were originally a shock force formed and trained in the *madrasas* (Koranic schools) of Pakistan and with the economic support of Pakistan, the United States, and Saudi Arabia. Many of their members came from refugee camps and orphanages operating in Pakistan with Saudi money. Their supreme leader is Mullah Muhammad Omar. They have neither a political ideology nor a program of government. Their objective is "to liberate the country from corruption and convert Afghanistan into the purest Islamic state," the Islamic Emirates. In reality, they serve Pakistan's interests in the region. Their first public appearance occurred in Afghanistan on November 5, 1994, when they freed a Pakistani convoy of some thirty trucks that, in crossing the country, heading from Quetta to Turkmenistan, had fallen into the hands of armed bandits.
- Shortly thereafter they occupied the city of Kandahar.
- They begin to spread rumors of their own invincibility.
- On September 5, 1996, the Taliban occupy the city of Herat that, since 1992, had been under the control of Ismail Jan, one of Rabbani's allies.
- During the winter of 1995–96, the two-pronged blockade imposed by the Taliban and Hekmatyar's troops plunge Kabul into one of the city's worst humanitarian crises, while Massoud and Rabbani dig in.
- On September 11, the Taliban occupy Jalalabad.
- On September 26, the Taliban enter Kabul, drag Najibullah out of his refuge in the U.N. headquarters, and execute him. They proclaim the decrees that they will impose on all cities they conquer. Massoud's troops withdraw into the northern provinces, where the fighting continues between the Taliban and what remains of the Northern Alliance, backed by France, Russia, Iran, and India.
- By September of 2000, the Taliban control roughly 95 percent of

Afghanistan. In the north, where the war continues, Pakistani regulars fight alongside Saudi forces against the Taliban.

- Foreign interference and the interests of the different powers giving support to the many warring factions mark and determine the Afghan situation.

- The U.N. imposes sanctions on the Taliban in November of 1999 and December of 2000 as punishment for granting asylum to the Saudi terrorist Osama bin Laden, sought by the United States.

- At the time of this writing, the only countries to have recognized the Taliban as the legitimate government of Afghanistan are Pakistan, Saudi Arabia, and the United Arab Emirates.

- The Taliban's primary objective is to gain the legal recognition of the international community, and they have started talks with several countries toward this end. The international community is favorably disposed toward recognizing the Taliban, given that they already control almost the entire country, and there are many pending interests and projects that depend on resolving the Afghan conflict.

- The United Nations, trying to ferret out Osama bin Laden, issues a decree in December of 2000 that places a unilateral ban on weapons and arms deals with the Taliban. The decree goes into effect on January 19, 2001, but it does not seem likely that it will put an end to the fighting and allow Massoud to reclaim territory.

- Spain deals arms to Saudi Arabia, Pakistan, and Iran—countries directly implicated in the war in Afghanistan.

- Mohammad Zahir Shah, exiled in Rome, continues his attempt to convene a *Loya Jirga*.

- In March of 2001, the Taliban destroy all statues in the country, including ancient historical pieces in the Kabul Museum, sites in Ghazni, and the famous Bamiyan Buddhas, which dated from the fifth century.

- In April, the U.N. accuses Pakistan of not allowing adequate supplies of food and medicine to reach Afghan refugees at the Jalozai camp near Peshawar.

- On September 9, Massoud is killed by suicide bombers posing as Arab journalists.
- On September 11, terrorists hijack four airliners and crash them into the World Trade Center, the Pentagon, and in Stony Creek Township, Pennsylvania. The attacks were orchestrated by Osama bin Laden, who later (on a videotape released by the Pentagon on December 13) described the results as being "all that we had hoped for."
- The Taliban refuse to extradite bin Laden to the United States, prompting the U.S. to launch air strikes against them and to increase their support (financial and otherwise) to the Northern Alliance and other opposition groups.
- Most Taliban and Al Qaeda forces have been driven from urban areas by November, at which point U.S. ground forces begin entering the country to hunt for bin Laden and Taliban leader Mullah Muhammad Omar.
- On December 22, a pan-Afghan conference held in Bonn, Germany, appoints Hamid Karzai, a Pashtun, as chairman of the Afghan Interim Authority, or AIA. The Bonn Agreement asserts "the right of the people of Afghanistan to freely determine their own political future in accordance with the principles of Islam, democracy, pluralism and social justice."
- The largest battle of the war erupts near the city of Gardez and involves U.S. forces fighting alongside soldiers from seven other nations—including France, which had several thousand troops in the region and whose warplanes flew reconnaissance and bombing raids during every day of the battle.
- The exiled king Zahir Shah returns to Afghanistan and convenes a *Loya Jirga* on June 9, 2002. Karzai is elected to a two-year term as president, while the king's position is retained for symbolic purposes as the "father of the nation." A few months later, one of Karzai's vice presidents is assassinated and an attempt is made on his own life.

- On October 5, 2002, President Karzai establishes a nine-member Constitutional Drafting Commission. Two of the nine members are women. According to the Secretariat of the Constitutional Commission of Afghanistan, "The Commission will be working closely with the Ministry of Women Affairs, which together with UNIFEM, is collecting inputs, holding seminars and other public education programs about the constitutional rights of women. Further, the Commission will establish a liaison with the women civil society organizations that will put at the disposal of the Commission a broad network of their grassroot organizations. Gender balance is also a priority for the selection of the regional consultation teams."

- Afghanistan's constitution is ratified on January 4, 2004. Although earlier drafts were criticized by such groups as Amnesty International for not sufficiently protecting women's rights (among other things, the right to choose a spouse freely), the new document asserts that women will hold at least 64 out of 250 seats in the *Wolesi Jirga*, the lower house of parliament. This percentage is higher than in most Western democracies.

- At the time of this book's English-language publication, an estimated two million Afghan refugees have repatriated since the overthrow of the Taliban's regime, with most of them returning from Pakistan. Still, the country continues to suffer from guerrilla warfare, crushing poverty, a shattered infrastructure, and deadly land mines. The United Nations has estimated that it will require $15 billion and at least a full decade to rebuild Afghanistan.